BETTER OFF FORGETTING?
ESSAYS ON ARCHIVES, PUBLIC POLICY,
AND COLLECTIVE MEMORY

Throughout Canada, provincial, federal, and municipal archives exist to house the records we produce. Some conceive of these institutions as old and staid, suggesting that archives are somehow trapped in the past. But archives are more than resources for professional scholars and interested individuals. With an increasing emphasis on transparency in government and public institutions, archives have become essential tools for accountability.

Better Off Forgetting? offers a reappraisal of archives and a look at the challenges they face in a time when issues of freedom of information, privacy, technology, and digitization are increasingly important. The contributors argue that archives are essential to contemporary debates about public policy and make a case for increased status, funding, and influence within public bureaucracies. While stimulating debate about our rapidly changing information environment, *Better Off Forgetting?* focuses on the continuing role of archives in gathering and preserving our collective memory.

CHERYL AVERY is a professional archivist at the University of Saskatchewan Archives.

MONA HOLMLUND is an assistant professor in the Department of Art and Art History at the University of Saskatchewan.

EDITED BY CHERYL AVERY
AND MONA HOLMLUND

Better Off Forgetting?

Essays on Archives, Public Policy,
and Collective Memory

UNIVERSITY OF TORONTO PRESS
Toronto Buffalo London

ISBN 978-1-4426-4167-9 (cloth)
ISBN 978-1-4426-1080-4 (paper)

Printed on acid-free, 100% post-consumer recycled paper with vegetable-based inks.

Library and Archives Canada Cataloguing in Publication

Better off forgetting?: essays on archives, public policy, and collective memory / edited by Cheryl Avery and Mona Holmlund.

Includes bibliographical references and index.

ISBN 978-1-4426-4167-9 (bound). – ISBN 978-1-4426-1080-4 (pbk).

1. Archives – Canada.   2. Archives – Access control.   3. Digital preservation.
4. Public records – Management.   I. Avery, Cheryl   II. Holmlund, Mona

CD3621.B47 2010   025.17'14   C2010-902793-0

The authors gratefully acknowledge support from the University of Saskatchewan Publications Fund.

This book has been published with the help of a grant from the Canadian Federation for the Humanities and Social Sciences, through the Aid to Scholarly Publications Program, using funds provided by the Social Sciences and Humanities Research Council of Canada.

University of Toronto Press acknowledges the financial assistance to its publishing program of the Canada Council for the Arts and the Ontario Arts Council.

 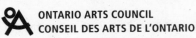

University of Toronto Press acknowledges the financial support of the Government of Canada through the Canada Book Fund for its publishing activities.

Contents

PART THREE: THE DIGITAL AGE

PART FOUR: ACCOUNTABILITY AND THE PUBLIC SPHERE

PART FIVE: RESOURCE FOR THE PRESENT

Contributors

Tom Adami is the information manager at the United Nations Mission in Sudan. Prior to this he was the chief archivist at the International Criminal Tribunal for Rwanda.

Cheryl Avery is an archivist at the University of Saskatchewan. Previously, she worked at the National Archives of Canada and at the Diefenbaker Canada Centre. She served as vice-chair of the Canadian Council of Archives and was co-chair of the Steering Committee for the Canadian Archival Information Network.

Marion Beyea is director of the Provincial Archives of New Brunswick. She was founding president of the Canadian Council of Archives and has served as president of the Association of Canadian Archivists. She currently chairs the International Council of Archives section on professional standards.

Robert Cole is Peel bibliographer and digital content coordinator at the University of Alberta Library. Previously, he was a graduate student in history at the University of Saskatchewan and the University of Alberta and served as a researcher and copy editor for Chinook Multimedia in Edmonton.

Terry Cook taught archival studies at the University of Manitoba. Earlier, he worked at the National Archives of Canada, specializing in the appraisal of government records. He is a fellow of the Society of American Archivists.

Terry Eastwood is professor emeritus in the School of Library, Archival and Information Studies at the University of British Columbia, where he was the founding professor and chair from 1981 to 2000 of the master's of archival studies program.

Jo-Ann Munn Gafuik has worked at the University of Calgary for twenty-two years – as university archivist from 1992 to 2003, as freedom of information privacy coordinator (FOIP) since 1998, and as policy coordinator since 2003.

Chris Hackett is a historian and formerly one of the principles in Chinook Multimedia, a company specializing in the development of digital teaching resources. He has written extensively on the impact of new media on the teaching of history and is currently graduate student ombudsperson at the University of Alberta.

Yvette Hackett has been with Library and Archives Canada since 1980, working initially with moving images and shifting to digital records in 1993. She has participated in the Rules for Archival Description, the National Data Archive Consultation, and, beginning in 1999, the InterPARES projects on authenticity in electronic records.

Mona Holmlund is an assistant professor of art history at the University of Saskatchewan. Her previous publications, *Women Together* and *Inspiring Women*, and her PhD research at Cambridge have impressed upon her the importance of archives and the valuable expertise and professionalism of archivists.

Martha Hunt has been the audio-visual archivist for the United Nations International Criminal Tribunal for Rwanda since June 2003.

Tom Nesmith is an associate professor, founder, and director of the University of Manitoba's master's program in archival studies. He was an archivist at the National Archives of Canada from 1978 to 1990 and editor of *Archivaria* from 1984 to 1986.

Robert Steiner is currently assistant vice-president of the University of Toronto, in charge of strategic communications. He is a former *Wall Street Journal* foreign correspondent, and a former senior communications adviser in the campaigns of two Canadian prime ministers.

Doug Surtees is an assistant professor of law at the College of Law, University of Saskatchewan. He specializes in elder law, law and disability, wills, contracts, insurance law, and trusts. He was co-director of the Public Legal Education Association of Saskatchewan from 1994 to 2005.

Shelley Sweeney is head, University of Manitoba Archives and Special Collections. She was in the first class of the master's of archival studies program at the University of British Columbia and has a PhD in archival enterprise (Austin). She has served as president of the Association of Canadian Archivists and secretary general of the Bureau of Canadian Archivists.

Bill Waiser, professor of history at the University of Saskatchewan, is the author of several books, including the award-winning *Saskatchewan: A New History*. He is a member of the Saskatchewan Order of Merit and a fellow of the Royal Society of Canada.

Introduction

CHERYL AVERY and MONA HOLMLUND

We are all archivists. Throughout our lives we select, store, and review. We keep documents, photographs, video and audio tapes as mementoes and souvenirs. Even if one is not a keeper of such memorabilia, we are all implicated in the archival project. We leave a trail of academic transcripts, medical records, job applications, and tax forms in our wake as we move through society. Even graffiti is a record that someone was there, an attempt to project one's presence into the future. We seem to have a compulsion to document.

Throughout the country, provincial, federal, municipal, and other archives exist to house the records we produce. We even draft legislation to govern how we manage these records. Nevertheless, archives have a relatively low public profile. The level of funding most archives receive is insufficient. The legislation that governs the records archives hold is often contradictory and confusing especially in terms of access versus privacy and copyright versus public use. There seems to be a disconnect between the apparent impulse to preserve and how we manage the material we produce. It would appear that no one is thinking about the fundamental question of archives: What value do these records have for us?

In many respects, it is easy to look back and assume that archives originated in simpler times. Especially in western Canada, eager collection of any documentation reflected a recently transplanted European society anxious to memorialize its pioneering exploits. Later came the perception that archives were untapped resources for professional historians to fuel their summers writing Canadian history. And more recently, archives have become a treasure trove for individuals researching their genealogy. However valid, all of these examples suggest a resource trapped in the past.

But that kind of thinking has shifted. Instead of seeing archives as a means to illuminate various histories, archives are now seen as a tool for institutional-records management. This is a product of the increasing emphasis on accountability felt by government and public institutions. This change is not necessarily negative, but it is significant. It shifts the record into the realm of the present rather than the past. It is about the public's perceived and immediate 'right to know.' This sense of entitlement also places the record in a more legalistic risk-management framework. It is preserved primarily for administrative purposes and then only as long as the benefits outweigh the risks. The attendant pressures of space and financial constraints have meant that some archives and institutions have narrowed their focus, favouring administrative records over collections documenting personal histories or social change. As managing institutional records becomes a larger and larger task, it becomes more difficult to argue for a broader mandate in a world that increasingly values only the 'bottom line.' Personal archives, the records of 'ordinary Canadians,' of grassroots social movements, for example – all might be at risk if institutions increasingly move towards managing their own information to the exclusion of everything else.

Our cross-cultural and trans-historical compulsion to document everything from pictographs to graffiti has never been solely about preserving the past nor recording the present. The broader aim has always been to help inform the future. This, in essence, is what archives are: a storehouse for the future. However, an increasing amount of material is now born digital. There is a widespread expectation that whatever we need to find will be at our fingertips – if those fingertips are on a keyboard. This expectation in turn does two things. First, it enhances the impression of archives as ancient repositories of 'old dusty paper,' despite the fact that archives must also appraise and manage new media. Second, it drives the push to digitize and make accessible all kinds of records. The net result could be a society with a truly ephemeral memory. Digital media are not stable. Their durability and longevity are yet to be tested. The immediacy of access belies the fragility of the system. The particular medium through which a document is recorded, be it a floppy disc or a memory stick, regardless of its own stability, relies upon some *other* technology, such as a compatible computer or software system or other playback device, in order to be retrievable. The chain of technology that individuals rely upon to access information is continually in a state of flux. Something as simple as a broken part that is now obsolete may make a document permanently inaccessible. Going forward, the path we are currently on will mean that we simply will not have kept records to the extent that we did in the past.

The implications of this are not simply theoretical or philosophical. The essays in this collection link the current state of archives to pragmatic concerns ranging from human rights to democracy, from residential schools and the Rwandan genocide to the Jamaican bank failure and CIA-sponsored drug testing. They enable the thoughtful reader to question assumptions about the gathering and preservation of information. There is a stark exercise of power inherent in archival decisions. The archivist must be a disciplined witness, attuned to multiple and shifting pressures and purposes of documents. What we do with records is just one of the many fascinating and complex quandaries that are inherent in the very nature of the business of collecting memory.

We have divided the chapters in this collection into five thematic areas: the history of funding; access and privacy; the digital age; accountability and the public sphere; and resource for the present. Archival practice, however, is by nature holistic. The most comprehensive understanding of the problems facing archives today will come from a reading of these essays that sees them as intersecting parts of the whole. They range from the practical to the philosophical, which we view as both a strength of the collection and a reflection of archives themselves.

In Part One, 'The History of Funding,' the aim is to place the contemporary issues that follow in their historical context. Marion Beyea's essay, 'Pennies from Heaven: The History of Public Funding for Canadian Archives,' provides a sense of the lobbying efforts that have resulted in the current levels of funding. In 'Lady Sings the Blues: The Public Funding of Archives, Libraries, and Museums in Canada,' Shelley Sweeney compares archives' financial resources to those of other cultural institutions and explores the implications of underfunding of the archival sector. Taken together, these two essays provide the basis for the public-policy issues presented by our other authors. In short, if the value of archives is the preservation of the past for the future, do we have the public will to provide for that accountability?

Undoubtedly, two of the most important public-policy areas affecting archives are the subject of Part Two, 'Access and Privacy.' One could easily assume that the proliferation of records and record keeping means that we are living in the age of accountability. The purported intent of legislation surrounding access and privacy would appear to be a well-intentioned attempt to enhance democratic rights. However, the legislation certainly doesn't always do what people think it does. Access legislation identifies broad swaths of materials that should be open or closed, but interpretation of the details is largely subjective. As Jo-Ann Munn Gafuik notes in 'Access-to-Information Legislation: A Critical Analysis,' it is not enough simply to accept the legislation and hope for the best. One has to reassess continually how well it functions and whether it continues to serve its original intent. Is information being illegitimately withheld or is it being bandied about in a frivolous, or even malicious, way?

Accountability is understood to mean *responsibility* where guardianship of personal information is concerned. Indeed, Doug Surtees's essay, 'Privacy: A Look at the Disenfranchised,' emphasizes how ethical approaches to the management of information are often anchored exclusively in the present. His concerns regarding misuse are a genuine and helpful reminder to the practitioner and theorist of archival policy. The problem facing archivists in the privacy debates, however, is how to decide when personal information makes the transformation into historically necessary information. Terry Cook and Bill Waiser explore that issue in their account of the 'census wars': 'The Laurier Promise: Securing Public Access to Historic Census Materials in Canada.'

Our definition of access, moreover, has been redefined by 'The Digital Age,' the subject of Part Three. A lesser-known recent policy of the Canadian government encouraged archives to make their holdings accessible online. The intent is certainly good: easier access to material across the country, and enhanced opportunities to learn about Canadian history and culture. Nevertheless, in 'Search vs. Research: Full-Text Repositories, Granularity, and the Concept of "Source" in the Digital Environment,' Robert Cole and Chris Hackett challenge us to consider how this might be influencing research. Does digital access affect the way we view the archival record? In the first instance, archivists must mediate the research experience by selecting which materials will be available online. This in turn is affected by legislation governing privacy and copyright. Finally, there is a fundamental difference between doing research online and the tactile and often serendipitous experience of research done physically in an archive.

In addition to its possible effects on research, digitization also presents practical implications for archives. In her essay, 'Preserving Digital History: Costs and Consequences,' Yvette Hackett clearly outlines the long struggle archives have had in finding appropriate and affordable solutions to manage the wealth of digital information. Given our current reliance on electronic records, it is astonishing that there is no public policy addressing this vital aspect of records preservation.

In Part Four, 'Accountability and the Public Sphere,' the essays by Tom Nesmith and Terry Eastwood take up this question by asking us to consider what role archivists ought to have in promoting and defining their own function. Nesmith quotes Ian Wilson, librarian and archivist emeritus of Canada: 'Archivists, as custodians of social memory, cannot be spectators, we take part in the creation of memory by the records we preserve. We are active participants.' In 'Archivists and Public Affairs: Towards a New Archival Public Programming,' Nesmith suggests that archivists must move 'more fully into the public square.' He argues for the more active promotion of archival holdings to shake loose the sense of dusty inconsequence that hovers over archives.

Regardless of any other mandate that one might assign to the archival enterprise, there is the fundamental effort to retain as accurate and authentic a record of our actions as possible, if only so that our future selves might know us. In 'Archives, Democratic Accountability, and Truth,' Terry Eastwood quotes Bernard Williams's statement that there is a need to 'make sense of one's situation, and that requires an appeal to the past. If it is not the historical past, then it will be to some kind of myth about it.' Do policy makers have a vested interest in myth making? When it comes to freedom of information and its widespread dissemination, not many governments *want* to be wholly accountable, and they are, of course, the ones making the laws. In his exploration of the paradoxes of accountability, Eastwood is cautioning us not to lose sight of the foundational work of *objectively* collecting and *adequately preserving* the past.

Accountability is the undercurrent to this collection. We see it in Surtees's and Cook and Waiser's concerns surrounding privacy and access. We see it in Nesmith's and Eastwood's call to reflection. And we see it explicitly in the final part of the book, 'Resource for the Present.' In horrific circumstances, when the stakes are enormously high, Tom Adami and Martha Hunt's essay – 'Reconciliation in Regions Affected by Armed Conflict: The Role of Archives' – identifies the consequences of offering greater and immediate access *regardless* of what we assume to be the costs. Their account charts a fundamental shift, from retribution to the pursuit of truth, from creating myths to understanding history.

And so we conclude with Robert Steiner's poetic mediation on the realpolitik of the intersection between archives, journalism, and the pursuit of power: 'Bridging Us to Us: An Argument for the Importance of Archivists in Current Politics and Journalism.' His is a subtle and nuanced argument for the importance of archives and thoughtful, principled archivists: 'It seems society itself works hard to help us *avoid* the frank encounter with the source materials of our current experience. Whole industries invest billions of dollars and employ thousands upon thousands of people to create *simple* stories.' One has to assess, critically and continually, whether archives are being best used to help give the whole story in all of its complexity. Inadequate funding, a black-and-white reading of our current legislation, and the impact of digital information could result in a very simple story for the future, or indeed no story at all. Are we building search-and-access systems that ensure future generations are content with only the most rudimentary and superficial understanding? Is digitization a quick fix that misses the complexity of preservation? Particularly in the electronic age, guarding privacy can be tenuous and difficult, but is there a value to personal material that can transcend individual concerns? Finally, how can archivists better position all these issues on the public stage?

In the title to this collection we have asked if we are simply 'better off forgetting.' Clearly, neither we nor any of our contributors believe that we are better off neglecting the archival enterprise. However, we feel strongly that we must confront the losses that will result from the ongoing omissions in archival public policy. Through a sustained failure to fund archives properly and to approach policy initiatives holistically, a series of governments and other funders have implicitly acted as if we *are* better off forgetting. Benign neglect is still neglect. There are costs to the paths that we are on and there is much at stake. We don't feel that this is the best course. We don't believe that we are better off discarding and forgetting the aspects of our past that archives preserve for the future. For example, Cook and Waiser's essay identifies exactly how difficult effective policy can be and the consequences of its failure. By following access/privacy legislation to the letter, as they interpret it, Statistics Canada is demanding that only certain information in their census data be made available to researchers. Later generations will be able neither to review nor to enhance that data. This is not an argument for other values trumping the 'right to know,' or a disagreement between statisticians and historians or archivists about where the bar should be set in terms of how much we should know, when we should know it, or how we should find things out. It is an argument for the complete erasure of certain information, for knowing only 'what we want you to know' and forgetting the rest. Similarly, Hackett's essay demonstrates quite clearly that considerable investment is required if our 'born digital' records have any hope of being retained for future generations. The failure or neglect to fund this enterprise will mean that much is lost and forgotten.

So we must indeed confront the question our title asks: whether current public policy implicitly suggests we are 'better off forgetting.' This is a view the essays in this collection would counter. They all imply, or make explicit, that the matters under discussion involve a complex balancing act. Indeed, the richness of the essays collected here amply demonstrates the nuanced complexity of the archival project and the hopefulness of those engaged in it. We have tried to make the case for more status, funding, staffing, and influence for archives in society. This is the first collection of its kind which filters public-policy concerns through the archival lens. We hope it is a useful beginning to a broader debate that will stimulate interest among decision makers and inspire professionals in the field to consider how best to bring their concerns to a broader audience. It is that broader audience – public-policy makers, public administrators, journalists, historians, and indeed the general public – whom we wish to inspire to take up the debates presented here.

The neglect of the archival function in society will have an impact far beyond the profession. Archivists, like all members of our fast-changing and tumultuous world, need to live with complexity. We all need to grow comfortable with being uncomfortable and be willing to grapple with difficult and thorny issues. The role of information in contemporary society is extremely complex and continually changing. All of the essays in this collection deal in one way or another with the implications of this for archives and society. We must take the debate forward and ask ourselves whether the decisions we are currently making, the policies we are enacting, and the dollars we are spending reflect our values.

Do we believe we are better off preserving our collective memory, or better off forgetting? It is our hope that this collection of essays, expressing different viewpoints and points of concern – and, above all, reflecting the dynamism of the debate surrounding archives' role – will help those who care about our collective memory as they consider how best to preserve and promote it.

PART ONE

The History of Funding

1 Pennies from Heaven: The History of Public Funding for Canadian Archives[1]

MARION BEYEA

It has been thirty-five years since the *Report on Canadian Studies* was published, thirty years since the *Report of the Consultative Group on Canadian Archives* was delivered, and twenty-five years since the Canadian Council of Archives (CCA) was established. This essay, in the course of reviewing the archival scene in the 1975–85 period, looks at the thinking that informed these undertakings, the situations they identified, the recommendations they made, their impact, and what all this said about financial support for archives.

The idea of a commission to study, report on, and make recommendations relating to the state of Canadian studies was conceived in 1970 and its members were appointed by the Association of Universities and Colleges of Canada in June 1972. Dr Thomas B. Symons, a historian and faculty member at Trent University, was appointed chair of the commission. At the time of its deliberations, the commission would have observed a nascent, developing archival scene in Canada.

People taking jobs in archives were usually not making a deliberate career choice – archives provided employment for ex-journalists, military veterans, the occasional political appointment, and university history graduates who often intended to return to their studies. Indeed, ties with historians were strong: one senior archivist stated during a 1973 debate that he hoped he would never see the day when archivists, rather than historians, would be in charge of education for archivists. Several years later, another archivist, also a senior member of the profession, tearfully questioned how archivists could leave their historian colleagues behind.

The (then) Public Archives of Canada (PAC) played a leading role in the Canadian archival community. For instance, the majority of people being employed in archives learned on the job and through a month-long course many attended at the PAC. The course was important in introducing working archivists, not only to archival theory and practice and the holdings and operations of the PAC and colleagues there, but also to each other and to archives as a profession.

The PAC assisted archives in other ways as well. Chief among these was the production of the *Union List of Manuscripts*, a guide to archival collections across Canada. This initiative provided archival institutions with standardized techniques for description at the collection level. It also provided the funding to prepare the entries and in some cases to do the arrangement and description of records. This was the first instance of non-institutional public funding for archives in Canada.

Meanwhile, meetings of the Archives Section of the Canadian Historical Association were becoming regularized with agendas that treated archival topics. The section newsletter had been transformed into a journal reporting news and addressing technical matters as well as broader issues in archival development. The section set up a Committee of the Future in 1973 to look at the options for a more vigorous and relevant association for archivists in Canada. Archivists began to meet locally and regionally, discussing issues and organizing and holding training workshops. At the same time, senior archivists, needing more robust archival activities, participated in the Society of American Archivists (SAA), even as presidents. Additionally, archivists arriving from Britain, such as Allen Ridge, Hugh Taylor, and Gordon Dodds, brought to Canadian practice their knowledge that a tradition, even a profession, of archival work existed, along with their ideas about archival education and theory.

In terms of theory and practice, Canadian archivists (particularly those in university settings) were exercised over library methodology being imposed on the arrangement and description of records. Another burning issue was acquisition, although this was more the fact that there was competition for records rather than that archives might not be preserving all they should. In part, the acquisition controversy was fallout from the PAC's introduction of the Systematic National Acquisition Program (SNAP). The national institution's acquisition of regionally important records was a sore point for archivists outside the nation's capital.

Records management was increasingly becoming an integral part of archival operations, especially at the PAC and provincial archives. There was also gestating concern about conservation – the fact that some records were in poor shape and that the friendly door-to-door laminating machine salesman had not done archivists any favours. However, only a few institutions had conservators and these were European-trained and worked in the tradition of treating individual items as treasures, rather than constructing a holistic conservation environment.

This Canadian archival scene is what the Commission on Canadian Studies responded to in its recommendations. The commission's report in 1975 (the 'Symons Report') was a landmark for Canadian archivists, not least because it devoted a chapter to archives and attached great importance to them – indeed, called them the foundation of Canadian studies.[2]

Among other matters, the Symons Report discussed university education for archivists, revision of legislation for the PAC, and mandatory deposit of Canadian Broadcasting Corporation (CBC) and National Film Board (NFB) productions at the PAC. It recommended revision of the Copyright Act, establishment of archives by all universities, and the proper care of university records. Further concern was expressed for the neglect of business archives and records of ethnic groups. Finally, the Symons Report supported completion of the *Union List of Manuscripts*.

A primary concern of the Symons Report was for those records that archives had *not* yet collected. It recommended that the archives of Canada undertake a program to 'promote public awareness of the potential value of private papers and other archival material.'[3] The Symons Report stated that locating material must precede systematic collections development, and proposed the preparation of a national guide, funded by the federal and provincial governments, for records not already in archives. Further, the Symons Report understood the increase in resources this would demand: 'If all archival material of interest to Canadian studies were to be located and briefly described in a manner proposed, proper repositories would be required to provide for its acquisition, preservation, cataloguing and facilities for consultation [and] such facilities [do] not exist in sufficient numbers.'[4] The Symons Report attributed a major role to universities in this project. The university archive would take in more records and lead in the creation of other archives. It was recommended that universities 'be funded specifically for this important facet of the university's work'[5] by federal and provincial governments.

Although the commission recognized the importance of archives, its report did not demonstrate an understanding of the Canadian archival landscape or of archival theory. Indeed, Dr Symons later revealed he was faced with difficulties in placing archives on the commission's agenda at all. The report paid short shrift to provincial archives and the solution to the development and rationalization of Canadian archival resources was not seen as lying in the extension of their services. Instead, the report stated that the acquisition of archival records by universities was 'yet another of the important ways in which the universities can and should assist their own immediate communities to achieve the self-knowledge that, as this Report has urged throughout, is essential for health and growth in the lives of both individuals and societies.'[6] The report's emphasis on the acquisition and preservation of records to meet the needs of the scholar and on a pivotal role for universities is not surprising given that the report was commissioned by universities and its members were university professors. The concentration on universities may have been to counter those commission members who would have preferred to leave archives out of the report altogether.

While acknowledging that more resources were needed and mentioning that cataloguing would be necessary, the Symons Report did not indicate an awareness of the labour-intensive work involved in making records ready for use, or of the fact that the meagre budgets of Canadian archives could be a reason for the passive state of acquisition. Archivists agreed with the report's view that the widest possible range of documentary materials should be preserved for future research. They also agreed with the report's identification of low or negative public awareness of Canadian archives, inadequate reference tools, and the absence of university programs to educate archivists as problems for Canadian archives. But the newly formed Association of Canadian Archivists (ACA) strongly took issue with the Symons Report's statement that at archives 'materials ... can be collected according to a subject or regionalization or be divided in terms of theme and format.'[7] The ACA evoked Jenkinsonian theory,[8] defining a direct relationship between organizations or individuals and the records of their activities, which meant that organizations should keep their own records insofar as possible. The ACA concluded that the Symons approach was inappropriate for archives. Instead it advocated the 'development of archives based whenever possible in an institutional setting where valuable records are created ... [since] only archives run by knowledgeable custodians capable of instituting standard procedures will ultimately bring us to our goal of linking repositories and their holdings in co-operative networks and systems.'[9]

Arising from Symons's recommendation for a national inventory of records not already located in archives, and his lobbying for this with support from Dominion Archivist Dr Wilfred Smith, was the allocation of money to complete a survey – the second instance of public funding for archives. The Department of Employment and Immigration granted $330,267, and the PAC added another $10,000, to cover the first phase of a national survey of archival resources involving 138 students working in 20 locations. The program continued for several years and, while it is unknown how many records it listed ended up in archives, it raised the profile of archives and highlighted the importance of records.

Yet a more important impact of the Symons Report was its galvanizing effect on the archival community and its fledgling professional body, the ACA. Archivists greeted the Symons Report with great interest. They were stimulated to think about their practice and theory and how that theory would play out during the implementation of the report's thirty-one recommendations. This in turn provided the impetus for the creation of the Consultative Group on Canadian Archives.

Ian Wilson, probably one of the few archivists at the time who realized that action in regard to the Symons Report would not come automatically or easily, approached the Canada Council for funding of a more exhaustive look at Canadian archives.[10] The Canada Council determined that the motivation for a new study by the Consultative Group came primarily from two sources: requests over the years for various forms of archival assistance and the council's feeling that it had neither the budget nor the mandate to respond; and the Symons Report.

Between the Symons Report of 1975 and the Consultative Group's work, which began in 1978 and concluded in 1980, there had been significant changes on the archival scene. The ACA was well under way: by 1980, the annual meeting in Montreal broke the 100-member registration mark and concurrent sessions were offered. Archivists were communicating regularly through their newsletter and had an impressive new journal, *Archivaria*. Committees addressed publications, finding-aid systems, and business archives, and an education committee developed guidelines for graduate archival-studies programs.[11] More archives were being established, and existing archives were taking on new staff and new specializations.

The Consultative Group, chaired by Ian Wilson, was comprised of nine historians and archivists. A first step was to develop statistics on archives in Canada based on responses received from 185 archives (and explanatory letters from a further 31) to a survey questionnaire. In addition, 73 briefs were received from archival associations, historical societies, the dominion archivist, five provincial archivists, individual archivists, and creators of records, as well as the ACA and three of its committees. The data revealed a sense of crisis in Canadian archives: 'Even in the largest archives, basic facilities or equipment was lacking ... few archives with full record management programs ... only a handful have developed conservation programs ... archives collections are disintegrating, educational opportunities open to archivists ... non-existent.'[12]

The resulting 'Wilson Report' made nineteen recommendations, which were well conceived and substantiated and directly pertinent to the current and longer-term funding needs of archives. Several covered the same ground as the Symons Report: university-level education of archivists; preservation of business records; and revision of copyright legislation. New recommendations concerned security and establishment of a national register of stolen documents, extension of the Cultural Property Export and Import Act to private institutions, the addition of archival science to the Social Sciences and Humanities Research Council of Canada (SSHRCC) list of eligible disciplines for research grants, and the involvement of archivists in assessing applications in the humanities and social sciences. Perhaps most important was the group's designation of an appropriate amount of funding in SSHRCC grants to assist archives in providing services.

The report was introduced with a discussion of archival theory, including an updated definition of archives that now moved beyond the strict Jenkinsonian definition of records 'drawn up or used in the course of an administrative or executive transaction ... of which itself formed a part; and subsequently preserved in their own custody ...' to encompass the reality that records of archival value would not always, or even often, be kept by their creator.[13] To this was added an extension of the principle of provenance to one of territoriality, aimed at keeping the context of records intact. This envisaged the locale or milieu of records as part of their context.

This laid the foundation for the major theme of the Wilson Report: the development and coordination of archives in Canada. The report recommended that 'all public archives re-evaluate their overall programs to achieve an appropriate balance between their traditional institutional programs and new programs designed to provide leadership to a co-operative system of archives in their region.'[14] New funding was urged for provincial archival associations: $100,000 to $200,000 annually from provincial governments; and $2.5 million annually from the

PAC at the federal level. The purpose of this would be to coordinate a national archival information system, share responsibility with provincial associations for providing smaller archives with access to consultants and specialized facilities, assist in the development of the archival profession, and, perhaps most important, establish a grants program for projects of national significance. The Wilson Report also called for a Canadian Association of Archives, under the mantle of the PAC, that would hold a regular meeting of heads of all archives over a certain size for planning joint programs, expressing collective opinions on public policy as institutions, and disbursing funding.

The ACA, led by President Kent Haworth, endorsed the Wilson Report's advocacy of a coordinated network in each province to establish priorities, recognizing that these might not be the same in all areas of the country. But it opposed doing so under a new branch of the PAC, arguing that this was redundant and a waste of public funds. It favoured instead an independent National Archival Records Commission (NARC) made up of representatives from the PAC, the ACA, and the Association des archivistes du Québec (AAQ), from institutional archives on a rotating basis, and from associations of users of archives (namely, SSHRCC). The ACA also saw the Canadian Association of Archives proposed by the Wilson Report as elitist and an expense that could be eliminated with NARC.

The Symons and Wilson reports, and the responses, discussion, and reflection they provoked, provided an invaluable basis for proposals made by senior archivists who lobbied provincial and federal ministers of culture and heritage. Through Quebec's interest in the pending revision of public archives legislation, archives finally gained a place on the agenda of a ministers' meeting in 1982. The archival lobbyists presented a complete status report on archives – including the issue of archival associations and federal funding – at that meeting. The ministers in turn tasked the national/provincial/territorial archivists to develop the issue further.

The provincial archivists continued to apply pressure on the federal government until 1985, when Ottawa responded with an endorsement of the Canadian archival system and a commitment to fund archives. This commitment was realized in 1986 with the infusion of $1.8 million into the Canadian archival system. Intensive and extensive lobbying by archivists and archival associations and users from across the country brought an additional $1 million in funding for preservation.

The result was the establishment of the Canadian Council of Archives in 1985 to coordinate the Canadian archival system. Its membership represented provincial and territorial associations, the ACA, the AAQ, and the PAC, then renamed the National Archives of Canada (NAC).

The ideas, principles, and recommendations from the various reports and the archival community's responses are reflected in the CCA's structure, objectives, and programs. The CCA is based upon provincial associations, as the Symons Report and all subsequent reports and responses advocated. It is also 'NARC'-like, as the ACA insisted it should be. Its makeup is inclusive, with rotating institutional representation achieved by the normal progression of executive roles within the provincial associations. Echoing the Wilson Report's recommendations regarding federal funding, the CCA's formula for provincial-funding allocations minimizes disparities among the networks. The flexibility to accommodate difference in the regions, the importance of which was emphasized by the ACA, was built into the structure of the CCA through the creation of several granting programs, the allowance of movement of funds between programs, and the provision of scope for the consideration of special projects.

The types of projects historically funded by the CCA were those recommended by the Wilson Report. These included standardized description for all archival media and the preparation of guides to archival resources, and grants for local, provincial, and national planning studies. As seconded by the ACA response, eligible projects also included training programs and travel bursaries, publications, and research. Despite being recommended by the Wilson Report and the ACA, exceptions to fundable projects were special facilities or capital construction of conservation storage vaults.

The inadequate planning for Canadian archives noted by the Wilson Report was addressed with the establishment of a two-year comprehensive planning process under the leadership of Planning and Priorities Committee Chair Brian Speirs, working with ACA representative Jean Dryden. This led to the setting of national goals and objectives. The planning process was formally repeated in 1992–3 and in 2004–5 and is also regularly undertaken by CCA committees. Grants were made to the associations and to institutions, as advised in the Wilson Report. Often, as that report foresaw, these grants are carried out by organizations in different combinations and arrangements with the NAC, now renamed yet again Library and Archives Canada (LAC).

Additional funding was forthcoming as recommended in all the reports and responses. Federal funding came as a result of long lobbying
efforts. Provincial governments have all provided significant indirect
support such as the use of offices, meeting rooms, conservation labs,
computers, copiers, and telephones. In many cases, provincial governments have also made direct financial contributions to provincial associations, as have individual institutions. The grant programs are all
cost-shared: applicants must contribute 50 per cent of project costs,
through either in-kind or direct funding.

Promoted by both Symons and Wilson, the national guide to archival
holdings has now been realized in the website Archives Canada in a
way not dreamed of in their reports. Technology and descriptive standards make the guide easier to use and richer and more widely accessible than the paper *Union List*, and the continuing energy and commitment of the Canadian archival community ensure its growth. All that is
wanting is the funding necessary to support the technological fix that
will permit this tool's value to be fully realized through the addition of
finding aids, digitized records, and enhanced access through web
search engines. Additional funds are also required to arrange and describe records so millions more entries can be included.

The Symons Report discussed the necessity of raising the profile
of archives through promotion and advocacy so as to ensure that
records were placed in archives. The Wilson Report also drew attention to the image problem of archives with the public and called on
Heritage Canada to 'reassess its responsibility for all heritage matters
and specifically that it begin programs to involve the public in archival concerns.'[15] In the first round of goal setting, the CCA identified advocacy as its first strategic approach to fulfilling its vision, with
the idea that, without the public's knowledge of archives, archives
will not be funded. Politicians must hear about archives and the
voting public must tell them. Some examples of advocacy initiatives
launched by the CCA include: the coordination of a sustained
communications strategy across institutions; the 'Archives and You'
conferences; and the 'My Archives, My Government' addition to the
CCA website.

The difference between what was envisioned by the Symons Report
and what has been achieved by the establishment of the CCA stems
from the latter organization's leadership. In the CCA, leadership is
exercised not by the universities, not by the federal government, not by
any one institution, and not by the larger institutions. Rather, the CCA

is led collaboratively by a Board of Directors whose members come from provincial associations.

The CCA has been efficient and successful. In the first ten years of CCA grants, 1,265 arrangement and description projects were funded to deal with the backlog of unprocessed archival material; at the end of that period, a total of 34,468 linear metres of textual records, 3,941,289 photographs, 159,794 maps and architectural drawings, 68,028 sound recordings, 36,353 moving images, and a few electronic records had been processed. Descriptive standards were developed and training in the creation of descriptive standards was supported, the standards themselves being introduced by archival advisers and liaison officers in the provincial associations. This initiative eventually led to 51,000 fonds-level descriptions being added to Archives Canada. Two hundred and thirty-three professional training events received financial support. In addition, preservation assessments were carried out in every province, conservation manuals and tools were developed, and internships for master's of archival studies (MAS) students and graduates in the early years of these programs provided employment for students and brought recent graduates into the workforce.

The work of the 1970s and 1980s – the studies, reports, and responses to them – laid the infrastructure which has supported the development, advancement, and cooperative action of archives in Canada. In the years since then, this infrastructure, informally known as the 'Canadian archival system,' has served the profession, archival institutions, and society well. Archives have grown and gained capacity, associations of archivists have developed and produced well-respected journals and programs, schools of archival studies have been established and have thrived, and Canadian archivists have contributed on the international scene. The CCA, a unique creation, has been a central and important force in the Canadian archival system.

The CCA has proven to be a robust organization able to adapt to government's changing priorities and trends in administrative styles and to respond to evolving circumstances. It embodies still the principles that the reports, and responses to them, identified as important in a country as large and diverse as Canada and for a profession with its own diversity.

Still pressing and urgent is the matter of funding – funding the system we have and its constituent parts. A significant infusion of money for the CCA is critically needed. The association's budget has decreased in real dollars since its establishment. The $2.8 million originally allocated in

1986 has been reduced to $1.7 million. The resources allocated to support individual archives, whether from institutions such as universities or from governments, have been and remain scant.

Research is required in many areas of archival practice to find ways to better address long-standing demands and to meet new ones. Best-practices guides and training for implementation are needed. Standards are needed. Archivists' work is never done and grants are required still to permit archives to address the backlog of work in many areas of archival practice, ranging from processing records to preserving them as well as for innovative initiatives and for pilot projects. Expensive new challenges face archives. Preserving electronic records and making archival holdings available in digital form on the web are not inexpensive undertakings. Electronic records will not wait. Finding a floppy disc discarded in the back of a desk drawer is not like finding a diary that has been left in an attic for years. Electronic records require considerable ongoing expenditure of resources if they are to be preserved and made accessible. Archivists are also dealing with increased user expectations. The same electronic technology that is attracting new users is causing all users to want a response faster and to expect responses that have a greater level of specificity. Where should this funding come from?

Archives have sought or been forced to devise and apply new ways of self-support with mixed results. Some have been successful in obtaining *funding* as well as *records* from donors. These funds have been used to support the conservation or description of the records donated. Yet obtaining money from private donors is not likely or possible in many cases. User fees have also been suggested as a way for archives to raise funds. There are many sound arguments against such fees. They deter users, favour people with money while placing students and seniors at a disadvantage, are contrary to the notion of open access, extract a fee twice from taxpayers who already pay for archival services through the public purse, and inhibit scholarship. Moreover, archives are a public good. They protect citizens' rights and the public's memory, and so should be funded by government. The most convincing argument against user fees in our public institutions, however, is that although archivists *are* making money from services such as sales of copies, it is difficult to think that such fees could ever generate enough revenue to have much impact in funding an archive's operations.

While the CCA has succeeded in leveraging funding from all levels of government, archives have never received their share from the public purse as compared to funding for galleries, museums, the film industry, and other cultural pursuits.[16] The records an archives strives to make available may be used by these very recipients of funds *denied* archives. The educational and cultural uses of archives are clearly within the purview of what government supports. Why, then, has funding for archives been so woefully inadequate? Would an improved profile for archivists help rectify the situation? In 1984 the Society of American Archivists commissioned a study into 'The Image of Archivists: Resource Allocators' Perceptions,' a qualitative exercise aimed at understanding how those who sponsor archives perceive and characterize archives and archivists. One of the descriptors used for archivists was 'mousey' but also scholarly and amazingly good at finding what was wanted from the archives. The archives tended to be 'out of sight, out of mind.' If they were seen, they were considered to hark back to the past, play a passive role compared to more current, ongoing, aggressive demands on the budget, and lack political clout. The archives' needs were seen to have a relatively low priority compared to other budgetary demands.

Archivists' carrying out of their traditional roles in a competent manner has not led to adequate support for their work. Their contribution in safeguarding the rights of citizens to information is rarely popular with government. And, given that cuts to bureaucracy are always popular, their administrative role of promoting the benefits of good management of records is vulnerable. In terms of preserving records for posterity, posterity does not vote, and so the government is not inclined to pay attention to its demands. Archives are the foundation of culture, but in tough times culture and heritage are considered frills, and therefore expendable. Yet in better times museums and galleries have bested archives in acquiring government dollars because they are *frillier*, and therefore seen as more deserving of funds.

Improvements in the perception of archives and in resources for them were outcomes of the Symons and Wilson reports. However, the circle of support was somewhat limited and has been eroded since the reports were issued. Whether another major report would have such results is a moot point in the face of the larger conundrum of how archivists would trigger such a major undertaking.

This makes it all the more important for archivists to assemble and maintain up-to-date information on their programs, on their contributions to Canadian society, and on their needs. The CCA has taken on this responsibility by recently conducting a survey of Canadian archives, and it can continue to do so on an ongoing basis. Archivists could use targeted studies to help meet the challenge of preserving electronic records. It would be helpful to know which archives are bringing in electronic records and keeping them accessible and to have case studies of their experiences. A study could identify what is required to implement electronic-records programs, including the costs, the planning, implementation strategies, and so on, and on the basis of this data apply the necessary targeted funding.

Archivists can benefit from sharing their experiences in seeking funding. Archivists have become more astute in learning the ropes of government for funding requests and justifications. While certain approaches to budget justification or defence of current budgets are place-specific, sharing tactics and successes could be beneficial. At the very least, archivists may be tipped off to trends in management theory or policy initiative that will have an impact on what may appeal to those who make decisions on resource allocation. The CCA and its provincial and territorial councils provide a forum for such sharing. Clearly, there is no ticket to success, no magic wand, no silver bullet. Archivists must pursue opportunities to promote themselves. They must be creative and energetic and politically astute in seeking resources. And they certainly must avoid defeatism and negative second-guessing.

NOTES

1 This essay was initially prepared as a talk to a meeting of the Association of Canadian Archivists held in Saskatoon in 2005. The author and the editors would like to acknowledge the editorial contributions made by Shelley Sweeney.
2 T.H.B. Symons, *To Know Ourselves: The Report of the Commission on Canadian Studies* (Ottawa: Association of Universities and Colleges of Canada 1975). Hereafter referred to as Symons Report.
3 Symons Report, 82.
4 Ibid., 71.
5 Ibid., 74.
6 Ibid., 74.
7 'The Symons Report and Canadian Archives,' *Archivaria* 11 (winter 1980–1): 7.
8 Sir Hilary Jenkinson (1882–1961), a Cambridge-educated classics scholar, began his archival career in 1906 at the British Public Records Office (PRO), eventually becoming the PRO's deputy keeper. He had an enormously influential career and is perhaps best known in Canada for his *Manual of*

Archive Administration (1922, rev. 1937), one of the first major theoretical approaches to archival practice written in Britain.

9 Ibid., 11.

10 The Social Sciences and Humanities Research Council of Canada, or SSHRCC, was eventually split off from the Canada Council to support academic endeavours.

11 The 'ACA Guidelines towards a Curriculum for Graduate Archival Training Leading to a Master's Degree in Archival Science' was published in 1976.

12 Consultative Group on Canadian Archives, *Canadian Archives* (Ottawa: Social Sciences and Humanities Research Council of Canada 1980), 9.

13 Ibid., 15.

14 Ibid., 109.

15 Ibid., 110.

16 Editors' note: see Shelley Sweeney's essay in this volume, 'Lady Sings the Blues: The Public Funding of Archives, Libraries, and Museums in Canada,' for a discussion of this funding comparison.

2 Lady Sings the Blues: The Public Funding of Archives, Libraries, and Museums in Canada

SHELLEY SWEENEY

'Money is certainly not all there is to policy ... but most policy implementation will languish without it.'[1]

It is difficult to paint an accurate picture of public funding for culture in Canada. Part of the difficulty lies in comparing funding between libraries, museums, and archives. By reviewing variations in spending over time, however, this essay provides the basis for comparing relative changes and trends in priority.[2]

Total federal, provincial, and municipal government funding for all three sectors fluctuated from 1984 to 2004, but generally over the 1990s heritage institutions saw a 14 per cent reduction in government spending.[3] For example, even though the majority of federal spending on culture goes to broadcasting, in 1990 the Canadian Broadcasting Corporation had to close eleven of its regional stations as a result of budget cuts. Although government reports released in 1986 and 1992 recommended increases in government funding for culture, by 1995 the federal government had reduced its spending on several cultural programs; and the budget of the Department of Canadian Heritage was reduced by $675 million. Heritage institutions were not the only ones to suffer from these cuts. The publications distribution-assistance program and the book publishing industry-development program were reduced by 61 per cent in 1997. Priorities also shifted; in 1998 multimedia productions received a greater share of the dwindling Department of Canadian Heritage budget.

This trend to reduction reversed towards the end of the 1990s, during which time funding for culture in general began to increase.[4] For instance, after adjusting for inflation, between 1996 and 2006, the smallest museums and galleries in Canada experienced an 80 per cent increase in government funding. Most recently, however, in 2008 funding to the arts has been under attack again, with cuts of more than $44 million.[5]

With regard to the museum sector specifically, museums currently obtain a significant amount of their funding from the federal government. This was not always the case. Budgets for museums in Canada were relatively modest until the 1970s. The 1972 announcement of the National Museums Policy introduced the Museums Assistance Program (MAP), the National Inventory Program (which became known as the Canadian Heritage Information Network or CHIN), and the Canadian Conservation Institute.[6] The first two programs were responsible for pouring millions of dollars into museums across the country. Even at the height of cutbacks in the 1990s, the MAP distributed approximately $13.5 million in grants to non-federal museums and other related institutions in 1993–4.[7] In 1999 the minister of Canadian Heritage increased MAP grants by $2 million. Even with this increase, *A Sense of Place – A Sense of Being*, a report by the House of Commons Standing Committee on Canadian Heritage, recommended that Canadian Heritage increase funding for more cross-Canada tours and exhibits.[8]

A portion of federal funding also goes to cover federal museums. There are four official national museums (the National Gallery of Canada, the Canadian Museum of Civilization, the Canadian Museum of Nature, and the National Museum of Science and Technology), and three affiliated/component museums (the Canadian Museum of Contemporary Photography, the Canadian War Museum, and the Canadian Aviation Museum). These seven museums will soon be joined by an eighth, the Human Rights Museum in Winnipeg. Although private funds have essentially built this museum, the federal government of Canada will provide ongoing operating funds. The creation of the Portrait Gallery of Canada, which would have provided for both storage and exhibition space for portraits held by Library and Archives Canada (LAC), was axed as of November 2008.

By contrast, libraries in Canada have not received much in the way of federal funding. What federal funds exist have been used to pay for the various federal library programs. These would include, for example, the Library of Parliament, the Canada Institute for Scientific and Technical Information (CISTI), libraries of government departments and crown corporations, the regional library services of the Northwest

Territories, Nunavut, and Yukon, and library services to Indian bands. There has been a strong interest by the library community to access federal funds but so far this has not resulted in any significant grant or transfer programs outside the federal system.

Turning to archives, federal funds support LAC and eight federal Records Centres. Federal funding has also provided what little additional support archives receive beyond that of their sponsoring institution. Archives in Canada began to receive direct government grants beginning in 1986. In addition to providing secretariat support for the Canadian Council of Archives (CCA), a sustained grant program was introduced and funding was set at $1.4 million annually. In 1991, $1 million was added for a three-year period for the Conservation Plan for Canadian Archival Records (CPCAR). These new archival grants required a matching 50 per cent contribution from applicant institutions. During the cutbacks of the 1990s, there was an overall reduction in funding of 38 per cent to these programs.[9] From 1998 on, funding levels stabilized at approximately $1.7 million per year.[10]

Additional funds were provided for work on the Canadian Archival Information Network (CAIN) in October 2000. CAIN, now Archives Canada, was envisioned as a searchable database of all archival fonds across Canada. Funding for 2001 was $2.3 million, with $1.7 million approved for 2002,[11] provided by Canadian Heritage. However, the purpose of this funding changed during the grant program to support primarily a digitization program. It has now been cancelled altogether.

On the provincial side, funding of culture across Canada received a major boost when exemptions were made to the Criminal Code of Canada in 1969. This gave provincial and federal governments the ability to use lotteries to fund charitable activities such as the 1976 Montreal Olympics.[12] A 1985 amendment to the Criminal Code gave the provinces and territories exclusive control over gambling. Since then, substantial revenues have accrued from the provincial and territorial governments' virtual monopoly on gambling in Canada. This helps explain the increase in provincial support for culture during the lean 1990s. Although funding for culture varies enormously from province to province, in general this funding has been gradually increasing. Ontario, for example, provided its first grants to five local museums in 1953. Over the years, it established a complete system of financial support consisting of grants to develop museums and to assist in their operating budgets. In order to encourage activity and generate revenue, the operating grants were based on the museum's income. By 1979, $1.7 million was granted by Ontario's Ministry of Culture and

Recreation to over two hundred museums.[13] While funding for archives in Alberta and Quebec has generally been more generous than in the rest of Canada, most provincial monies have been aimed at supporting province-wide initiatives – such as archival advisers and provincial web portals to descriptions of archival records.

Libraries, by contrast, derive most of their funding from municipalities. This is a reflection in part of funding for schools – and, by extension, school libraries – through taxes on property. But, in general, a significant amount of municipal funding goes to fund public libraries. Municipal funding for museums has been relatively modest in comparison. Municipal funding for archives has been negligible, and probably only accounts for spending on the small number of municipal archives that exist in Canada. Remarkably, in the 1990s, when the federal government was wrestling down the deficit and funding for culture was in a free fall, municipal funding of culture actually increased. The recipients of this increase, however, were mostly libraries. Actual expenditures on libraries increased by $144 million, or 15 per cent, between 1991 and 1994, while archives experienced a 67 per cent drop in funding during the same time.

The inevitable conclusion from all this is that, in terms of overall funding, archives have not been well served by the public purse. Figure 2.1 shows the funding for the three sectors at all levels of government.[14] Libraries receive the most funding from all three levels of government combined. Thirty per cent of all public expenditure on culture goes to libraries. They consume 40 per cent of provincial/territorial and 80 per cent of municipal expenditures on culture.[15]

One might be justified in wondering whether archives receive the least amount of public funding simply because of their relatively small numbers. A quick overview paints a different picture (see Table 2.1). At one time the numbers of libraries in Canada completely overwhelmed those of archives and museums, and those archives that existed had very small budgets indeed. As late as 1978, only thirty Canadian archives had annual budgets of over $75,000, not a significant amount even by 1970s dollars.[16] The numbers of archives and museums have increased significantly since the late 1970s, however. Libraries, in contrast, have been decreasing in number as communities and hence public libraries decline in rural Canada and as government libraries are closed or consolidated. In 1978, according to the Consultative Group on Canadian Archives, there were 321 archives in Canada.[17] By 1987, when the provincial councils of archives gathered information for their needs-assessment and

Figure 2.1: Public funding of cultural institutions, 2003–4, by thousands of dollars

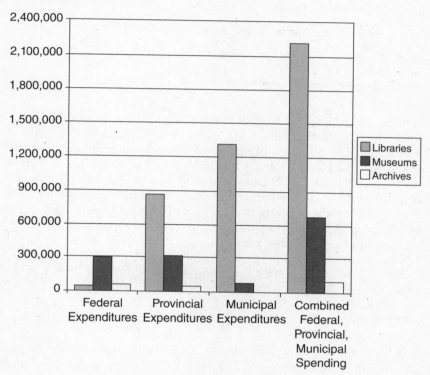

planning studies, there were 627 archives in Canada; by 1992, the number had risen to 700,[18] and in 2008, 800 archives had been identified, including ones residing in other types of repositories, such as libraries and museums.[19] This last fact – that archives are rarely stand-alone facilities but most often are part of other institutions such as libraries and museums – make it some-what difficult to tease out an accurate picture of the numbers.

In contrast, according to the *Canadian Almanac & Directory*, there were 631 museums in Canada in 1978; according to Statistics Canada, 1,164 museums in 1987 and 1,227 museums in 1992; and finally, as self-reported by the Canadian Museums Association (CMA), 2,500 mu-seums and related institutions in 2008. This number includes what one traditionally thinks of as museums, as well as art galleries, science

Table 2.1

	Archives	Libraries	Museums
1978	321	2,679	631
1987	627	3,557	1,164
1992	700	3,856	1,227
2008	800	3,685	2,500

centres, aquaria, sports halls of fame, artist-run centres, zoos, and historic sites. Confusingly, the CMA includes archives in its definition of a museum. The directory of museums includes such organizations as the Appaloosa Horse Club of Canada Museum and Archives as well as the University of Guelph Library's Archives and Special Collections.[20] It is not entirely clear whether the directory simply includes in their total number those archives that are part of a larger museum or whether it is counting archival sections of museums as separate institutions. As a comparison, another report suggests that there were just under 1,500 museums in 2002.[21]

There were 2,679 libraries excluding school libraries in 1978, 3,557 in 1987, 3,856 in 1992, and 3,685 in 2008, according to the *American Library Directory*. Of course, when one includes school libraries, the number is much higher: as the authors like to point out, more libraries than Tim Horton's and McDonald's restaurants combined![22]

If we look at public funding on a per-capita basis today, as per Figure 2.2, we can see quite clearly that, although archives occupy 11 per cent of the total numbers in the three sectors, they only receive 3 per cent of the total funding from all levels of government. The situation has not changed much over time. This is a particularly disturbing fact given that the largest archives in the country, employing the most archivists, are in fact government archives.

The nature of archives is that they are both cultural and administrative. One would think that such diversity of purpose would be a reason to celebrate. This means that archives are relevant to more than one audience, for different reasons. On the whole, however, administrators do not deal well with diversity. Diversity makes departments such as archives difficult to pigeonhole and administrators like to categorize their departments; it makes the process of administration easier.

In Canada, archives usually fall under departments of culture and heritage, which often has the unfortunate effect of causing the

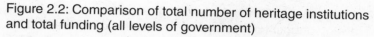

Figure 2.2: Comparison of total number of heritage institutions and total funding (all levels of government)

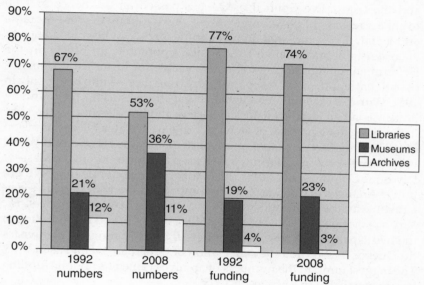

administrative nature of archives to be ignored. Likewise, many university archives report to library administrations, which ironically have traditionally treated archives as repositories for private papers and 'special collections' supporting the research interests of scholars. Yet archives are often responsible for records management, freedom of information, support of democratic rights, and other legal responsibilities that have little to do with two tasks generally associated with cultural institutions, supporting tourism and attracting visitors and scholars. And when it comes to the public funding of archives, the underappreciated administrative side of archives and the comparison of archives to museums and planetariums and zoos contribute to the underfunding.

Historic Development of Heritage Institutions

Understanding the current situation of funding for all heritage sectors in Canada requires a review of their historic development. Turning first to archives, their severe and chronic underfunding arises in part from their late development. Although the administration of New France proposed the appointment of a custodian of the official archives in 1724 and the Legislative Council of Quebec passed an ordinance in 1790 to collect records of the administration, 'such initiatives were sporadic and isolated.'[23] A national archives for Canada can be traced back to an order-in-council dated 1872 which appointed an officer in the Department of Agriculture to be responsible for historical documents of national significance. A separate department came into being only in 1912. With the exception of a few archival efforts, such as the founding of the Canadian Baptist Historical Society and its collection in 1865, the nationwide development of archives came much later.[24] The expansion of government archives took place particularly after the Second World War when the volume of records increased and the report of the Massey-Lévesque Commission of 1951 called for an increased role for the (then) Public Archives of Canada.[25] Further impetus came with Canada's centennial year, the publication of T.H B. Symons's *To Know Ourselves: The Report of the Commission on Canadian Studies* in 1975, and the founding of the two separate archival organizations, the Association des archivistes du Québec in 1968 and the Association of Canadian Archivists in 1975. The biggest jump in the numbers of archives came after public funding became available to archives in 1985.

In comparison, museums had a similar start to archives, but a different development. Unofficially, priests in eighteenth-century religious institutions in Quebec and the Maritimes employed natural-history collections in their teaching while the Université Laval had a mineralogical collection as early as the 1790s.[26] In the early 1800s, miscellaneous collections were assembled and periodically displayed in libraries or government buildings. The first museum in Canada seems to have been opened by a private citizen, Thomas Barnett of Niagara Falls, in 1831.[27] Federally, museums began officially in 1856, with the creation of a museum at the Geological Survey of Canada.[28] As with archives, the growth of museums was relatively slow, as noted in the Miers-Markham Report of 1932 and the Massey-Lévesque Report of 1951.[29] A major boost in the numbers of museums in Canada came with the one-hundredth-anniversary celebrations of Confederation in 1967. This was followed closely by the passing in 1970 of the UNESCO Convention on the Means of Prohibiting and Preventing the Illicit Import, Export and Transfer of Ownership of Cultural Property. The subsequent push to compile an inventory of all museum and art objects led to the Trudeau government's announcement in 1972 of the National Museums Policy and a significant injection of federal funds to develop museums. Within the following decade, nearly every province created its own grant programs for museums.[30] This policy was responsible for an explosion in the growth of museums across Canada. The Canadian Museums Association, started in Quebec in 1947, became a strong advocate.

Although the National Library of Canada was founded only in 1953, libraries in Canada can trace their history back to the libraries of early religious orders such as the Canadian Jesuit mission of 1632 and the Jesuit College in Quebec City which was established in 1635.[31] Libraries were also established at various settlements and fur-trade and military posts in the eighteenth and nineteenth centuries. Staff of the Montreal General Hospital founded what became the McGill Faculty of Medicine Library in 1823.[32] Also in Montreal, the Atwater Library, established in 1828, was the first so-called mechanics' institute in continental British North America.[33] These mechanics' institutes were patterned after ones that had sprung up in England and Scotland. As part of their programs, the mechanics' institutes provided libraries as well as some small museum collections in order to educate workers for developing industries. In Guelph, the first circulating library began operating out of the backroom of a city merchant's store in 1832. In 1882 Ontario passed the Free Libraries Act, which allowed municipalities to establish libraries using locally collected taxes.[34] This pattern was replicated across the country. And in the early part of the twentieth century, libraries in Canada, particularly in Ontario, received a strong boost from Andrew Carnegie of the United States. Carnegie, a philanthropist who had made his fortune through the steel industry, believed that every member of society was entitled to a free education and was convinced that libraries were a cornerstone of that effort. He donated $56 million during his lifetime to build 2,509 libraries throughout the world, of which 125 were built in Canada.[35] Carnegie did not give his grants for libraries without stipulation; all towns that received a grant were required to follow 'The Carnegie Formula,' with an annual subsidy equal to one-tenth of the cost of the library building. Municipal funding became and continues to be the most significant support for libraries. The Canadian Library Association, founded in 1946, has acted as an advocate for libraries in Canada.

Government Responsibility for Culture

Following this historical overview, the question may arise: Should governments even be responsible for funding culture? The answer from the many reports and commissions that have examined this question has been a resounding yes. There were several significant developments in the recognition of government responsibility for culture, particularly during the latter half of the twentieth century. The original constitutional division of powers that occurred in Canada in 1867 granted responsibility for both education and culture to the provinces. This quickly changed, however, into a shared responsibility with the federal government. Parallel structures within both levels of government handle this responsibility today. In 1973 the Culture Statistics Program was established at Statistics Canada to collect relevant statistics for this sector. In 1980 responsibility for cultural affairs was transferred from the secretary of state to the minister of communication. In 1980 the federal and provincial ministers responsible for culture met for the first time. Shortly after, in 1982, the Applebaum-Hébert Report was published; it encouraged the federal government to 'muster the political will to transform our cultural landscape.'[36]

There was a slight hiccup in the increasing responsibility that government took for culture. Amendments to the Income Tax Act in 1991 transferred the responsibility for determining fair-market value from what was then Revenue Canada to the Canadian Cultural Property Export Review Board. The 1992 *Report of the Standing Committee on Culture and Communications: "The Ties That Bind"* delineated a role for the federal government that envisioned a more integrated policy and planning function among all federal departments with responsibility for culture and a close relationship with 'other levels of government, the private sector and Canada's cultural community.' The Department of Canadian Heritage was created in 1993 from several departments to take major responsibility for Canadian culture. The 1999 federal report *A Sense of Place* stressed the need for interdependence and multisite planning and policy development. In other words, support for culture must move beyond the Department of Canadian Heritage. Thus, there has been a recognition that government is responsible, at least in part, for funding culture and, by extension, heritage.

Economic Advantages of Culture

In 2004 the Culture Statistics Program published a research paper entitled *Canadian Framework for Culture Statistics*. A careful reading of the report is illuminating. The report's goal is to adopt standard definitions of culture and to create a conceptual framework that will lead to the development of 'culture indicators based on approved conventions, yielding coherent and accurate analytical conclusions.'[37] This would be extremely helpful to the cultural community. Unfortunately, the report then goes on to add that the framework is to provide 'measures of the economic impact of the culture sector, the size and characteristics of the culture labor force, the value of international trade for culture goods and services, [and] the value of consumer spending on culture goods and services.' Reading the entire report makes it quite clear that these *economic* aspects interest the government the most. After their discussion of culture consumption, purchaser and consumer, and the 'creative chain' that includes manufacturing and distribution, the authors claim that 'the creative chain works best for physical goods.' They might well have added that the model works best for physical goods *that are sold.* Such culture goods include books, magazines, newspapers, postcards, films, videos, paintings, and so on. Archives provide content services that are not sold, for the creation of culture goods by others. Even though the report includes the preservation of human heritage as part of the definition of culture, it nonetheless claims that a special case must be made for this kind of heritage.

Heritage, particularly archives, is an uneasy fit in this framework, which classifies various culture activities and places archives under 'other information services.' This heading also oddly includes news syndicates under the 'creation' category, libraries and archives under the 'production' category, and grant services, social-advocacy organizations, and business, professional, labour, and other membership organizations under 'support services.' The authors struggle somewhat to wedge into the report an activity that does not lead directly to the flow of dollars.

The Statistics Canada report that grew from this framework was entitled *Economic Contribution of Culture in Canada.* Overall, the culture sector, which includes the heritage areas under discussion as well as industries such as publishing and film, contributed approximately 3.8 per cent of the Gross Domestic Product (GDP) to the Canadian economy in 2001. The value of the contribution went from a respectable $29 billion in 1996 to $38 billion in 2001, an increase of 31.7 per cent. A closer analysis however, shows that the largest contributors to culture GDP were written media, broadcasting, and the film industry. Libraries accounted for about 4 per cent of culture GDP on average over the period 1996 to 2001, and museums 3 per cent. Astonishingly, archives do not actually figure in this report. The report looks at admissions fees and services including duplicating, fees, and fines. It does not consider any such services as supplied by archives, probably because these statistics have not been gathered.

Nationally, most heritage sectors reported an increase in GDP growth rates in every year between 1996 and 2001, for an overall percentage increase of 24.4 per cent. Similarly, employment in the culture sector between 1996 and 2001 increased 18 per cent, exhibiting an average annual rate of 3.4 per cent, higher than the growth rate of the overall Canadian economy. Ironically, while libraries actually declined on both these measures during this period, they remain, overall, the best-funded of the heritage areas.

Provincially, the culture sector was an important contributor to provincial GDP from 1996 to 2001, with growth in all provinces.[38] The culture sector was of increasing importance to provincial economies if one considers numbers of employees. Employment in the culture sector grew in all provinces during this period except in New Brunswick and Nova Scotia. Culture GDP and employment accounted for just under 5 per cent of overall provincial GDP and employment.

What can we conclude from these figures? While museums, archives, and libraries cannot compare to the money-making capabilities of other players in the cultural sector, there is nonetheless some money-generating potential. Of the three sectors, museums are the most likely to succeed at generating income through admission fees and the sales of items relating to their collections. Although museums have been struggling to move from 'publicly supported cultural repository to market oriented private sector entertainment/tourism industry,' they have acknowledged that they must make this transition.[39] *A Sense of Place* goes further. The report stresses the relationship between production, distribution, marketing, and promotion and notes that museums understand the relationship and take advantage of it.

Whereas museums provide both information and entertainment, libraries and archives fall predominantly into the information industry. While the government realizes this, one has the sense that it is particularly unhappy about the fact that archives do not generate more revenue. An article from Statistics Canada notes that heritage institutions 'increasingly find themselves competing with other players in the entertainment sector for audiences and discretionary dollars.'[40] Archives, the article says with a hint of disapproval, obtained only 3.1 per cent of their funds from earned revenues in 1997 whereas the equivalent figure for aquariums was 80.5 per cent. Clearly, this is a new twist on the old adage about comparing apples and oranges – in our case, archives and aquariums.

The Use of Archives

In relation to heritage services, the authors of *Canadian Framework for Culture Statistics* point out that there is an issue with the fact that there may be heritage objects that will never be displayed. If one considers this applied to archives, the vast majority of archival materials will never be 'displayed' or used yet the material needs to be kept as evidence. This goes directly against the statement the authors make that the production of culture goods and services 'has no impact unless they are used.' Democracy depends upon authentic and reliable evidence held in archival records that are potentially available regardless of whether it is ever actually used or not. Its very existence is mute testimony to the activities of various levels of government and organizations. This argument for keeping archival materials, however, has never been particularly compelling to many outside the archival field. Keeping evidence makes governments and organizations accountable, which can work against their interests.

Given archives' unique holdings, what would constitute a reasonable measure of use? Libraries can point to their number of visitors. As the *National Core Library Statistics Program* pointed out, 'in 1999 more Canadians went to libraries than to movie theatres.'[41] Museums can also count numbers of visitors. In 1995, for example, museums and galleries counted 26,882,000 visitors, while archives claimed 641,000.[42] Both libraries and museums are fortunate to have large numbers of students of all ages to boost their in-person statistics. Students have never been, and some might argue may never be, a significant part of the traditional audience for visiting archives. Without mediation, even some of the most experienced researchers may have difficulty in successfully navigating all the complexities of an archives, let alone inexperienced students. Preservation issues actually work against large numbers of individuals of any age and experience handling fragile materials. Archives can toy with some of the methods their sister institutions employ to lure users to their institutions, such as creating both physical and virtual exhibits, sponsoring readings or lectures, or selling reproductions of choice archival materials in their repositories. Unfortunately, no amount of outreach will ever produce for archives the numbers of users that libraries and museums have. The materials are just too challenging to use.

However it is looked at, counting the number of visitors to an archives is almost meaningless. In-person visitors constitute a very small fraction of the users of archives. Archives are routinely accessed by other means such as e-mail, fax, and telephone. In fact, visits to archival websites and use of e-mail for reference enquiries have skyrocketed. Statistics Canada, however, continues to use numbers of visitors as the yardstick to compare heritage sectors, which leaves it to conclude that 'museums are consistently the most popular type of heritage institution in Canada.'[43]

Sometimes, archivists point to the fact that archives foster knowledge among people who never enter the archives. For instance, a single user may produce a film, a television program, or a book that is enjoyed by many thousands. This is a true, but not exclusive, argument. It is in fact also true of every library. No reputable researcher or writer would produce a product for which they had not consulted some sort of published or secondary source. In fact, all too often, researchers consult *only* secondary sources and ignore primary archival material when creating their 'culture good.'

However, the Massey-Lévesque Commission of 1951 advocated that '"cultural defenses" deserved as much attention as military defense to secure our borders.'[44] The support of the idea of a sovereign nation resisting the flood of American culture is considered to be a critical function of museums.[45] This will become only more important in today's global marketplace and information society. There is also the expectation by the government that 'culture goods' and services exhibit desired characteristics such as 'Canadianness' and provide Canadian content. This is something that Canadian archives, with their store of unique materials created by Canadians over the course of the nation's history, are ideally suited to provide.

Conclusion

Archivists have long desired better core funding. They have been constantly frustrated that they are unable to keep up with core activities: acquiring records and making them available through arrangement and description. The *Report of the Advisory Committee on Archives* in 1985 encouraged archives to be active in seeking grants, interacting with funding agencies, and lobbying for public funding.[46]

But archives cannot compete with libraries at the municipal level. While they have definitely improved their funding at provincial levels, federal funds will likely always be unstable, growing or decreasing as different governments with different agendas, indeed different ministers of culture and heritage, come and go. Without a major catalyst, such as occurred with the passing of the UNESCO Convention on Cultural Property in 1972, it is not likely that the funding will substantially increase in a permanent way. The conclusion of *A Sense of Place* was that 'the Government of Canada cannot be the sole source of funding for cultural initiatives.' Although the cultural sector will continue to grow as it has in the past fifty years, the authors note that the rapid growth rate in the cultural sector in Canada will not be funded entirely by the government: 'Public funding will continue to play an important part, but the bulk of the financial resources will have to come from individual Canadians, either as members of an audience, as volunteers or as patrons.'[47] This sentiment has been repeated in report after report and accurately reflects the new reality. Archivists need to accept this.

From a developmental point of view, archivists have now moved past the stage that Canadian museum curators were at in the 1950s. At that stage, museum curators thought that the true work of the museum was research in order to produce knowledge; the visiting public was merely tolerated. Likewise, many archivists in the 1960s and 1970s, perhaps as late as the 1980s, saw their work as producing elaborate finding aids for a select scholarly clientele. The general public was merely tolerated. But now that archivists appreciate the importance of a broad clientele, how will they attract more patrons? They will be forced to market themselves the same way as all the other cultural sectors. This means that archives must understand their audiences better, and they must 'tailor policies, programs, products and services to meet changing consumer expectations.'[48] Archives have already begun to do this without even realizing it; by digitizing their resources they have made these records accessible to a new generation which relies more heavily on the Internet and in turn have introduced these users to the concepts related to archives so that they have the skills to pursue their research interests further should they desire. This does not mean that archives should 'dumb down' their product, as once feared by archival theorist Terry Cook: 'Archives must not be turned into the McDonald's of Information, where everything is carefully measured to meet every customer profile and every market demographic.'[49] Only a small segment of the general population will ever avail themselves of archival material; the trick is ensuring that all those who need and wish to avail themselves do so. Every effort to bring archives to the attention of new users usually results in some gain.

Not only must archives broaden their user base, they must properly and convincingly document this phenomenon.[50] The CCA and LAC have both determined that they must better document not only how federal funds are spent by their constituents but how the products that are created by these funds are employed. This will assist in assessing the success of any grant programs. In the late 1970s, collection of data on Canadians' leisure activities proved that 'participation in cultural activities was as widespread as participation in sports.'[51] This resulted in substantial amounts of lottery funds being allocated to the arts. Archives must also document their successes.

Obtaining better support from sponsoring institutions requires a different sort of effort than what archivists have been used to in the past. Archivists not only need to support their institutions' information needs as they have always done; they also need to be active in winning recognition for these efforts. Each institution will value these efforts in a different way. Archivists will have to work within the organizational culture in which they find themselves, rather than bemoaning the fact that they are not in a more congenial situation. Part of the lack of profile of archives rests with the fact that they are often not stand-alone repositories but rather are small parts of larger, better recognized institutions. Thus, it is more difficult for them to carve out a separate identity. But their materials are unique and their services are distinct, which makes a good basis for creating a positive profile.

Raising the profiles of archives with the public is equally essential. It is not the fault of archivists that society does not appreciate archives as a public good and fund them to the extent necessary for archivists to do their jobs adequately. But, if archivists do not promote archives, no one will do it for them. It is only with a greater appreciation of archives by society that governments will provide better support. Governments respond to voter interests. Archivists must stop lingering at the stage where they feel 'their project is so worthwhile they assume that once the public is aware of it, they will patronize it.'[52]

Raising public profile and private funds will not be easy. Archives are entering the fund-raising game just as all other charitable and non-profit organizations have increased their efforts. Arts and heritage organizations have typically not been the targets for charitable giving. A survey conducted in 2000 among Canadians over fifteen years of age found that culture was the lowest-ranking charitable cause in terms of numbers of donors.[53] Nevertheless, during the 1990s, private donations to heritage organizations grew by 23 per cent.[54] Archives have much to recommend them as a potential recipient for charitable giving. Archivists, however, do not have the training to do fund-raising on their own and this will be difficult, even if they come to accept that it is a necessity. For those wishing to make a significant contribution, the trend likely will be smaller numbers of donors giving larger donations.[55]

However much it goes against the grain, the funding situation will not change without the active promotion of archives by archivists. This necessitates doing less in other areas of work, however unpalatable that may be, as well as changing how things are done. Finally, archivists need to stop singing the blues and change their song to a new tune. Only then will the funding situation improve.

NOTES

1 Richard I. Hofferbert and Ian Budge, 'Patterns of Postwar Expenditure Priorities in Ten Democracies,' in Louis M. Imbeau and Robert D. McKinlay, eds., *Comparing Government Activity* (New York: St Martin's Press 1996), 30.
2 Ibid.
3 *Canadian Encyclopedia*, 'Arts, Heritage and Cultural Industries Funding,' http://www.thecanadianencyclopedia.com/index.cfm?PgNm=TCE&Params=A1ARTA0000341 (accessed 28 September 2008).
4 Statistics Canada, *The Daily: Government Expenditures on Culture*, 7 January 2004, http://www.statcan.ca/Daily/English/040107/d040107a.htm (accessed 28 August 2008).
5 'Make the Case for Culture to Ordinary Canadians, Artists Told,' http://www.CBC.ca/arts/story/2008/09/11/arts-panel.html (accessed 28 October 2008).
6 Canadian Heritage Information Network, 'About CHIN,' http://www.chin.gc.ca/English/About_Chin/index.html (accessed 18 November 2008).
7 Danielle Cliche and Terrence Cowl, 'Canada,' http://www.culturelink.hr/culpol/Canada.html (accessed 17 November 2008).
8 *A Sense of Place – A Sense of Being: The Evolving Role of the Federal Government in Support of Culture in Canada*, http://www2.parl.gc.ca/HousePublications/Publication.aspx?DocId=1031610&Language=E&Mode=1&Parl=36&Ses=1 (accessed 19 September 2008).

9   Canadian Council of Archives, 'CCA Response: Evaluation of the Grants and Contributions Program, LAC,' 24 June 2004, http://www.cdncouncilarchives.ca/whnew2.html?7 (accessed 30 December 2008).

10 Library and Archives Canada (LAC), 'Formative Evaluation of the National Archival Development Program Final Report,' http://www.collectionscanada.gc.ca/about–us/014/012014–209–e.html (accessed 7 September 2008).

11 LAC, *Evaluation of the Canadian Archival Information Network (CAIN): Final Report*, http://www.collectionscanada.gc.ca/about-us/014/012014-201-e.html (accessed 4 September 2008).

12 Rhys Stevens, 'Legalized Gambling in Canada,' http://www.abgaminginstitute.alberta.ca/pdfs/Gambling_in_Canada.pdf (accessed 14 September 2008).

13 *Community Museums Policy for Ontario* (1981), http://www.culture.gov.on.ca/english/heritage/museums/mupolicy.htm (accessed 7 September 2008).

14 Statistics Canada, *Government Expenditures on Culture: Data Tables 2003–04*, http://www.statcan.ca/english/freepub/87F0001XIE/2006001/method.htm (accessed 11 October 2008).

15 *Canadian Encyclopedia*, 'Arts, Heritage and Cultural Industries Funding.'

16 Anne MacDermaid, 'Applications of Computers in Canadian Archives,' in International Council on Archives, *Second European Conference on Archives: Proceedings* (Ann Arbor, Mich.: ICA 1989), 95.

17 *Canadian Archives: Report to the Social Sciences and Humanities Research Council of Canada by the Consultative Group on Canadian Archives* (Ottawa: Social Sciences and Humanities Research Council of Canada 1980), 30.

18 Marcel Caya, ed., *Canadian Archives in 1992* (Ottawa: Canadian Council of Archives 1992), 17.

19 Canadian Council of Archives.

20 'Canada's Museums,' Canadian Museum Association, http://www.museums.ca/en/info_resources/canadas_museums/ (accessed 4 September 2008).

21 AEA Consulting, *Museums, Libraries and Archives Council: Research Project 'Cultural Spend and Infrastructure: a Comparative Study,'* 47.

22 Ralph W. Manning, 'Counting Libraries: Reading between the Lines,' *Focus on Culture* (summer 1997), http://www.statcan.ca/english/ads/87-004-XPB/pdf/fcis1997009002s2.pdf (accessed 18 November 2008).

23 Ian Wilson, 'Archives,' *Canadian Encyclopedia*, http://www.thecanadianencyclopedia.com/index.cfm?PgNm=TCE&Params=A1ARTA0000290 (accessed 1 September 2008).

24 http://www.macdiv.ca/students/baptistarchives.php (accessed 1 September 2008).

25 *Report – Royal Commission on National Development in the Arts, Letters, and Sciences 1949–51* (Ottawa: King's Printer 1951).

26 George Lammers, 'Art Galleries and Museums,' *Canadian Encylopedia*, http://www.thecanadianencyclopedia.com/index.cfm?PgNm=TCE&Params=A1ARTA0000329 (accessed 1 September 2008).

27 Ibid.

28 http://cgc.rncan.gc.ca/hist/logan/museum_e.php (accessed 1 September 2008).

29 Sir Henry Miers and S.F. Markham, *The Museums of Canada* (Edinburgh: T. and A. Constable 1932).

30 Lammers, 'Art Galleries and Museums.'

31 Margaret Beckman, Moshie Dahms, and Lauren Bruce, 'Libraries,' *Canadian Encyclopedia*, http://www.thecanadianencyclopedia.com/index.cfm?PgNm=TCE&Params=A1ARTA0004674 (accessed 24 November 2008).

32 http://www.health.library.mcgill.ca/OSLER/exhibits/175th/begins.htm (accessed 1 September 2008).

33 http://www.atwaterlibrary.ca/en/taxonomy/term/8 (accessed 1 September 2008).

34 http://www.library.guelph.on.ca/about/history.cfm (accessed 1 September 2008).

35 'Andrew Carnegie,' Ontario Ministry of Culture, http://www.culture.gov.on.ca/english/library/carnegie/carnegie_bio.htm (accessed 4 September 2008).

36 Federal Cultural Policy Review Committee, *Report* (Ottawa, 1982), 12.

37 Statistics Canada, *Canadian Framework for Culture Statistics* (Ottawa: Statistics Canada 2004) (accessed 5 September 2008).

38 Vik Singh, 'Economic Contribution of the Culture Sector in Canada – a Provincial Perspective' (Ottawa: Statistics Canada 2004), 15.

39 Leighann C. Nielsen, 'The Development of Marketing in the Canadian Museum Community, 1840–1989,' http://jmk.sagepub.com (accessed 19 September 2008).

40 Fidel Ifedi, 'Changing Times for Heritage Institutions,' *Focus on Culture* 12 (winter 2000): 8.

41 Alvin M. Schrader and Michael R. Brundin, *National Core Library Statistics Program*, 'Statistical Report, 1999: Cultural and Economic Impact of Libraries on Canada 2002.'

42 *A Sense of Place.*

43 Ifedi, 'Changing Times,' 8.

44 Quoted in Nielsen, 'The Development of Marketing.'

45 Quoted in ibid.

46 Ian E. Wilson, chair, *Report of the Advisory Committee on Archives* (Ottawa: SSHRCC 1985).

47 *A Sense of Place*.

48 Ibid.

49 Terry Cook, 'Viewing the World Upside Down: Reflections on the Theoretical Underpinnings of Archival Public Programming,' *Archivaria* 31 (winter 1990–1), http://journals.sfu.ca/archivar/index.php/archivaria/article/view/11725/12674 (accessed 18 November 2008).

50 LAC, *Evaluation of the Grants and Contributions Program: Final Report*, http://www.collectionscanada.gc.ca/about-us/014/012014-202-e.html (accessed 4 September 2008).

51 Terry Cheney, 'Golden Nuggets: Striking It Rich with Cultural Data,' *Focus on Culture* 2 (summer 1990): 3.

52 Quoted in Nielsen, 'The Development of Marketing.'

53 AEA Consulting, *Museums, Libraries and Archives*, 54.

54 *Canadian Encyclopedia*, 'Arts, Heritage and Cultural Industries Funding.'

55 AEA Consulting, *Museums, Libraries and Archives*, 55.

PART TWO

Access and Privacy

3 Access-to-Information Legislation: A Critical Analysis

JO-ANN MUNN GAFUIK

The authors of *The Culture Shift to Transparency* argue that 'the last decades of the 20th century saw a dramatic shift in the values, norms, and cultures of information.'[1] Few would disagree. Although opacity and outright secrecy are still powerfully entrenched in some spheres and in some domains, a culture shift towards transparency, to the open flow of information, and to accountability has clearly advanced worldwide. Indeed, the rise of transparency in pursuit of the ideal democratic society is so persistent and so widespread that it is considered by many to be a 'social fact.'[2]

Freedom-of-information (FOI) legislation, where it exists, has played a critical role in supporting this shift toward transparency because it provides a mechanism for access to information that has traditionally been managed and controlled by government. It inevitably recognizes and expands the notion of the government's 'duty to disclose' and the public's 'right of access' to information in the custody of authorities in centres of power. Furthermore, since information asymmetry between a government and its citizens limits democratic participation and accountability, removing the asymmetry – that is, increasing the flow of information to the public – allows for meaningful popular participation and oversight of government. Access to information is, therefore, considered to be a precondition for informed public participation, and effective freedom-of-information legislation is regarded as the hallmark of a strong democracy.[3]

Some critics have argued, however, that freedom-of-information legislation has not had a positive impact on transparency in Canada, at least not at the federal level. In an article published in 2005, Alasdair Roberts described a 'government-wide pattern of resistance'[4] intended, in his view, to minimize the disruptive potential of the Access to Information Act[5] and, in effect, diminish the relevance of the legislation as a tool for providing a transparent view into the operations of government. Matthew Yeager goes further. He asserts that the phrase 'freedom of information' represents 'a certain kind of public myth.'[6] He writes: 'So-called liberal, democratic governments keep a lot of information secret, or prevent its disclosure through obfuscation and delay, but use the ideology of access to government information as a means of shoring up the state's legitimacy.'[7] He comments that it would be 'false advertising'[8] to suggest that private citizens use the law to access government information so that they can participate more fully in the democratic process. He notes, and others concur, that because of the complexity of the law and the difficulty of navigating the internal procedures set up to access government information, access requests are more typically filed by those who have developed some expertise in the field such as advocacy and special-interest groups, the media, and opposition politicians.[9] Furthermore, as John Crosbie said in 1997, 'in the vast majority of instances, embarrassment and titillation are the only objects of access-to-information requests.'[10] The end result, according to this group of analysts, is that the law is, at best, a 'pointless irritant'[11] and, at worst, a threat to the government's ability to govern effectively.

In this essay I reconsider this pessimistic conclusion by examining the role of the FOI legislation in contributing to and supporting changing cultural norms surrounding the public's right of access to information and the government's duty to disclose. I explore the inherent tension between public expectations of transparency on the one hand and concerns about governability on the other and examine the challenge of balancing the duty to disclose with the need to protect privacy. I argue that the process of transformation has, indeed, begun among the variety of actors who manage, control, and seek access to government information, but I also acknowledge that accountability and transparency may not become a matter of routine at the federal level until the transition from a 'highly centralized, command-and-control style of government to one in which public authority is distributed across a wider number of citizens and organizations'[12] is more advanced.

Canadian Context

The Canadian Access to Information Act (ATIA) was proclaimed in force on 1 July 1983, almost twenty years after New Democratic Party

MP Barry Mather first introduced the concept as a private member's bill. The legislation established a right of access to government-held information, subject to limited and specific exceptions, and provided a new mechanism by which citizens and permanent residents could access government information.[13]

In 2001 policy analyst Mary Franceschet wrote that 'it is fair to say that accountability [was] the driving force behind access to information legislation in Canada. The process to introduce access legislation was initially sparked by the belief that stronger accountability mechanisms were required in government and promoting the Act in the early 1980's was all about accountability.'[14] The government of the day clearly recognized that access to the 'information and options available to the decision-makers'[15] was important for effective accountability, public participation in decision making, and increasing public knowledge. Some politicians, however, suggested that it was also, and maybe essentially, about power. Joe Clark, then leader of the Official Opposition, said: 'We are talking about the reality that real power is limited to those who have facts. In a democracy that power and that information should be shared broadly. In Canada today they are not, and to that degree we are no longer a democracy in any sensible sense of that word. There is excessive power concentrated in the hands of those who hide public information from the people and Parliament of Canada.'[16]

The timing may have had a lot to do with circumstances in the political arena in the late 1970s. Roberts writes that 'a combination of circumstances – frustration over the declining power of Parliament, deteriorating economic performance, constitutional instability, fiscal indiscipline, and abuses of power by the national police force – contributed to disillusionment with central government in Canada.'[17] He suggests that this disillusionment led to a groundswell of support for freedom-of-information legislation along the lines of American legislation which had been passed into law in 1966.

The timing was also a reflection of political realities increasingly evident as the twentieth century drew to a close. It is not necessary here to trace the transition from the industrial to the information age; it is sufficient for our purposes to highlight the fact that we live in a society that is very different from the one inhabited by our grandparents and great-grandparents – 'different physical infrastructure, human geography, access to knowledge and information, economic relationships and technology.'[18] Indeed, changes in both the private and public sector have led to or resulted from other organizational and cultural changes that

have had a significant impact on the character of the relationship between citizen and government. Three merit highlighting in this context.

Most remarkable is the decline in deference and respect for authority, especially political authority. In 1998 Antonio Lamer, then chief
justice of the Supreme Court of Canada, commented: 'Fifty years ago,
judges came down with decisions and didn't get into the reasons why.
They just said here's the law and you don't have to understand it, you
just have to abide by it. Today, anybody wielding any authority is
much more accountable and this is a healthy thing. Awe in the face of
power has disappeared.'[19] This unwillingness to passively accept decisions that appear as proclamations from on high has been documented
by a number of analysts.[20] People want to 'have a say' on matters of
public interest and, in fact, assert their right to contribute to public-
policy decisions.

The second societal change is the explosion of not-for-profit and
civil-society organizations. The Crossing Boundaries/Canada 2020
Working Group comments: 'Voluntary organizations, linguistic and
cultural groups, professional associations, community organizations,
advocacy groups, websites and blogs, information networks, and new
international institutions ... form large national and international
networks that link people in new and often surprising ways. As a result, they also often cut across the boundaries of Canada's traditional
communities, as well as its international borders. Many are highly engaged in public policy issues and/or the delivery of public services.
Over the last two decades civil society has emerged as a powerful new
force in democratic politics.'[21]

Globalization has had a similar kind of impact. In a global world,
people, corporations, and political entities are forced to interact across
boundaries, requiring 'new norms and new solidarities that operate
beyond national boundaries.' 'Information cultures,' according to
Burkart Holzner and Leslie Holzner, 'are at the center of these changes.'[22] Providing proof and having access to reliable information is
essential for honest transactions among strangers and across cultural
boundaries whether those transactions are economic or political in
nature. Transparency, therefore, becomes a necessary condition for
building confidence and creating trust at a distance.

These three factors in particular have fuelled what Roberts calls a
'transparency revolution' that has affected 'all major social institutions ... [and has been] manifested in the rapid diffusion of FOI laws'[23]
in Canada and among other liberal democracies. The idea is that

mechanisms, such as a formal access-to-information program, will support and promote transparency by improving the ability of citizens to hold government to account.

Bureaucratic and Political Obstruction

Many critics claim, however, that the political objectives that provided the impetus for freedom-of-information legislation have not yet been met in Canada. Roberts, who has written extensively on the implementation of access legislation in various jurisdictions, suggests that although Canada has served, with some justification, as a 'model of good practice,'[24] it also illustrates the 'difficulties that beset a mature access regime.'[25] He sees two main challenges. The first he calls adversarialism, by which he means the development of administrative routines or strategies deliberately designed to minimize the disruptive potential of the Access to Information Act. The second relates to the scope of the act.

Roberts breaks down administrative adversarialism into three categories: procedures for sensitive requests, disclosure of identities, and problems in record keeping. He describes in detail an internal review process, employed in several federal departments, which has been designed to handle those requests that are considered by staff to be politically sensitive.[26] Sometimes called the 'amber light' process, it involves a series of consultations between ATIA staff and other administrators and frequently leads to frustrating delays in processing a request or delivering records. Roberts is unwilling to say that the amber light process ultimately affects the amount of information disclosed but he does cite examples of cases wherein ATIA professionals were subjected to pressure from other officials to apply a generous interpretation of exceptions to access. He also admits that it is difficult to assess how well these strategies work for government but indicates that it should be clear that the process protects the values that are important to government, that is, control over the policy agenda and consistency in policy creation, at the expense of transparency and accountability.

Government officials also try to manage the political risks of disclosing information by asking ATIA staff for information about the applicant. Disclosing the identity of the applicant is considered to be a violation of the Privacy Act but some departments will ask anyway because, in their experience, there is a greater possibility that information will be misused or abused if the applicant is a journalist or opposition politician – and if they know ahead of time who they are dealing with, they can be prepared for what follows. Again, Roberts provides evidence that names of applicants have been disclosed by ATIA staff to ministerial staff.[27]

Problems with respect to record keeping can be quite complex – ranging from avoiding the creation of a document to actually destroying records. Evidence presented before Justice John Gomery's Commission of Inquiry into the Sponsorship Program and Advertising Activities confirmed what critics had long suspected, that is, that civil servants sometimes made deliberate decisions not to record potentially controversial information to avoid disclosure under the ATIA. Testifying on the evolution of the Sponsorship Program in April 2004, Charles Guité told the Standing Committee on Public Accounts that 'we kept minimum information on the file in case of an access to information request ... There was a discussion around the table during the referendum year, 1994–95, when I worked very closely with the FPRO [Federal-Provincial Relations Office] and the Privy Council ... We sat around the table as a committee and made the decision that the less we have on file, the better. The reason for that was in case somebody made an access to information request.'[28] In Guité's words: 'A good general doesn't give his plans of attack to the opposition.'[29]

Roberts also points to evidence provided to the Gomery Commission that Public Works and Government Services Canada officials tried to deal with potentially embarrassing access requests by fabricating records. Apparently, there is evidence that staff in the department drafted expenditure guidelines which had no operational significance but which were released to applicants to give an impression of bureaucratic regularity within the Sponsorship Program.[30]

Less common but no less serious is the destruction of records. Roberts references the most egregious case: the 1989 destruction of tape recordings and transcripts of meetings held in the 1980s during which public servants debated how to manage threats to public safety posed by the contamination of the blood supply, when officials knew or ought to have known that there was a pending access-to-information request. Following is an excerpt from the information commissioner's report on his investigation into document destruction by the Canadian Blood Committee (CBC):

> At the May 16–18, 1989 meeting (held in Winnipeg) of the CBC, a decision was taken by the CBC directing the Secretariat to destroy audiotapes and verbatim transcripts of all of the previous meetings of the CBC in the

possession of the Secretariat since its inception in 1982. The official minutes of that meeting record the decision as follows: 64 'Dr. Hauser informed the Committee that, following each CBC meeting, a verbatim transcript is prepared from the tapes. Both the verbatim transcripts and tapes of all previous meetings of the Committee have been retained by the Secretariat. According to him, if the verbatim transcripts were requested under the *Access to Information Act*, they may have to be released. It was agreed that once the minutes of a meeting are approved by the Committee, the verbatim transcript will be destroyed, including all previous transcripts, and the tapes erased.'[31]

Roberts's final issue with respect to record keeping involves manipulation of the record. Again, he cites the most notorious example: the mishandling of records relating to the 1992–3 Somalia mission by National Defence officials in 1995 when journalists filed a request for access under the Access to Information Act. Following is an excerpt from the Report of the Somalia Commission of Inquiry: 'Official reporting and record-keeping requirements, policies, and practices throughout DND and the Canadian Forces are inconsistent, sometimes ineffective, and open to abuse. We have seen that, in some cases (for example, Daily Executive Meetings records and minutes), as publicity regarding Somalia matters increased, records were deliberately obscured or not kept at all, in order to avoid later examination of views expressed and decisions made.'[32]

The second main problem identified by Roberts and, in fact, echoed by most commentators relates to the exclusion of crown corporations and other quasi-governmental organizations that conduct business in the public sector or on behalf of the public sector. The presumption has been that records under the control of a private-sector company contracted to deliver a public service or program are outside the scope of the legislation and are therefore not accessible under the act. Nevertheless, there is general agreement that Canadians ought to have access to records relevant to the government's accountability for a service or program whether government delivers the service or program directly or through an alternative service provider. In June 2002 the Access to Information Review Task Force[33] agreed, reporting that transparency of new service-delivery bodies is a challenge in Canada as it is in other jurisdictions but that the scope of the federal act was more restrictive than comparable legislation in other countries and in the Canadian provinces. The task force commented that 'there are no

criteria for consistent and principled decisions on coverage of new institutions.'[34] It should be noted that this concern has been at least partially addressed by amendments to the Access to Information Act which
came into force on 1 September 2007. Under the Federal Accountability
Act, passed 12 December 2006, coverage of the act will be expanded to
include crown corporations and any wholly owned subsidiaries, seven
agents of Parliament, and a number of foundations.

I cannot dispute this evidence of bureaucratic and political obstruction although I do think that it has been somewhat overstated. Case in
point: in 2000 staff at the National Archives were commissioned by the
Access to Information Review Task Force to examine the allegation that
the Access to Information Act had had a 'chilling effect' on records creation and record keeping. An assessment of record-keeping practices in
seven different areas of government led the archivists to conclude, in
fact, that the ATIA had not had a negative impact on the creation or
management of government information.[35] In the files they sampled,
records were, for the most part, created and maintained in accordance
with applicable legislation as well as departmental standards and
policy. In fact, in some cases, record-keeping practices appeared to have
improved during the period under review as a result of factors quite
independent of the ATIA. Likewise, where there were persistent record-
keeping problems, it was usually caused by organizational factors as
opposed to a reaction against the possibility of disclosure. For example,
the fragmented nature of the Banff National Park filing system led to
equally fragmented and incomplete files.

This makes sense from an operational point of view. The archivists
point out that 'a culture of secrecy notwithstanding, records manage to
get created. For many public officials, the principle of accountability
remains important; officials still have to answer to Parliament and the
Canadian public for the substance of their decisions. In other words,
the records need to be created to accomplish day-to-day business ...
Regardless of ATI concerns, the records had to be created, and they had
to be detailed. Thus, there would be little to gain and much to lose from
not creating full and detailed records.'[36] Anecdotal evidence collected
by the research team through interviews of information and privacy
officers substantiates conclusions drawn from the empirical analysis.
The results are, therefore, quite compelling despite the preliminary nature of the study.

Nevertheless, it is fair to say that, even though the act has been in
place for twenty years, it is still not well understood by the public, by

those who supply information to the government, by those who want to access information held by the government, or even by members of the public service.[37] In addition, while I do not agree that there is a systemic problem of non-compliance, I will accept the assessment of many political insiders that the system is 'deeply entrenched in bureaucratic routine,'[38] at least at the federal level, and that there is a 'stubborn persistence of a culture of secrecy'[39] within government.

Tensions and Challenges

Beyond rather obvious organizational explanations, why would a culture of secrecy persist? Why, when most agree that freedom-of-information legislation provides an important mechanism by which people can access information about the priorities, intentions, capabilities, and conduct of public bodies; when most understand that it creates an environment that encourages the routine disclosure and active dissemination of information in the custody of public bodies; when technological innovations such as the Internet have reduced the cost of transmitting information and increased the ability of governments, news media, and non-governmental organizations (NGOs) to distribute it; and when the explosion in the number of not-for-profit and civil-society organizations and the adoption of access legislation in more than seventy nations have meant that people have access to more information and more transparency than at any other time in history?

There is no question that transparency and therefore access to information is valued by those who seek freedom and the ideal of the open society. Transparency gives people and NGOs new tools of influence and 'when wielded appropriately can be a force for good governance, freedom, and democracy.'[40] However, it would be naive to think that transparency is a stand-alone value or that it is an unalloyed good. Kristin Lord, reflecting on the complexity of the trend towards greater transparency, writes that 'it is not an unmitigated good. In all likelihood, the trend toward greater transparency will be at once positive and pernicious.'[41] Her point is that, while the increasing availability of information can reduce the power of authoritarian governments, it may also 'strengthen illiberal regimes and increase their legitimacy.' She continues: 'To the extent that transparency empowers transnational NGOs, it does so indiscriminately, aiding terrorist networks as well as human rights advocates.'[42]

Indeed, increased access to information creates challenges and introduces tensions that bear a quick review before we draw any conclusions on how far cultural transformation has progressed. I will highlight six.

The Meaning of Information

Technology has led to a dramatic increase in the volume and diversity of documents produced by government. Paper consumption has risen steadily ever since the introduction of the photocopier into the workplace and the storage needs for structured and unstructured electronic data seem to grow exponentially. The numbers are almost inconceivable. For example, the Office of the Chief Information Officer reported in 2002 that the 150,000 public servants who work for the federal government exchanged an estimated six million e-mail messages every working day that year.[43] As transparency increases the flow of information, there is a real risk that it may simply be 'too complex, too incredible, too demanding to be intelligently received.'[44]

There are two issues here. First of all, the sheer volume of information is more than we may be capable of or interested in assimilating. Who has the time to sort through millions of e-mail messages or boxes of files? Or figure out if there are any significant differences between various drafts of a report? Second, our understanding of information is shaped by our own frame of reference. According to Holzner and Holzner, 'it is part of the social construction of reality.'[45] Furthermore, they note, 'the sources of information ... have their own interests and perspectives'[46] and it is up to the individual to evaluate the piece of information and determine its significance and meaning. Lord writes: 'Optimists focus on how the availability of information will transform world events, but where people seek information, what information they trust, and what meaning they draw from that information will be more powerful.'[47]

Cost/Benefit

It costs money to provide access to information. The law inevitably generates its own administrative routines and bureaucracy. Staff are needed to retrieve and review records, to make copies, and to provide advice on disclosure decisions. There are office expenses and costs attached to the training of public servants. In 2000 the Treasury Board Secretariat estimated that the annual cost of administering the Access to Information Act for the fiscal year 1998–9 was approximately

$24,945,000, exclusive of the $3,900,000 involved to support the Office of the Information Commissioner. The Secretariat also indicated that, based on the 14,340 requests completed in 1998–9, the average total cost of handling a request for access to information was estimated at $2,010. This is not an insignificant amount and costs are escalating as the volume of information and complexity of formats increase. The greater the number of institutions covered, the higher the cost, and for departments that deal largely in sensitive information, the cost of processing a request for information may be disproportionate to the amount of information that may ultimately be disclosed.

Governability

Excessive openness can lead to a corrosion of the government's ability to maintain a decent degree of control over the business of government. Roberts talks about 'overload,' which he defines as 'the problem of too many voices making too many demands on government.'[48] There appears to be a widespread perception among elected officials and public servants that this is a very real problem and that it is getting worse over time. The 'anxiety was manifest at a conclave of OECD [Organization for Economic Co-operation and Development] ministers held in Paris [in 1996],' Roberts writes. 'Governments, the ministers agreed, were facing "intense pressure from citizens, transmitted or provoked by the media, and demanding rapid responses." Mechanisms for prompting responsiveness – "policies of consultation with the public, freedom of information, and transparency" – could be abused, blocking constructive governmental action. It was important, the ministers concluded, to resist "excessive pressure" from the media and pressure groups. Governments needed "to pursue more active communication policies, to keep control of their agendas and not just react passively to the pressure of events."'[49]

Democratic governments must maintain broad popular support to stay in power and this makes them susceptible to populist demands for change. The need to respond to pressure can derail a government's agenda; the need to react quickly can render the formal decision-making processes obsolete.[50]

Commercial Interests

There is also a real risk that the objective of freedom-of-information legislation can be corrupted by commercial interests. Data aggregators or commercial data brokers, for example, have developed the capacity to exploit large stores of digitized data collected by government agencies by combining data collected at the taxpayers' expense with information collected by the private sector. Journalists also take advantage of the availability of structured data. Information acquired under disclosure laws regularly provides the foundation for investigations into government operations.

Commercial interests may also militate against disclosure. Governments have been known to resist the disclosure of information that has commercial value, that is, information that either has been or could be packaged and sold by government itself.[51] The University of Calgary recently refused access to an applicant who requested access to information that is collected and used by the university on a regular basis for its own commercial purposes. This individual wanted the information so that she could operate a competing business, a more affordable option for the client, she said. She argued unsuccessfully that she had a democratic right to acquire the information and use it for her own personal profit and that competition would ultimately help the university improve its own operation.

Secrecy/Security

Heightened concerns with respect to security have generated a real tension between transparency and secrecy. The events of 11 September 2001 prompted a number of countries including Canada to implement national-security legislation which authorized new restrictions on information that could potentially assist terrorist activity or otherwise interfere with national security. A number of academics, however, are beginning to ask questions about the basic assumption that 'information about national security and defence warrants unqualified protection.'[52] They wonder if there has been sufficient debate about the level of compromise citizens are willing to tolerate in the name of security. Lee Strickland writes that 'in fact, the [United States] today faces a classic conundrum of how to balance the rights of the members of a democratic society, the need for information exchange among the members of the academic community, and the requirement of the state to protect the people by denying the tools of destruction to national enemies.'[53]

Privacy

The information-technology revolution creates new opportunities but also introduces new threats, particularly to privacy. There are two basic issues here. First, there are issues with respect to the adequacy of measures taken to protect the security of information stored in public databases or transmitted by government officials. These are largely technical problems that can be solved by people with appropriate expertise. Second, there are issues with respect to the way that government collects, uses, and discloses personal information. This is the more complex problem because privacy is a value that is protected by transparency in that it 'protects individuals from intrusion by the state or by others and prohibits the unauthorized use of personal information.'[54] At the same time, though, the right to privacy limits the right of access, thereby limiting transparency.

In addition, by lowering the cost of accessing and distributing information, technology has had the effect of 'liberating data that had once existed in obscurity.' Anne Wells Branscomb writes that information, 'whose value could once be protected by guarding against those who would try to copy from the paper on which it was recorded, can now be compromised in ways invisible to the human eye and at speeds almost unintelligible to the human mind.'[55] This transformation has led to greater sensitivity to potential abuses, and subsequently new controls on access. There are some who suggest that it may be time to reconsider the long-held view that public bodies have no right to consider the motives of the applicant when making a decision about whether or not to release information.

Transformation

The reality is that access to information can be abused, information can be manipulated or misunderstood, and support for an access-to-information program can draw resources away from other government priorities. It is also not difficult to imagine the impact of compliance on civil servants who struggle with the demands of responding to increasingly large and complex requests while dealing with several oversight bodies policing their work, a more aggressive media, other operational responsibilities, and pressure from political superiors;[56] or discount the effect on ministers who are trying to maintain control of the policy agenda in an era of twenty-four-hour news and ever increasing numbers of special-interest groups.

And yet even Roberts admits that, although the Canadian government has not 'adopted a culture of openness ... the rules that govern the conflict over information have shifted in favour of openness, and ... government officials (as a rule) recognize their ultimate obligation to submit to the rule of law.'[57] I would argue further that the obligation to comply with access legislation will lead to that elusive culture of openness at all levels of government in the end. Access law already permits the disclosure of government information, indeed sensitive government information, to journalists, opposition members of Parliament, and civil-service organizations. It has led to procedures for routine disclosure of information that is considered to be in the public interest. Most important, the very existence of legislation that gives people, regardless of their status in society, the right to information about knowledge held and actions taken by authorities in centres of power awakens the public's imagination and weakens the influence of those who would try to exert power in a discretionary way.

I would also argue that the transformation to a culture of openness is well under way. We may not immediately see dramatic change, particularly at the federal level, because 'more than a century of governing from the top down has created a culture of control and secrecy within government that will be hard to break.'[58] Still, as Donald Savoie writes: 'One can hardly introduce one reform measure after another without important implications for the relationship between public servants, ministers, Parliament, and citizens. The impact of Access to Information and whistleblowing legislation, and the delegation of statutory responsibilities to deputy ministers can never be self-contained. Unintended consequences flow out of such measures. They can have a profound impact on different parts of the machinery of government and they can also serve to reshape how our political and administrative institutions function.'[59]

We know that access legislation gives media and, by extension, the public access to information about public servants – what they are working on, where they stand on policy issues, how they carry out policy directives, and even whom they had lunch with if the expense is filed as a claim on the public purse. We see that ministers, particularly of late, have been quite willing to identify public servants who have had a role in the success or failure of a program or policy.[60] We also have more than one example of an individual who is willing to risk career and reputation to file an allegation of wrongdoing within the public service.[61] Indeed, the intricate interplay of new law and changing conventions is exemplified in the way results from the Gomery Commission on the Sponsorship Program and other such recent inquiries have been reported. Savoie writes: 'Public inquiries ... serve to make public servants visible and expose their personal failures to public view. The

Gomery inquiry made Chuck Guité as highly visible and well known as any minister in either the Chrétien or Martin cabinet. As experience shows, public inquiries from Gomery to Walkerton do not limit themselves to political failures; they also point to administrative failures and the final reports do not hesitate to single out the activities of particular public servants.'[62] It is clear that employees in the public service have had to accept direct personal responsibility as servants of the state and not simply to the government of the day.

In addition, the cultural environment within which business operates and within which public servants and politicians conduct their personal lives has already gone through a paradigm shift which some have likened to Ford's invention of the assembly line.[63] The language of openness and expectations with respect to accountability and transparency has become part of their vocabulary. These expectations are brought to the workplace and affect attitudes on the job. As the University of Calgary's access and privacy coordinator, I have handled numerous personal calls from university employees who want information on how to access information held by other public-sector organizations and many more calls from employees who object to a workplace information-management practice on personal as well as professional grounds.

Even so, it may be hard to collect evidence of this cultural transformation in a bureaucracy such as that which exists in government at the federal level. According to current institutional change theory, organizations are transformed 'through a process by which the logics of action that parties bring to the exchange are aligned, misaligned, and realigned.'[64] Essentially, the idea is that actors within an organization take action and justify decisions based on a conventional understanding of what is appropriate and reasonable. The introduction of a new logic leads to a temporary misalignment of the logics of action but ultimately new rules and institutions are developed, resulting in a re-alignment or a reformed logic of action.

Going Forward

Freedom-of-information legislation has played a pivotal role in supporting the transformation of cultural norms surrounding the control and management of knowledge and information held by authorities in centres of power, but that is not to say that the legislation is working well in every jurisdiction. I would agree, in fact, that the federal law, in particular, is not working as well as it should and that it needs to be updated. There has been some solid work on how the law should be changed and there seems to be some consensus developing, at the very least, on issues that need to be addressed.

However, I submit that revisions to legislation may not remove all of the obstacles that frustrate the objective of the open society. A supply of information is only as good as our ability to process it and use it. When we have too much information, or the wrong information, or no information, or when we have difficulty organizing, validating, or deciphering the information we do have, we are no further ahead. Some of this can be handled by revising the Access to Information Act although in my view it is better dealt with in subject-specific legislation. My sense is that, while it would not be terribly helpful to have a section in the Access to Information Act admonishing record creators to record 'appropriately,' a requirement, for example, to conduct all electronic communications through government servers would mean that government would have the ability to audit, monitor, and record business traffic and that relevant records would be available in the event of an access request.

I also think that archivists and other similarly trained information professionals have an important role to play in making some sense out of the record-keeping and information-overload issues that confound the movement towards greater transparency. Archivists have relevant expertise in managing records and it is time, as Canadian archivist Terry Cook puts it, for archivists to 'take charge and move from being passive custodians to active documenters, from managing the actual record to understanding the conceptual context, business processes, and functional purpose behind its creation.'[65]

It is also time for archivists to take a more active role in teaching the general public how to use the information that is accessible. Increasing transparency requires that individuals accept greater responsibility for their personal and collective well-being. With this responsibility comes the duty to be informed and to know where to find information, what information to trust, and how to judge its meaning. It is so easy to get information that I think we forget that the skills needed to judge the quality or veracity of information and even to find the right information have to be learned. The archivist is the ideal teacher to lead researchers through an exploration of content and concepts such as record bias, credibility of sources, the importance of context, and the authenticity of documents. Archival sources are an ideal medium to learn to decipher meaning. Educational psychologist Sam Wineburg writes:

'The comprehension of text reaches beyond words and phrases to embrace intention, motive, purpose, and plan – that is, the same set of concepts we use to decipher human action.'[66]

Holzner and Holzner make the point that governments and corporations will choose to implement transparency programs for purely pragmatic reasons but that the right to access information held by public bodies still needs to be enforced by law, by investigations, by codes of conduct, and by the pressure of social movements.[67] My own experience supports this view. The University of Calgary moved towards a culture of openness in the first instance because the law required it but ultimately the culture was sustained by the need to bind departments to organizational goals, to build institutional loyalty among staff, to improve the student experience, to encourage collaboration across programs, and to create opportunities for greater community engagement. In short, transparency was supported by the need to adopt a new style of governing – a style that allows the institution to respond to change quickly and effectively and to thrive in the twenty-first century.

While the federal government has responded to demands for transparency with talk of greater openness, collaboration, partnerships, and democratic renewal, it remains 'bound by the hierarchical, controlling and secretive culture of the past.'[68] I suspect that, until this changes, revisions to freedom-of-information legislation will have little impact on political and bureaucratic efforts to obstruct compliance. Until the organizational structure of government recognizes citizens, organizations, and communities as partners in governance, changes to improve the ability to share government information will not be made. The question that we cannot avoid asking is whether democracy can be achieved without this fundamental change.

NOTES

1 Burkart Holzner and Leslie Holzner, *Transparency in Global Change: The Vanguard of the Open Society* (Pittsburgh: University of Pittsburgh Press 2006), 6.
2 Ibid., 5. Alasdair Roberts, 'Spin Control and Freedom of Information: Lessons for the United Kingdom from Canada,' *Public Administration* 83, no. 1 (2005): 20, http://www.blackwell-synergy.com.ezproxy.lib.ucalgary .ca/loi/padm?cookieSet=1 (accessed 15 January 2007).
3 Alasdair Roberts, 'Closing the Window: How Public Sector Restructuring Limits Access to Government Information,' *Government Information in*

Canada 17 (March 1999), http://www.usask.ca/library/gic/17/roberts
.html (accessed 1 April 1999).

4 Alasdair Roberts, 'Two Challenges in Administration of the Access to Information Act,' 2005, 119, http://www.aroberts.us/documents/chapters/
Roberts_Gomery_2006.pdf (accessed 22 January 2007).

5 Ibid., 118.

6 Matthew Yeager, 'The Freedom of Information Act as a Methodological
Tool: Suing the Government for Data,' *Canadian Journal of Criminology and
Criminal Justice* 48, no. 4 (2006): 500, http://ww.utpjournals.com/cjccj/
cjccj484.ytml#1 (accessed 16 February 2007).

7 Ibid.

8 Ibid.

9 Ibid.; Alasdair Roberts, *Blacked Out: Government Secrecy in the Information
Age* (Cambridge: Cambridge University Press 2006), 84, 116; Roberts, 'Spin
Control,' 6.

10 Roberts, 'Spin Control,' 6.

11 Ibid.

12 Crossing Boundaries/Canada 2020 Working Group, *Progressive Governance
for Canadians: What You Need to Know* (Crossing Boundaries National
Council, March 2007), 12.

13 The government extended access rights to all individuals and incorporated
entities resident in Canada in 1989.

14 Mary Franceschet, 'Report 6: Access to Information Review Task Force'
(Government of Canada 2001), 3, http://www.atirtf-geai.gc.ca/paper-
account1-e.html (accessed 16 February 2007).

15 Government of Canada, 1977 Green Paper, cited in 'Access to Information:
Making it Work for Canadians; Report of the Access to Information Task
Force' (June 2002), 17.

16 Cited in Roberts, *Blacked Out*, 87.

17 Ibid., 86–7.

18 Crossing Boundaries, *Progressive Governance for Canadians*, 14.

19 Cited in Rae Corelli, 'Facing a Supreme Challenge,' *Maclean's*, 111, no. 7
(16 February 1998): 24.

20 For example: Roberts,'Spin Control,' 20; L.K. Boserup et al., *An Introduction to Openness and Access to Information* (Copenhagen: Danish Institute for
Human Rights 2005), http://www.humanrightsinitiative.org/programs/
ai/rti/articles/handbook_intro_to_openness_&_ai.pdf (accessed 19 January 2010); Neil Nevitte, *The Decline of Deference: Canadian Value Change in
Cross-National Perspective* (Peterborough, Ont.: Broadview Press 1996).

21 Crossing Boundaries, *Progressive Governance for Canadians*, 21.

22 Holzner and Holzner, *Transparency in Global Change*, 6.

23 Roberts, 'Spin Control,' 20.

24 Roberts, 'Two Challenges,' 117.

25 Ibid.

26 Roberts, 'Spin Control.' His research also provides evidence of the same kind of tactics employed at the provincial level.

27 Roberts, 'Two Challenges,' 125.

28 Cited in ibid., 127.

29 Working Paper II for the Standing Committee on Public Accounts – chapters 3 (The Sponsorship Program), 4 (Advertising Activities), and 5 (Management of Public Opinion Research) of the November 2003 Report of the Auditor General of Canada – Based on Evidence Received up to and including 30 April 2004, Prepared for the House of Commons Standing Committee on Public Accounts (11 May 2004), 26.

30 Cited in Roberts, 'Two Challenges,' 127.

31 Annual Report of the Information Commissioner, 1996–7, submitted to Parliament, June 1997, 63–4.

32 Report of the Somalia Commission of Inquiry, 2 July 1997, published by the minister of Public Works and Government Services Canada, 14.

33 The Access to Information Review Task Force was established in August 2000 with a mandate to review the legislative and administrative issues relating to access to information.

34 Government of Canada, 'Access to Information: Making it Work for Canadians,' 4.

35 The research team compared files created before the proclamation of ATIA with files created after. Records reviewed had been deposited in the National Archives for permanent preservation.

36 Kerry Badgley, J.J. Dixon, and Paulette Dozois, 'In Search of the Chill: Access to Information and Record-Keeping in the Government of Canada,' *Archivaria* 55 (spring 2003): 18.

37 Government of Canada, 'Access to Information: Making it Work for Canadians,' 3.

38 Roberts, *Blacked Out*, 49.

39 Annual Report of the Information Commissioner, 2004–5, submitted to Parliament, June 2005, 4.

40 K.M. Lord, *The Perils and Promise of Global Transparency: Why the Information Revolution May Not Lead to Security, Democracy, or Peace* (Albany, N.Y.: State University of New York Press 2006), 3.

41 Ibid.

42 Ibid.

43 Michelle d'Auray, Presentation to CIPS Breakfast: Annual Federal CIO Update (Ottawa: Office of the Chief Information Officers 2002), http://www.tbs-sct.gc.ca/cio-dpi/pres/cips/cips_e.pdf (accessed February 2007), 4.

44 Holzner and Holzner, *Transparency in Global Change*, 105.

45 Ibid., 6–7.

46 Ibid.

47 Lord, *Perils and Promise*, 4.

48 Roberts, *Blacked Out*, 100.

49 Ibid., citing OECD, Ministerial Symposium on the Future of Public Services (Paris: OECD 1996), Session 2.

50 Cited in Roberts, *Blacked Out*, 101.

51 In 1994 British Columbia refused access to environmental data, arguing that the information was available for purchase. The government's decision was overturned on appeal.

52 Cited in Paul Hubbard, 'Freedom of Information and Security Intelligence: An Economic Analysis in an Australian Context,' *Open Government: A Journal on Freedom of Information* 1, no. 3 (2005): 6, http://www.opengovjournal.org (accessed 17 January 2007).

53 Lee Strickland, 'The Information Gulag: Rethinking Openness in Times of National Danger,' *Government Information Quarterly* 22 (2005): 552, www.sciencedirect.com (accessed 22 January 2007).

54 Holzner and Holzner, *Transparency in Global Change*, 97.

55 Anne Wells Branscomb, *Who Owns Information? From Privacy to Public Access* (New York: Basic Books 1994), 4.

56 Roberts, 'Two Challenges,' 132; Donald Savoie, 'The Canadian Public Service Has a Personality,' *Canadian Public Administration* 49, no. 3 (2006); Donald Savoie, *Breaking the Bargain: Public Servants, Ministers, and Parliament* (Toronto: University of Toronto Press 2003).

57 Roberts, 'Two Challenges,' 136.

58 Crossing Boundaries, *Progressive Governance for Canadians*, 10.

59 Savoie, 'The Canadian Public Service Has a Personality,' 11.

60 Ibid., 10.

61 For example: Myriam Bédard (sponsorship scandal) and Staff Sergeant Ron Lewis (RCMP pension fraud).

62 Savoie, 'The Canadian Public Service Has a Personality,' 10.

63 Crossing Boundaries, *Progressive Governance for Canadians*, 20.

64 Samuel Bacharach, Peter Bamberger, and William Sonnenstuhl, 'The Organizational Transformation Process: The Micropolitics of Dissonance Reduction and the Alignment of Logics of Action,' *Administrative Science Quarterly* 41, no. 3 (1996): 477.

65 Cited in Magia Ghetu, 'Two Professions, One Goal,' *Information Management Journal* (May/June 2004): 2, http://findarticles.com/p/articles/mi_qu3937/is_200405/ai_n9366912/print (accessed February 2007).
66 Sam Wineberg, 'On the Reading of Historical Texts: Notes on the Breach between School and the Academy,' *American Educational Research Journal* 28, no. 3 (1991): 499–519.
67 Holzner and Holzner, *Transparency in Global Change*, 341–2.
68 Crossing Boundaries, *Progressive Governance for Canadians*, 21.

4 Privacy: A Look at the Disenfranchised

DOUG SURTEES

Access to information is an important tool in our never-ending quest to preserve and perfect democracy. As the ability of governments (and private actors) to gather and use information grows to levels previously inconceivable, the right to access at least part of that information is an important democratic tool. Existing in a somewhat symbiotic relationship with access to information is our right to privacy. Sometimes we think seriously about privacy as a result of our thinking about access to information as a valuable democratic tool. We almost instinctively realize that, as information is made available to individuals, corporations, or democracy's tattlers, the press, it becomes necessary to safeguard personal information about an identifiable individual.

Privacy rights however are not just the 'B' side of access-to-information initiatives. The Supreme Court of Canada has quoted Alan Westin in saying, 'Society has come to realize that privacy is at the heart of liberty.'[1] What do we mean when we say 'privacy'? One trait of the concept that makes it confounding is that we don't necessarily mean the same thing as our neighbour does when we each use the word. We mean many different things when we say 'privacy.' Indeed, defining privacy has posed a problem for many authors.[2] The problem with conceptualizing privacy may be that we simply mean too many different things by the term.

We need some common language to examine how this malleable concept affects all of us. Yet, although we need to agree on common language, we don't need to develop a definition or theory of privacy which will be approved of by all suitors. We need not conceptualize privacy in a manner that is most useful to those who are examining the privacy implications of the Internet or store loyalty programs (although those are both very important issues). Specific examples can help bring this into focus.

In 1988 the Supreme Court of Canada decided a criminal law case which provides a useful framework for understanding privacy. A Mr Dyment was involved in a motor-vehicle accident and received a cut on his head. A doctor and a police officer saw Dyment at the accident scene. He was seated in the vehicle's driver seat. The police officer drove Dyment to the hospital. Neither the doctor nor the police officer observed anything which would indicate that Dyment had been drinking alcohol. As a result, the police officer did not request a voluntary blood sample (or take steps to compel a blood sample to be taken) to determine a blood-alcohol reading.[3] Since the police officer did not observe any signs of Dyment having consumed alcohol, he would have had no grounds to seek a blood sample.

The doctor in the course of treating Dyment held a vial to his head wound and collected some blood. Dyment was unconscious at the time. The doctor collected the blood in order to conduct some medical tests to see if there was a medical cause to the accident. Later, Dyment told the doctor that 'he had consumed a beer and some antihistamine tablets.'[4]

Although the police officer never did request a blood sample, the doctor turned the sample that was collected over to him. The officer had it analysed and it was determined that Dyment had a blood-alcohol ratio in excess of the legal limit. He was charged accordingly.

The issue in the case was whether or not the turning over of the blood sample by the doctor to the police officer was an unreasonable search and seizure and therefore contrary to section 8 of the Canadian Charter of Rights and Freedoms. Seven judges heard the case in the Supreme Court of Canada. Of these, one judge retired prior to the decision and so took no part in the decision. With one judge dissenting, the majority of five judges determined that the blood-sample evidence should be excluded because it was obtained by an unreasonable seizure. There were two majority judgments. Mr Justice Antonio Lamer, writing for himself, Mr Justice Jean Beetz, and Madam Justice Bertha Wilson, held that the transfer of the blood in the vial from the doctor to the police was an unreasonable seizure because it was a violation of Dyment's privacy interests.[5] It was unreasonable because it was obtained without a warrant in circumstances where there was no evidence of a reason justifying the seizure without a warrant. Mr Justice Gérard La Forest, writing for himself and Chief Justice Brian Dickson, likewise focused on privacy interests as the basis of his finding that the transfer Dyment's blood sample was an unreasonable seizure. He held that the Charter protection against unreasonable search and seizure is 'concerned ... with the protection of the privacy interests of individuals from search and seizure.'[6] It is the person's reasonable expectation of privacy that is being protected, and in these circumstances 'Mr. Dyment was entitled to a reasonable expectation of privacy.'[7]

In deciding the privacy aspect of this case, La Forest adopted and explained a concept of three realms or zones of privacy.[8] These are:

1 Claims to privacy involving territorial or spatial aspects;
2 Claims to privacy related to the person; and
3 Claims of privacy that arise in the information context.

Real-life situations, including the one Dyment found himself in, can involve a claim to privacy which involves all three areas.

Spatial claims developed largely as protection for one's home and were often explained in property terms. Courts in Canada and the United States have made it clear, however, that 'what is protected is people, not places.'[9] Common law and constitutional rights against unreasonable search and seizure are rights to protect one's privacy interests. The space within which a person clearly has a reasonable expectation of privacy may vary from person to person and situation to situation. But some places will generally be presumed to be protected by privacy. The house one lives in is a traditional example. The room one lives in within an institution also fits the description. In Dyment's case, the hospital, a place he was taken for care and treatment, was such a space.

Claims to privacy related to the person are typically stronger claims than spatial claims.[10] 'A violation of the sanctity of a person's body ... constitutes a serious affront to human dignity.'[11] The doctor who treated Dyment did not violate his right to privacy when he collected a vial of blood for medical purposes. The violation, here cast in terms of an unlawful seizure, occurred when the blood collected for one purpose was given to another person to be used for another purpose. A person does not lose his reasonable expectation of privacy at the moment a sample is taken from him. The authority to take a sample for certain purposes does not give others the right to use the sample for other purposes. Science makes all sorts of tests possible but our reasonable expectation of privacy limits which tests may be conducted.

Claims of privacy in the information context arise because of the special interest we possess in information about us. Each of us has a special interest in information about ourselves because that information reveals who we are. We have a reasonable expectation of privacy when we divulge information for a specific purpose or in confidence. The information we divulge is our own, and it is for us to choose if it may be used for any purpose other than the purpose for which it was divulged. Possessing information for one purpose may provide the ability to use that information for other purposes, but it does not provide the right to do so. That would offend the dignity of the one whose privacy is violated.

These three zones of privacy are protected by an array of laws including the common law, aspects of the Criminal Code, the Charter, and privacy legislation. The extent of protection afforded by the law is often difficult to determine. It is the concept of privacy, as illuminated by the three zones of privacy, that the law is seeking to protect. The three zones serve as a helpful analytical structure with which to examine legitimate privacy interests. They provide a guide for understanding privacy interests. This is important not only to understand our own privacy interests but also (and more significantly) to help us recognize when we may be impinging on the privacy interests of others. The duty we owe others to respect their reasonable expectations of privacy is most critical when we have responsibilities towards those who are, in a privacy sense, disenfranchised.

Who are society's disenfranchised? Here, I am using the word 'disenfranchised' to refer to people who, as members of a group, are to be the beneficiary of some programmatic or institutional initiative but who do not have the ability to control the use of the information collected about them for the purpose of that initiative. The type of initiative I am referring to is one delivered by someone other than the members of the group itself. Typically, but not necessarily, the programmatic or institutional initiative will be delivered by government. Elementary school students are an example of a group whose members are disenfranchised. These students share a unifying characteristic. They all receive the benefits of an educational program. As a legitimate part of delivering the educational program, information is gathered and developed. For example, a student's elementary school records may disclose the student's elementary school-achievement record, information regarding the living arrangements of the student and the student's parents, results of tests like the Canadian Test of Basic Skills, conclusions regarding learning disabilities, and so forth. The students, however, do not have a voice in determining what information will be developed, recorded, or maintained. Their right to privacy requires limits on the information holder's right to use the information.

While all of us to some extent find ourselves in this position, two groups in particular are profoundly in danger of having each of their protected realms of privacy invaded. These two groups are people with a disability and the elderly. The individuals who make up these groups, I would suggest, are exposed to a greater likelihood of inappropriate intrusion into their proper realms of privacy because of their membership in the group. There is a long history of decisions being made for, and things being done to, persons with a disability and the elderly. This history and the high level of involvement that members of these two groups have with institutional service providers puts their privacy rights in greater jeopardy relative to the rest of the population.

Who is a person with a disability? The appropriate way to determine whether a person is someone with a disability varies according to the reason why we want to know. Consider two basic reasons to ask how we identify whether or not a person is a person with a disability: provision of a benefit and prevention of a harm.

Where we intend to prevent a harm, such as discrimination, we want to define the group in such a way so as to include all those who are perceived to be within the group. A social model of disability (modified to include those who are *perceived* to be a person with a disability) would be the typical model adopted. A social model of disability views disability as the end product of a complex interaction between the individual's abilities, society's attitudes, and the social, vocational, and physical environments.[12] A person may be missing part of one foot. This is without doubt a reality which affects the person's ability to do some tasks. However, whether such a person has a disability depends upon the environments the person lives in. For example, do others in the society assume a disability? Does the person live in a modern city with good mass transportation, or in a place where long walks are necessary to haul water and gather food? Is the person able to earn a livelihood by working as an author or must she tend fields? Answers to questions like these will determine if the person has a disability according to a social model of disability. If our goal is to prevent discrimination against this person, then we ought to design our law or program so as also to include people who, though not actually disabled, are seen as disabled. This is to prevent an apparent (though not necessarily 'real') disability from being a cause of discrimination.

Where we want to identify individuals as having or not having a disability in order to provide a benefit, the medical model of disability remains the typical model. Resources are typically allocated on the basis of a medical diagnosis. An individual becomes entitled to assistance in the form of money, subsidies, special equipment, living accommodations, or programs only upon establishing a medical need. The provision of services to people with a disability in this way is similar to the provision of services to the elderly. Some people who are elderly receive services or inclusion in a program because they have been identified as disabled. Other elderly persons receive services or inclusion in a program because of their age, either solely or in conjunction with other criteria.

There are two types of information gathering that I believe pose a risk to the privacy and therefore the dignity of persons with a disability and the elderly. These risks are greater than the risks faced by members of society generally. I do not claim that there are no others who are similarly situated. I am simply asserting that people with a disability and the elderly are placed in an at-risk position, and that all service providers therefore ought to evaluate their actions in this light. Of course, there will be some members of these groups who are positioned so that they are well protected from such risks. Their wealth, education, and family may combine to offer a great deal of protection to the individual. My point is simply that, on average, being a person with a disability or elderly greatly enhances these risks.

The first type of information gathering is the usual sort of information gathering which bureaucracies, like service providers, undertake. I call this 'bureaucratic-desire information gathering.' It is the gathering of information that the bureaucracy perceives as convenient or necessary for the provision of services. The second type of information is gathered not because it is necessary or convenient for the provision of services but because it can be used to overcome other perceived harms. It is the kind of information the service provider can use 'for the individual's own good.' I call this 'benevolently intrusive information gathering.'

I believe that people with a disability and the elderly share a fundamental characteristic which will tend to place them in a disenfranchised position. It is not the state of being a person with a disability or an elderly person which results in the disenfranchisement. Rather, people with a disability and the elderly are at a high risk of having their privacy rights violated because, on average, they are more likely than the general population to receive a program or benefit from a service provider.

The program or benefit is provided to them because of their membership in the group. It is required in order to facilitate full, active participation in society. In order to receive the program or benefit, members of these groups typically have to establish their eligibility. For a person with a disability, this may involve a medical-model diagnosis. This could involve a medical examination and various tests. For the elderly, entrance to a program or benefit may involve the provision of age-establishing information, sometimes combined with other information related to income or service in the military or elsewhere. In each case, while there has not necessarily been a violation of the individual's privacy rights, the potential exists. Just as in Dyment's case, the interference with privacy may occur when information legitimately gathered for one purpose is shared with another party or used for another purpose.

Every service or program an individual uses requires information to be collected. When an individual uses a greater number of programs and services, the amount of information collected, and the number of people with access to it, increases. As the provision of programs and services becomes broader, the opportunity for privacy infractions caused by bureaucratic information gathering increases.

As programs and services become more fully integrated into an individual's life, they can be thought of as growing deeper. Perhaps the most deeply integrated situation occurs when an individual lives in a long-term care facility. For some, life in such a facility means that program and service delivery is omnipresent. As the provision of programs and services increases, so does the opportunity (and perhaps temptation) for privacy infractions caused by benevolently intrusive information gathering.

The types of programs and services provided vary dramatically. Let me provide some examples to illustrate the potential for privacy infringements in each of the three realms: the spatial realm, the personal realm, and the information realm.

Suppose Joe is an adult with a disability who lives alone. Joe may have home-care workers come into his home daily to assist him with getting out of bed, dressed, and into his wheelchair. This will occur at a fixed time – let's say 7:00 each morning. Service providers may have supplied special seating, footwear, and braces to Joe. Home care may also provide Joe with assistance in bathing a fixed number of times per week; certain house-keeping services may be provided as well. Joe may wish to bathe more frequently than the existing arrangements allow. If he has a sufficient income to permit him to hire others, Joe may arrange for others come into his home to provide him with additional baths.

Whether Joe is a student, or employed, he has likely arranged for regular transportation to be provided by the service available in his community. Let's suppose it picks him up at 8:30 each morning. If Joe is a university student, he has likely arranged for the assistance he requires to accommodate his disability. This may involve another person's assistance as a note taker or attendant. Joe may meet this person at 9:00 each morning. Whether Joe is a student or employed, he may be provided with technical devices such as those that convert the spoken word into type, or the typed word into speech.

Joe's leisure time may involve the provision of services as well. Of course, transportation may be involved. He may attend an organized recreational program or even a residential recreational program with services designed to meet his needs.

I have just laid out the barest skeleton of activities in Joe's life. Think how many people and organizations have gained access to private information about Joe simply because of the services he uses. The home-care providers will have invariably gathered information regarding Joe's medical condition. They may have gathered financial information as well. In the course of providing services, they also learn when Joe gets up every morning, when he goes to bed, when he bathes, and so on. The transportation provider will also have gathered information regarding Joe's eligibility for the bus service. This will include medical information. Likewise, the university will have gathered medical information from Joe to ensure that he is eligible for the services it provides. The assistant will learn Joe's course schedule and his attendance record in the process of providing services. Even the suppliers of special equipment will collect information from Joe prior to supplying the equipment. The recreation provider will also gather information. Like some of the others, it, too, will develop information. If a typical camp is involved, for example, it is likely that, in addition to requiring medical and other personal information to be provided by Joe and his doctor, the camp staff will develop a file on Joe. Often this is used for the guidance of staff in the future. The file may contain information such as staff observations of Joe's habits, his likes and dislikes, his deportment and demeanour, and so forth. On and on it goes. Every provider of a service engages in bureaucratic-desire information gathering. Some will require the information to be updated regularly. The cumulative effect is that many organizations have collected, and are retaining, information that Joe provided, someone else provided on Joe's behalf, or someone created for the purpose of delivering a service to Joe.

Joe's claim to privacy regarding this information arises in all three spheres. The largest amount of information involves claims to privacy in the information realm. In the course of obtaining some of the information, Joe would have to give blood samples and submit to some testing, so Joe's claim to privacy would also arise in the personal realm. Additionally, Joe has a claim to privacy arising in the spatial realm, both where he invites or permits others to come into his 'space' (such as his home) and where he is provided space by the service provider (such as at camp). In all these realms, the duty of the information holder is to respect Joe's reasonable expectation of privacy.

This information is what I call bureaucratic-desire information. The actor who is providing a service or program wishes to obtain information for the purpose of administering the program or service. This is a legitimate reason to collect information. The issue, however, is whether Joe's reasonable expectation of privacy will be respected. It will be respected if only information reasonably likely to be required is gathered, if information is not shared unnecessarily, and if information is retained only as long as required for the original purpose or a subsequent purpose that has been authorized by Joe.

Upon gathering or developing information, the collectors ought to ask themselves if the information is actually required. Most people have encountered forms which ask for information which cannot possibly be relevant to the matter at hand. Sometimes one gets the idea that some questions are asked merely because they appear on a form, and they appear on the form merely because they appeared on some previous form. The proper use of information is related to the purpose for which the information was gathered and other reasonably incidental purposes.

The retention of information results in a continuing duty on the information holders. I once worked at a camp where 'camper files' were created for every camper who attended. Some campers attended for many years, and so each year more information was added to the file. The files grew thick. They contained information about each camper intended to guide the staff the following summer. One of the former campers became a counsellor and then the camp director. He joked that the first thing he did as camp director was to pull his own camper file and destroy it. From that point forward, much less information was retained in those camper files. The camp director was keenly aware that campers had a reasonable expectation of privacy that included an expectation that their personal information would not be available to others when it no longer served the purpose of administering the camp program. Information that is no longer required for a proper purpose is a liability to the organization holding it. Logically, such information will either not be used at all or will be used for an improper purpose. In this area, a proper purpose means the original purpose or a subsequent purpose that has been authorized by person who is the subject of the information.

Like people with a disability, the elderly also may require programs and services to facilitate full, active participation in society. For some, this means assistance in daily living tasks like snow removal, grass cutting, and meal preparation. For others, it means living in a long-term care facility. Claims to privacy for residents of long-term care facilities will involve all three realms. They will involve claims based on the spatial realm to a greater extent than most other activities. The collector of bureaucratic-desire information will have to be vigilant to ensure that the residents' reasonable expectation of privacy is respected. In addition, the depth of the relationship may provide a temptation for well-meaning service providers to gather information to overcome perceived harms. This benevolently intrusive information gathering should be carefully and thoroughly examined to ensure that privacy rights are respected. An example of this type of information gathering is the so-called 'granny cams' which transmit video surveillance of a resident to a password-protected website.[13] Such technology may be helpful in reducing abuse of residents of long-term care facilities, but vigilance must be exercised so that admirable goals do not blind the actors to the risks. Privacy rights should not be abused in the pursuit of reducing the risk of other abuses.

Those who collect, use, and maintain information about others in the delivery of a program or service have a high duty to meet the reasonable expectation of privacy of those about whom they are collecting information. This duty can be met. Prudent information collectors will understand the realm in which this expectation of privacy arises. They will gather only information reasonably likely to be required. They will not share information unnecessarily. They will retain the information only as long as required for the original purpose or a subsequent purpose that has been authorized by the one the information relates to. This is not an easy task. Such important tasks seldom are.

NOTES

1 *R. v. Dyment*, [1988] 2 S.C.R. 417 at 427.
2 For a useful review, see Daniel Solove (2002), 'Conceptualizing Privacy' 90 Cal. L. Rev. 1087–1155. esp. 1088–9. After summarizing the thoughts of many academics, Solove says (at 1089): 'The widespread discontent over conceptualizing privacy persists even though concern over privacy has escalated into an essential issue for freedom and democracy.'
3 Since the date of the case, the Criminal Code has been amended so that a police officer who has reasonable and probable grounds to believe that a person has driven while impaired may compel the person to provide a blood sample, if the taking of a breath sample is not practicable. See Criminal Code, s. 254(3). Therefore, under current law, the police officer could have demanded a blood sample if he believed Dyment was impaired.
4 *Dyment*, at 422.
5 Ibid., at 440–1.
6 Ibid., at 435.
7 Ibid., at 434.
8 Ibid., at 428.
9 Ibid., at 429.
10 Ibid., at 439, where Mr Justice La Forest quotes Mr Justice Lamer from *R. v. Pohoretsky*, [1987] 1 S.C.R. 945 at 949: 'A violation of the sanctity of a person's body is much more serious than that of his office or even of his home.'
11 *Dyment*, at 429.
12 See generally: Jerome E. Bickenbach, 'Disability and Equality' (2003) 2 J.L. & Equal. 7.
13 For an interesting review of this issue, see Lisa Minuk, 'Why Privacy Still Matters: The Case against Prophylactic Video Surveillance in For-Profit Long-Term Care Homes' (2006) Queen's L.J. 224.

5 The Laurier Promise: Securing Public Access to Historic Census Materials in Canada[1]

TERRY COOK and BILL WAISER

> The Census is intended to be a permanent record, and its schedules will be stored in the Archives of the Dominion.
>
> – *Canada Gazette*, 23 April 1911

Prime Minister Sir Wilfrid Laurier's promise of census confidentiality has become an unlikely flashpoint in Canadian society in the past decade. Opponents clashed in parliamentary hearings, through the media, and at public forums held across the country. How did this obscure bureaucratic instruction, directed by Laurier a century ago at census takers, become such a hotly contested battleground in contemporary Canadian society? This ongoing struggle pitted combatants arguing for access to non-sensitive government records against those believing that the lasting protection of personal information in such records must come first. Nor was it an arcane war fought between researchers in the ivory tower and bureaucrats in the backrooms of Ottawa, but rather one that evoked issues that go to the very heart of twenty-first-century Canadian public life.

Archivists and historians found themselves on one side of this battle, allied with the well-marshalled forces of the genealogists, in lobbying the federal government to release historic census materials in accordance with current Canadian law. Arrayed against them were the forces of various privacy advocates, who picked the historic census returns as a convenient and symbolic target to flex their growing strength to change the law. This essay tells the story of the ensuing conflict, of important battles won and lost, in a war still far from over. The struggle goes to the heart of our identity as Canadians and to the value we place on a just and accountable society. At stake is the very definition of what it means to be Canadian: to have a balanced rather than ideological approach to formulating public policy arìd to achieve in tone and substance better standards for Canadian governance.

Prelude: The Background to the Census Wars

In 1983 the Liberal government of Pierre Trudeau proclaimed the Access to Information Act and the Privacy Act. Together, these twinned pieces of federal legislation granted Canadians two fundamental and yet inherently contradictory rights. The Access to Information Act, often called 'freedom of information' in other jurisdictions, gave Canadians the right of open access to information created or collected by the government, immediately, subject to certain specific exemptions, rather than waiting three decades as under the former thirty-year-rule (enunciated in 1969). The central purpose for allowing such ready access to current information was to permit citizens to hold their government accountable for its actions. Accountability through reliable recorded evidence of government activities, as found in government documents and files, is essential to the functioning of democracy.[2] Of course, access to information in a timely way serves a myriad other purposes, from research in many academic disciplines to support for the arts, culture, and sciences, and for pleasure, profit, and social justice.

The Privacy Act, by contrast, gave Canadjans the right to protect personal information about themselves, collected and held by government, from unauthorized release. The purpose was to shield citizens in a democracy from a too-powerful state intruding unnecessarily in their lives. The collection of such personal information was accordingly limited to needing to serve a pre-specified government purpose. Once collected by the government, the information could be used only for that original purpose, unless the citizen consented to its subsequent use for another purpose. Information from an income-tax form could not be used to compile a voters list, to take one well-known example, unless the citizen specifically authorized such a secondary reuse of the information. The personal information, moreover, could be disclosed only according to careful and specific regulations.

The two acts, therefore, worked almost in contradiction to each other: one sought to open government information to public scrutiny, the other to prevent the release of government information, at least as it related to personal information held by the government. An access commissioner squared off against a privacy commissioner, both officers reporting directly to Parliament. Yet neither act granted their foundational rights as absolutes – some might argue, a typically Canadian compromise. The Access Act contained several exemptions, such as records relating to national security or third-party commercial interests, that precluded access to such information within records. There would be freedom of information, but only when it was judged that such immediate access to records would not inflict harm on individuals, organizations, or the state. The Privacy Act (and its related regulations) likewise did not establish an absolute right of privacy nor an open-ended protection of personal information. Such personal information, in an archival context, could be released 110 years after the birth or 20 years after the death of the citizen, provided no other exemptions applied.

Most germane to this study, the Privacy Act contained special 'archival' clauses (section 8.2.i and 8.3) that authorized government institutions to disclose any kind of records containing personal information to the National Archives 'for historical or archival purposes' (including provisions for what happens when such materials have been transferred to the custody and control of the Archives). In the case of the national census, the national archivist could disclose census records to 'any person or body for research or statistical purposes' ninety-two years after the census was conducted (section 6.d of the Privacy Regulations).[3] The ninety-two-year waiting period was, again in typically Canadian fashion, an apparent compromise between the U.S. practice (seventy-year waiting period) and that of Great Britain (100 years). There was the rational calculation at the time that the average age of Canadians was seventy-two, and so adding twenty years after the average death gave the ninety-two-year total. Of course, as with all such compromises, a few long-lived Canadians might still be alive when the census data was made public.

Decisions made by government institutions under both acts could be appealed to their respective commissioners, and, if satisfaction was not obtained at that level, further appeals up to the Federal Court of Canada were possible. The deliberate intent of these early 1980s public-policy changes, then, was for access and privacy to exist side by side in a kind of delicate balance: a creative tension between the two commissioners, the two communities they represented, and the two rights that Canadians had sought from their government and achieved through these two pieces of legislation.[4]

There was also a third federal law important to the census wars of the late 1990s and spilling over into the new century. In 1987 the National Archives of Canada Act was proclaimed. The new act articulated a whole range of activities that the archivist (with staff) 'may' undertake to deal with the complex recording media and professional and operational realities of archives and records management that were impossible to foresee when the original Public Archives of Canada Act was passed in 1912. Amid these many discretionary activities that the archivist 'may' undertake, there were only two non-discretionary clauses in the new act that 'shall' be followed. These were outlined in sections 5 and 6: 'no record under the control of a government institution ... shall be destroyed or disposed of without the consent of the Archivist,' and 'the records of government institutions ... that, in the opinion of the Archivist, are of historic or archival importance shall be transferred to the care and control of the Archivist in accordance with such schedules or other agreements for the transfer of records as may be agreed on between the Archivist and the government institution or person responsible for the records.' The act also clearly established that there would be no mini-archives across government: section 4, in setting forth the institution's four-part broad mandate, explicitly stated that 'the objects and functions of the National Archives of Canada are ... to be the permanent repository of records of government institutions.'[5]

The new National Archives of Canada Act, with the Privacy Act and the Access to Information Act, formed a triumvirate of integrated information policies of the government of Canada. Together, they combined the twin rights of accessibility to government information and protection of personal information with control of records destruction. Without control over records destruction, the other two rights were meaningless. Government agencies could not destroy or otherwise dispose of any record simply in order to preclude access to it or to shield the privacy of its subjects without the authorization of the national archivist: both the privacy and access acts as passed in the 1980s are therefore silent on records destruction, that power being exclusively assigned to the national archivist and to be exercised after appraising records for their historic or archival value. These linkages were made explicit in the Management of Government Information Holdings Policy (MGIH) issued in 1989 by the Treasury Board Secretariat of Canada, the central government agency responsible for the overall management of the public service. Records that might otherwise have historic and cultural value were equally important for facilitating efficient government, the rights of citizens, and accountability. This MGIH directive strongly reinforced the need for good record-keeping practices across government, so that all three pieces of legislation could work together effectively.[6]

Such was the legislative and policy framework in place on the cusp of the census wars. At the time, there was no hint of the acrimony that would come to dominate the census issue in the late 1990s. Indeed, the spirit of this triumvirate of federal policies reflected past practice when it came to archival transfers and public use of historic census materials. That practice is worth reviewing.

The Dominion Bureau of Statistics was created in 1918 (renamed Statistics Canada in 1971). The Statistics Act of 1918 formalized and consolidated the information-gathering activities of the government of Canada within the new agency, including taking the national census, which at Confederation had been assigned to the Department of Agriculture and then reassigned in 1912 to the Department of Trade and Commerce. In 1917, in light of this pending creation of the Dominion Bureau of Statistics, the Department of Agriculture transferred to the then-Public Archives of Canada the pre-Confederation census rolls for 1851 and 1861. The Archives also held various earlier censuses back to 1825 for Upper and Lower Canada, some Maritime colonies, Red River, and even further back for New France (including the first Canadian census conducted by Intendant Jean Talon in 1666).

After these transfers, the next major census record in line for transfer was the first decennial census taken by the new Dominion of Canada, that of 1871. It too was transferred in 1941 – seventy years from the date of the census – from the Dominion Bureau of Statistics to the Public Archives of Canada. This transfer followed an informal accord negotiated by the chief statistician and the dominion archivist, with the understanding that the census records would be made available only for scholarly research in the social sciences. But the arrangement was never regularized because some officials within the Dominion Bureau of Statistics believed that all census research should be done under the direct purview of Statistics Canada. The Statistics Act also muddied the waters. The 1918 legislation restricted the use of nominal (name-identified) census data, collected from that date forward, to employees of Statistics Canada; only they could view the name-specific material. Despite the 1941 precedent, then, there were those who maintained that any further transfers to the Public Archives would technically violate that clause.

Statistics Canada, however, hardly fell on the sword of principle over the matter. Starting in the late 1970s, there began intense lobbying for release of older historical censuses from the academic and genealogical communities, especially stimulated by the very popular 1977 television mini-series *Roots*, which generated enormous interest in family and personal history. Along with the 'Roots Syndrome,' there was also a new, growing interest in local, community, and social history during this period. Responding to these pressures, including questions in Parliament, Statistics Canada again followed the precedent of the 1871 census conveyance and transferred to the Public or National Archives of Canada the census returns for the next three decennial censuses: 1881, 1891, and 1901. At the same time, the apparent legal conflict between the two institutions' acts – one limiting viewing of post-1921 census data to Statistics Canada employees; the other requiring records of historical and archival value to be transferred (subject to negotiations regarding logistics) to the National Archives – was never resolved, despite this working compromise that had developed between the two agencies, and so tensions continued to simmer in the background.[7]

Upon transfer of the reels of census microfilm negatives (the voluminous original paper returns had long ago been destroyed), the Archives made numerous positive copies of the film for circulation and internal use, as well as for inter-institutional loan across Canada and indeed internationally. Intensive work was devoted to linking the many census cities, towns, and districts to census maps, and then preparing book-length lists of the districts to be found on each microfilm reel. These guides were so popular, and so essential to use of the records, that they were published as *Catalogue of Census Returns on Microfilm, 1666–1891 and 1901*.[8] Without doubt, many hundreds of thousands, and very likely millions, of Canadians, or those with Canadian roots, have used these historical census returns. And yet, even with such massive use, there was not a single complaint ever registered with the privacy commissioner about personal information being improperly disclosed through the National Archives' widespread dissemination of the microfilmed historical census records. A balanced approach had thus evolved historically over the century: releasing census data long after the census was taken, thus both protecting personal information while it was still sensitive and allowing for its eventual access by an eager public.

Into this fairly satisfactory modus vivendi strode Privacy Commissioner Bruce Phillips, a former CTV national correspondent, head of public affairs at the Canadian Embassy in Washington, and the communications director for the prime minister, who was appointed by the Conservative government of Brian Mulroney in 1991.[9] Rather than implement the law which he had sworn to uphold and for which he was accountable, Phillips launched in 1993 a puzzling and ill-informed attack on historical census data. On the bare evidence of thirty-three complaints that his office had received – out of millions and millions of Canadians filling in the 1991 census form – that some current census questions were too intrusive, Phillips came to the bizarre conclusion that the old historical censuses – in fact, all censuses – were a threat to personal privacy, despite not having a shred of evidence or single complaint to suggest that this was so. He believed, moreover, that the transfer of census data to the National Archives was a secondary and thus inappropriate use of the information, again contrary to his own law. He formally told the Archives that the destruction of nominal census data was the best protection of privacy, and he hoped that the Archives would destroy the census records.

Phillips seemingly did not know his own law and its related regulations. The Privacy Act explicitly countenanced the transfer to the National Archives and the public disclosure of personal information, appraised to have historical or archival value, after the regulated sufficient passage of time (ninety-two years in the case of census records) to remove the sensitivity of such information. Use of records containing personal information in the Archives was not a secondary use requiring either the consent of citizens or the approval of the privacy commissioner; it was a logical continuation or consistent extension of the primary or original use and long-term accountability of the record, as set forth not just in Phillips's own act but in the National Archives Act and the Management of Government Information Holdings Policy. How could it be otherwise when government law, regulation, and policy explicitly and repeatedly allowed, as seen above, for the transfer of records containing personal information to the Archives? The national archivist of Canada, Jean-Pierre Wallot, not surprisingly refused to authorize any such destruction of the census records, since they were among the most valuable and heavily used of all the holdings of the Archives.

Phillips never explained nor justified his attack on the archival acquisition of historical census records. While modern census questionnaires, such as those used in 1991, do indeed ask some highly personal questions, especially concerning religion and sexuality, and that caused some Canadians – thirty-three of them in this case – to complain about this line of questioning, Phillips should have targeted the current government of Canada as a whole, and Statistics Canada in particular, for designing such an intrusive form in the first place and for asking such questions of Canadians. And while he was at it, why not attack the government for the (even more) intrusive nature of some of the personal information it asks of (and gathers from) immigrants, or applicants for grants, or taxpayers, or participants in many other social programs? Could it be that Phillips was reluctant to criticize his political paymasters about their current information-gathering practices yet could still appear to march on as the very vocal champion of privacy by attacking a 'safe' target far removed from the current government activities: the long-ago historical census records?

One repercussion of Phillips's campaign was to make Statistics Canada much more reluctant than in the past to come to a negotiated agreement with the National Archives over the scheduling of census records for transfer. Dr Ivan Fellegi had been appointed chief statistician in 1985 (remaining in the post until 16 June 2008).[10] Internationally recognized in his field, Fellegi was a friend of the Archives in some key ways: he once spoke eloquently to the Archives' senior managers annual retreat, and he empathized with the role both institutions shared in fostering research and knowledge about Canada. Statistics Canada has two major functions: it collects mountains of data on a wide range of issues, including but going well beyond the census; and it engages in research and analysis of the collected data and then interprets and disseminates the results to Canadians. In many ways, then, its approach to statistical data was not unlike the Archives' approach to documents. But Statistics Canada ultimately deals with numbers and anonymized data sets to produce statistics; the Archives deals with real people, real historical figures, with real names and rich seams of personal information.

The essential core business for Statistics Canada, however, was collecting statistically valid data, upon which all its functions depended. For that to be successful, it required the trust of Canadians that their privacy, when cooperating with Statistics Canada's data collectors, would not be compromised. Without that compliance, the accuracy of the census or any other survey data would be severely compromised. Loose talk about census-confidentiality promises being broken, or Phillips connecting very sensitive current census data that Canadians by law must provide to their government with the historical census from a century ago that Canadians have used in great numbers with no recorded violations of privacy, deeply concerned Fellegi, as it did

National Archives officials. It was not in the interest of either agency or any researcher to have an inaccurate or incomplete census because Canadians, in the light of Phillips's negative publicity about the census, might refuse to complete the forms at all, or complete them incorrectly to protect their most sensitive personal information. For this reason, the National Archives deliberately spoke of the 'preservation' of census data, not its 'acquisition,' in light of Statistics Canada's nervousness over relinquishing control of sensitive personal information that might be perceived as compromising its confidentiality, and in light of 'the Privacy Commissioner's crusade to destroy all name-identified census records.'[11] Thus, the forces were set in motion for the drama ahead.

The Stakes: The Value of Historical Census Data for Research

Raw census data (that is, the census with the nominal identification still intact) are used by historians and many others in a myriad ways to understand ourselves as Canadians. The nominal information is critical to providing linkages across time and space, to tracing the evolution of the individual and his/her family throughout their lives. This is made possible through a census snapshot that is taken for Canada as a nation once every ten years, from 1871 onward and, since 1956, once every five years: 1951, 1956, 1961, 1966, and so on. (There were also regional censuses of the prairie provinces in 1906, 1916, etc.) The anonymized statistical version of the census that Statistics Canada produces serves well the needs of government agencies analysing broad population trends or needing aggregated totals of people by province, region, voting district, occupation, family size, and so forth. Anonymized data equally supports many types of academic research in such disciplines as political science, sociology, and geography, which are likewise interested in broad patterns and aggregate totals. That approach does not work, however, for historians trying to uncover other aspects of Canada's past reality, or for medical researchers and others needing to connect specific people and families.

Linking data by family name is essential for historical inquiry. Such linked data across time and space is needed to reconstruct family and local histories, discern employment patterns, understand mobility across time and place, spot disease occurrences and genetic disorders, comprehend marriage and fertility, learn of itinerant workers and boarders staying with families, and much else. Professor Susan Morton of McGill University, for example, has used nominal data from several censuses to reconstruct the African-Nova Scotian community in nineteenth-century Halifax. Community leader Peter McKerrow was listed in the census as Scottish (his paternal line), but only by accessing his name on the actual census returns did Morton discover that McKerrow lived and was recognized as Black.[12] Similarly, research using 1891 and 1901 census materials has found that the incidence of divorce in Quebec was much higher than reported in the aggregate data, that first-generation immigrants in 1901 earned more on average than did the Canadian-born, and that the percentage of single-parent Canadian families in 1901 was almost equal to the percentage in 1996.[13]

Such data from the censuses consequently allowed historians and other researchers to put average men, women, and children, and ethnic, occupational, and community groups, back into our history, as well as challenge common assumptions and stereotypes. Our identity as Canadians is not just the narrative of the elite in positions of power, or those conscientious enough to create and leave behind letters and diaries for our archives; it is also the stories of farmers, plumbers, teachers, and homemakers. Release of nominal historical census data – after the ninety-two-year period of restriction – is not a special privilege for a group of professional historians, as Privacy Commissioner Phillips was fond of asserting. It forms the very cornerstone of Canadian identity, of understanding who we are as a people and where we collectively have come from.

Of course, nominal census data is also absolutely essential for genealogical research, a pleasure enjoyed annually by tens of thousands of Canadians seeking to find their own roots in the distant past. Genealogy, one of Canada's fastest growing pastimes, is an occupation with a definite demographic, appealing overwhelmingly to people in their mid-fifties to mid-seventies, who are more than ever interested in their family history and who enjoy more leisure time as their formal working lives end. There is enormous emotional and psychological satisfaction in being able to connect oneself by genealogical research to a chain of past humanity, and to pass on the results to one's children and grandchildren. While many archival sources can and do contain genealogical information, the nominal census is its absolute backbone.

At a 1989 meeting of the International Council on Archives, a formal UNESCO body that represents the national archives of all countries, the world's archivists agreed that the census is an 'essential' record that every nation must preserve as a building block of its societal information infrastructure.[14] Today, Library and Archives Canada (LAC), as the National Archives has been known since 2004, has embraced this international protocol in its formal appraisal strategy and methodology, which is not just an internal procedural document to guide archivists in their work but also one published online to support transparency and accountability for archival work itself:

> Moving now from policy and subject operational records to case records, the first step is to consider the existence of all essential case file series, to ensure that no unnecessary duplication of general demographic information occurs between the records covered by the submission [describing all the records in all media for some government program being appraised] and the type of essential records normally targeted for preservation by many foreign countries. Several International Council on Archives (ICA) countries have identified essential records as belonging in four categories:
>
> a. those proving civil status (births, deaths, marriages, divorce, adoption, citizenship, naturalization, and aboriginal status);
> b. land registry records;
> c. certain legal records (wills, judgements, and decisions of many types of regulatory and semi-judicial tribunals and boards and agencies as well as courts); and
> d. the national census (and related survey material).
>
> … These records allow for the identity and status of Canadians now and their descendants over time [to survive], protect their rights and privileges as citizens, and provide a demographic profile of the nation, its people and organizations against which to judge program impact and variance.[15]

The census, then, is part of the baseline data on Canadians. But, unlike the other three essential categories above (to which LAC has added taxation records as the fifth essential appraisal target), it is not event-driven (a birth, a land sale, a court case) but rather a longitudinal series of multiple snapshots over time. Nor is the census just a source for historical and genealogical research in its nominal format. It also serves as a means of assessing program effectiveness and government accountability over the long term. One such example is how Statistics Canada itself manipulates or 'polishes' the raw census data to achieve statistical accuracy: in-filling unanswered fields or incomplete questionnaires, or editing out unlikely values, in order to get the 'final' version upon which scores of government public-policy decisions are based and thousands of private-sector social and economic decisions are made.

Archivists from the National Archives of Canada decided that the archival record in electronic form for the 1991 census (and all those following) should include sufficient evidence of this editing and imputation process to reflect the raw data provided by Canadians, as well as the final, polished version of the data. As the appraising archivists concluded, the nominal census is 'the only body of records in which all Canadians are named and numbered.' Canadians exist in history and across time because they are in the census.[16]

The First Campaign: Securing the Release of Post-1901 Censuses

The campaign to secure public access to post-1901 census materials was ironically kick-started by a 1998 federal government investigation into the future role of the National Archives of Canada and the National Library of Canada. Until that time, the archival, historical, and genealogical communities had been talking about what could be done to help bring about the release of nominal census data on a regular and continuing basis, but nothing formal had been decided upon and no particular steps had been taken. Then, in March 1998, Minister of Canadian Heritage Sheila Copps asked John English, a former Liberal MP and professor of history at the University of Waterloo, to head a public consultation on the future role of the National Archives and National Library, including how the two national cultural institutions 'can help preserve and provide access to the collective memory of the country.'[17]

The Canadian Historical Association (CHA) was one of several organizations and agencies to appear before the English committee in the fall of 1998. Working in concert with Dr Joanne Burgess of the Institut de l'histoire de l'Amérique française, the CHA deliberately used the opportunity, through its spokesperson, council member Bill Waiser of the University of Saskatchewan, to throw its support behind the National Archives in its efforts to secure access to historic census materials. The special 1906 western census, for example, should have been made public in 1998 according to regulation 6.d in the Privacy Act (ninety-two years after the census was taken), but it was being withheld by Statistics Canada contrary to the clear intent of access and privacy laws and regulations. The CHA followed up its presentation with several letters through the winter of 1998–9 urging Minister of Industry

John Manley to instruct Statistics Canada to release name-specific census returns for historical research and genealogical purposes. Further pressure on the minister came from the English consultation process, which recommended in its summer 1999 report not only that the national archivist play a more active role in access and privacy issues but that all historic census materials be released in their entirety seventy years after the information was collected (the U.S. practice).[18]

That same year, the federal government also introduced Bill C-54 (later C-6), the Personal Information Protection and Electronic Documents Act (PIPEDA), to extend the protection of personal information in the private sector and provide guidelines for the collection, use, and disclosure of that information in the course of commercial activity, especially the ever-expanding world of electronic commerce. When the bill became law, it brought Canadian international business practices on data sharing and data protection in line with the most advanced privacy protection in the world. The Association of Canadian Archivists (ACA) submitted a brief to Parliament, through a recently retired National Archives senior manager and now an archival educator at the University of Manitoba, Terry Cook, along with ACA partners from the Canadian Historical Association and the Institut de l'histoire de l'Amérique française. All three groups testified before a parliamentary committee in February 1999. The wording of the ACA brief clearly set out the formal position of these partners on privacy, access, and the census and formed the basis of future skirmishes over access to census materials:

Bill C-54 recognizes, as do (in combination) the federal Access to Information Act and Privacy Act (hereafter ATIP), that, in extending protection of personal information to the private sector, there remains the need to balance 'personal information protection' on one hand, and, on the other, both (7.3.g) 'conservation of records [containing such personal information that are] of historic or archival importance' (as contrasted with their destruction, as recently improperly recommended for the national census by the Privacy Commissioner), and (7.2.c) disclosure (if qualified) for 'statistical, or scholarly study or research, purposes.' The ACA very strongly supports this balance in public policy. Canadians have a right to privacy and protection of personal information about themselves that forms part of their interaction with the state and business, AND they have a right to know about their government, their country's history, and their collective identities and memories.[19]

The response of the government of Jean Chrétien to these and other pressures was to launch another federal investigation in November 1999 – this time, an expert panel to recommend how the impasse over access to post-1901 census material could best be resolved. On the one hand, Statistics Canada and the Office of the Privacy Commissioner maintained that census material in the past had been collected under the promise of confidentiality made by Prime Minister Wilfrid Laurier. On the other, the National Archives, in association with heritage, archival, and genealogical groups, argued that census records constituted a national historic treasure and should be made available for public consultation in keeping with the laws of Canada.

Given these very different positions, the actual wording of the 1906 census regulations, including the so-called Laurier promise, is instructive.[20] There was a confidentiality provision (instruction 23): 'to keep inviolate the secrecy of the information.' But this directive was specifically aimed at census enumerators, not the general public nor governments generations later. The Laurier government wanted to assure Westerners, especially those settlers of continental European descent, that census information would not be passed along to tax collectors or military conscription personnel, and instructed its census workers to emphasize this point in carrying out their work. The census enumerators, going house-to-house in local communities, were not to gossip about their findings concerning their neighbours' living conditions but rather keep such current, contemporary information confidential. The very same 1906 census regulations (instruction 36) also stated: 'The Census is intended to be a permanent record, and its schedules will be stored in the Archives of the Dominion.' If – as asserted by those who later opposed releasing the 1906 census – Laurier had indeed made a promise that the information would remain confidential forever, then why did his government in the very same 'promise' explicitly indicate that the census material would be transferred to the Archives? The purpose behind the 1906 census is also revealing. Because so many immigrants were pouring into western Canada in the early twentieth century, Laurier stepped outside the normal census cycle – every ten years – and ordered a special census of the three prairie provinces in 1906 to serve as a kind of statistical snapshot of the phenomenal growth. In short, it was an unprecedented exercise – hence the requirement that the data become a permanent record of the Archives, not destroyed at the whim of a privacy commissioner nine decades later or precluded from transfer by the nervousness of a chief statistician.

The five-member expert panel appointed by Chrétien, including a former Supreme Court judge and two university presidents, held several meetings with interested groups and individuals in early 2000, read 2,500 pieces of correspondence, and considered public-opinion research commissioned by Statistics Canada.[21] The public campaign, in the meantime, was not put on hold but gathered some momentum. On 8 November, just three days after the announcement of the appointment of the expert panel, Bill Waiser debated Privacy Commissioner Bruce Phillips on CBC national radio's flagship program *This Morning*. During the discussion, Phillips insisted that census returns had been collected for a specific, stated purpose and should be used only for that purpose and then destroyed. Waiser countered that researchers were not asking for any special privilege and that the prior release of historic name-specific census data had not resulted in a single complaint – including the special case of Newfoundland and Labrador, whose census returns up to and including 1945 had been made public when the province joined Confederation in 1949. Phillips's comments, both on the radio and in print, elicited a stern rebuke from the *Globe and Mail*. A lead editorial, 'The Past Belongs to All of Us,' suggested that Phillips's stance was 'anti-intellectual.'[22]

The new national archivist of Canada, Ian Wilson, appointed in the summer of 1999, also became vitally involved in the campaign. On 16 November 1999, with the expert panel just getting organized, Wilson asked the chief statistician of Canada, Ivan Fellegi, to transfer the 1906 and 1911 individual census records to the custody and control of the National Archives. 'The censuses of 1906 and 1911,' Wilson argued, 'must be preserved and made available to fulfill the promise Parliament made to Canadians early in the century.'[23] Fellegi did not see it that way. He responded that his department was legally prevented from releasing post-1901 census records because Prime Minister Laurier had made a pledge that the information would remain forever confidential.

The expert panel's report was submitted to the minister of industry, responsible for Statistics Canada, at the end of June 2000.[24] Dr Fellegi had previously claimed that the census deadlock would be resolved by the blue-ribbon panel. But Statistics Canada did not like its recommendations. The expert panel had reviewed all the evidence on the so-called Laurier promise and found not a single reference to perpetual confidentiality; rather, it affirmed that census material, according to the regulations, should be transferred to the National Archives as a permanent record. The panel also recommended that past and future census material should be released after an appropriate waiting period, noting that such a policy would bring Canada in line with the practices of Great Britain and the United States. Perhaps the panel's most telling finding, though, was that those who participated in a national poll and focus groups generally supported the release of their personal census information after 100 years. These survey results flatly contradicted Statistic Canada's repeated claim that the release of historic census materials would jeopardize future census-participation rates.

There was other bad news for Statistics Canada. While the Chrétien government sat on the report of the expert panel, it sought a legal opinion on the question of public access to historical census materials. This was not the first time that such an opinion had been sought. In fact, since 1978, the question had been considered eleven times. The latest one, dated 1 August 2000, and made available through an access-to-information request by Bill Waiser, was prepared by a senior counsel with the Department of Justice who was asked to consider whether pre-1918 census records could be legally released after ninety-two years without any legislative change. Ann Chaplin's opinion was an unequivocal 'yes' – noting that, if these records were meant to be kept secret forever, why did the Laurier government insist that they be transferred to the National Archives as a permanent record? Why, she might have added, had Statistics Canada itself transferred the 1871, 1881, 1891, and 1901 censuses to the Archives?

Statistics Canada still refused to budge on the issue. Instead, the agency scrambled during the summer of 2000 to develop a compromise proposal to provide limited access to century-old census data. Known internally as the Wilk option, Statistics Canada proposed that any genealogical research in the records be restricted to 'direct descendants of a direct ancestor.' Taking a peek at extended families on the census return, such as a spouse's grandparents, would have been taboo. Doing the kind of community and other linkages needed by historians (obviously not direct descendants) would also have been prevented. The Wilk option did recommend that 'reasonable' access to the records be granted for 'historical research,' but 'reasonable' and 'historical research' were never defined. Finally, the proposal severely limited public disclosure to certain basic census information: name, age, address, marital status, and birthplace. It would consequently have been illegal to publish data on any number of topics, from health and employment to education and religion.

When Statistics Canada sent the Wilk option to the National Archives for comment, the staff responded with a devastating critique, listing several substantial reservations. National Archivist Ian Wilson followed with his own letter on 1 September 2000 to Fellegi, asserting that the Wilk compromise was really no compromise but 'heavily bureaucratic and essentially unenforceable.'[25] It appeared that Statistics Canada was on the ropes. But, when the expert panel's report was finally released on 15 December 2000, Brian Tobin, the new minister of industry, in the best Mackenzie King tradition, called for more study. In particular, he indicated that future public consultation on the census issue would likely take place as part of a larger review of the access and privacy acts scheduled for some time into the future.

This delay suggested that Tobin preferred the advice of the chief statistician over the findings of his own expert panel. It also gave Statistics Canada some breathing room while its energies were focused on conducting the 2001 census that coming May. Those involved in the campaign to secure public access to historic census materials had other plans. In fact, Statistic Canada's continuing intransigence on the issue served to bring together various archival, history, and genealogical organizations in order to share information and develop a common strategy. Some of the key players, besides Terry Cook, Joanne Burgess, and Bill Waiser, included University of Ottawa history professor Chad Gaffield, a member of the expert panel and then the incoming CHA president, and genealogist Gordon Watts, co-chair of the Canada Census Committee and a tireless campaigner for access to the census for his genealogical constituents. Collectively, they decided to push for the immediate release of the 1906 special western census and a government commitment to resolve the larger issue after the 2001 census was taken.

This new census offensive was pursued on several fronts. Waiser, with advice from Cook, prepared three articles for the *Globe and Mail* in 2001 calling for the unqualified release of historic census materials and highlighting Statistic Canada's continuing failure to obey the laws of Canada.[26] He also submitted to Statistics Canada an access-to-information request for the nominal returns of the special 1906 western census, as well as another request to see copies of all recent correspondence regarding access to historic census records. The genealogists, for their part, decided to file a legal action (*Beatty v. Canada, Attorney General, 2003*) in the Federal Court of Canada to compel the chief statistician to turn over custody of the 1906 census to the National

Archives for immediate public release. The application was handled by Calgary family lawyer Lois Sparling, also a genealogist.

Statistics Canada countered these moves by contracting the Environics Research Group to convene a series of town hall and focus-group meetings across the country to secure yet more public input on the question of access to historic census material, in particular the 1906 and 1911 returns. And, in a bald-faced attempt to influence the objectivity of these forums, the agency also promoted the Wilk compromise as a way out of the census impasse. The response at the hearings, however, was a resounding 'no' to the compromise option. The majority of presenters, according to the Environics report dated 15 February 2002, supported the release of individual census returns after a reasonable waiting period.[27]

A further blow to Statistic Canada's position came later that year. When the agency rejected Bill Waiser's access request for the 1906 census, he appealed the decision to John Reid, the information commissioner of Canada. Reid issued his finding on 11 December 2002, after a sixteen-month investigation.[28] He upheld the complaint and called on Statistics Canada to release the material in its entirety. 'I have not been convinced,' he reported to Statistics Canada in advance of making his ruling public, 'that access to these records can be refused lawfully.'[29] Waiser celebrated Reid's decision at a national press conference at the University of Saskatchewan on 18 December. But the victory was a hollow one since Fellegi had already advised the information commissioner that he did not intend to accept his recommendation and turn over the census returns. Waiser instructed Reid to take Fellegi to the Federal Court of Canada over the matter, while calling on Statistics Canada in a newspaper article to do the honourable thing and respect the law of Canada and release the data.[30]

Over the next few weeks, Statistics Canada tried to limit criticism of its position by publicly insisting that there was 'ambiguity' regarding the release of historic census materials.[31] But, with the information commissioner about to take Fellegi to the Federal Court, the Chrétien government moved quickly to deal with the festering problem with a two-pronged solution. On the very day the court applications were to be filed, 24 January 2003 – coincidentally a Friday so that media coverage would be limited – Allan Rock, the new Liberal minister of industry, announced the immediate release of the 1906 census records.[32] Two weeks later, Liberal Senator Lorna Milne, a genealogist and long-time champion of the release of post-1901 census records, introduced Bill S-13 (An Act to Amend the Statistics Act), for which she had long advocated. The bill was worrisome on two counts. It sought to extend the waiting period for access to historical census records (1911–2001) another twenty years beyond the mandated ninety-two years. More alarming, though, was how future census returns from 2006 onward were to be handled. Each and every respondent would have to consent to the transfer of her/his individual census return to the National Archives for eventual release.

Public hearings on Bill S-13 were held in February 2003 before the Senate Committee on Social Affairs, Science and Technology. Terry Cook, speaking on behalf of the Canadian Historical Association and the Association of Canadian Archivists, noted that the 1911 and 1916 records were collected under the same legislative conditions and in-structions as the recently released 1906 census and could (and should) be made available ninety-two years after the census was taken without violating existing legislation. He also argued that a longer waiting period for other historic census materials from 1921 to 2001 was com-pletely unnecessary and that the current period of closure represented a kind of compromise between the slightly longer British (100 years) and much shorter American (70 years) periods. His most damning comments were reserved for the 'opt in' proposal for post-2001 cen-suses, declaring that such a requirement would undermine the integ-rity and usefulness of the census as a historical source even if only a small percentage of Canadians refused to give their consent.

Gordon Watts, co-chair of the Canada Census Committee, echoed Cook's remarks in his testimony. He, too, slammed the idea of an 'opt in' clause and said that, if genealogists were forced to accept a 'check box' option, then it should be an 'opt out' clause. But that was only a last resort if the legislation went forward. Watts, as spokesperson for tens of thousands of Canadian genealogists, did not like the proposed restrictions on access to census materials and called on his supporters to let parliamentarians know their displeasure with the bill. Indeed, the academic community probably does not fully appreciate to this day the vital role played by genealogists in the census campaign in flooding parliamentarians with e-mails, phone calls, and letters in record num-bers. And their vociferous opposition got results. Rather than being rushed through, Bill S-13 was allowed to die on the order paper when Parliament was dissolved for a general election.

The census situation in 2003 was, therefore, almost a mirror image of the situation five years earlier. In 1998, the year the special 1906 western census was scheduled for public release, it was being withheld by

Statistics Canada. Now, in 2003, researchers faced a similar situation with the 1911 census. But the difference was that they had been down this road before. The genealogists, marshalled by Watts, flooded Statistics Canada with formal access-to-information requests for the 1911 nominal census returns. When the agency refused to make the material available, ninety individual complaints, including one by Watts himself, were lodged with the Office of the Information Commissioner. John Reid once again recommended disclosure and, once again, Statistics Canada, through the new minister of industry, David Emerson, refused the request. It appeared that the matter was once again headed to the Federal Court in the fall of 2004. And it would not be the only census case under consideration. As a kind of insurance policy, the genealogists had filed a new claim (*Beatty v. Canada, Attorney General, 2004*) in June, calling on the chief statistician to transfer the 1911 census returns to the legal custody of the national archivist of Canada and to direct the national archivist to make the information available to the public for research purposes. Statistics Canada was once again obstinate, refusing to obey the law.[33] Clearly, in this stalemate, the time had come for a comprehensive resolution that would satisfy all parties.

The Second Campaign: Victory, but at a Cost

The solution to the census impasse was floated in the fall of 2004, three months after the Paul Martin Liberals had returned to office with a minority government. The deal broker was Senator Lorna Milne, the passionate advocate for the release of historical census materials who was equally anxious to see the matter resolved. In fact, Milne was now working with her fifth industry minister – in this case, still David Emerson – and was genuinely worried that there was a real danger of 'issue fatigue.' The minority Liberal government, she argued, might decide that the census issue was too intractable, the warring parties too far apart, and that it would be best under the circumstances to set the matter aside for a generation. Finding space on the crowded parliamentary agenda for new legislation is always difficult, and no new government, especially a minority one, invites trouble by tabling legislation for which there is not already a good consensus that it should pass. The bottom line, according to the advice that Milne was getting from the inside, was that the federal government wanted the issue to go away. It was tired of the thousands of letters, faxes, and e-mails, especially from the genealogical community. Nor was it happy with the internal bureaucratic tension, if not open wrangling, between Statistics Canada, Library and Archives Canada, the information commissioner, and the privacy commissioner. But the solution had to be clear-cut, one that contained no ambiguity and at the same time was palatable to all the major players, giving each 'side' something that it wanted.

What was proposed was a draft government bill, amending the Statistics Act, that would be formally introduced that fall but only after those key organizations involved in past census battles agreed to support the legislation – or, at least, agreed not to speak out against it. Senator Milne repeatedly emphasized during the consultation process that the Martin government wanted no messy parliamentary debates or negative divisions given its minority situation. Accordingly, she invited Ian Wilson, Terry Cook, and Chad Gaffield to her Ottawa office on 23 September 2004 for an off-the-record meeting to discuss the hardball compromise that had been hammered out. The new and much more judicious privacy commissioner, Jennifer Stoddart, and Chief Statistician Fellegi had agreed, in return for a consent clause, not to stand in the way of all the other demands of historians, archivists, and genealogists. Milne needed a commitment from the key individuals and, of course, their organizations involved in the census wars that they would be on side should such a bill to be tabled in the Senate. The attendees balked at the opt-in clause. Milne countered that anything else, including an opt-out clause, was unacceptable to the other side and would doom the draft bill. A compromise was consequently suggested: an opt-in clause, but with a mandatory statutory review added to the act. Milne said she would try for that.

Terry Cook agreed to take the proposal to the Canadian Historical Association and the Association of Canadian Archivists. He did so with the knowledge that Ian Wilson had done his own investigations in the Ottawa back corridors of power and found that the compromise was the best that probably could be secured for a generation. He also knew that Senator Milne had followed this brief longer than anyone else on the Hill and that she sensed that the influence of privacy interests was growing – hence the need to take what was now possible given the competing interests. It really came down to two choices: accept the package as is, without change (save trying for a statutory review of the opt-in clause if results were poor), or no legislation would be brought forward.

Both the CHA and ACA executive committees gave their approval to the deal, albeit, like Cook, Wilson, and Gaffield, with misgivings over the consent clause. A follow-up conference call was organized by

Milne's office on 20 October, this time including Gordon Watts and Lois Sparling's representative, among others. Cook delivered the verdict: the archivists and historians would accept – or at least not oppose – such a bill, and would recommend to their members that they do the same.

The new government bill dealt with all historical censuses (1911–2001) and all future censuses (2006 onward). In particular, the draft legislation called for the immediate release of the 1911 nominal census to the custody and control of Library and Archives Canada. This action probably would have happened anyway, given the precedent set by the release of the 1906 census, but it still represented a symbolic victory. The bill also provided for the regular and continuing release of all census returns from 1916 to 2001 after a ninety-two-year waiting period. The 1916 prairie census, for example, would be made available for public consultation in 2008. This legislated schedule for ongoing release of the censuses was a major victory, and an important one, since it effectively ended any dispute over how the provisions in the original 1918 Statistics Act should be interpreted. Everything that historians, archivists, and genealogists had been saying for years was vindicated. There was also to be no additional twenty years tacked on to the waiting period as had been proposed in the earlier Bill S-13 from February 2003. Finally, the bill was silent on the possibility of citizens controlling the destruction of sensitive personal information that they submitted to the government. This too was a victory, for it ensured that these and other records would not be lost forever – as has been the case in Australia, which decided in 2001 to destroy census records containing personal information. This was the key point for Wilson: the preservation of the entire census for all time. Access can be negotiated and renegotiated, but once a record is destroyed it is forever gone.

The price of these victories was accepting the opt-in clause – the other half of the hard-ball compromise. Starting with the 2006 census, participants would be asked to indicate, by checking a box, whether they consented to having their responses made public after ninety-two years. If respondents said 'no,' the form would not be destroyed, but access to it in its name-specific or nominal format would be prohibited. And, in cases where respondents did not answer the question, the default position was 'no.' Historians, archivists, and genealogists had strenuously opposed any consent clause, and, if forced to accept one, preferred an opt-out clause, but this was the price of the package deal.

The bitter opt-in pill was sweetened by two promises. The use of the opt-in clause and how Canadians responded would be formally reviewed by Parliament after two censuses (2006 and 2011), a significant victory that historians and archivists had pushed for at the September 2004 meeting. Both Statistics Canada and Library and Archives Canada also vowed as part of the 2006 census public-communications campaign 'to encourage Canadians to allow future access to their census records to preserve Canada's history for future generations.'[34] In the end, these promises, together with the knowledge that the package was the only census deal to be secured at the time, helped convince leaders of Canada's historical, archival, and genealogical communities to recommend acceptance of the compromise to their members. The decision was not an easy one, but clearly there were major gains in law to be secured. It was also made with the determination to push for an opt-in clause based on the concept of 'informed consent.' The consequences of providing consent had to be explained to respondents completing the census form – that their family history would be available to their descendants in the future and that it would be part of the larger historical record of Canada, and that their privacy would be protected throughout their lifetimes with no release for over nine decades.

Bill S-18, An Act to Amend the Statistics Act, was introduced in the Senate by the Martin government on 2 November 2004, with the intent of removing the 'legal ambiguity' that seemed to set the statistics and archives acts at loggerheads. While historical, archival, and genealogical organizations watched from the sidelines, as they had promised to do, and thus keeping any concerns about the implications of the opt-in clause to themselves, as they had promised to do, Fellegi told the committee hearings on the legislation that Statistics Canada supported this compromise and would promote and encourage a 'yes' answer to the informed-consent question. Other witnesses spoke favourably about the compromise. The only dissenting voice was that of Information Commissioner John Reid, who had never been consulted, let alone told, about the deal that had been brokered and learned about it only when he appeared before the committee hearings.[35] Reid maintained that the opt-in clause set a dangerous precedent and that it would actually make the situation worse, especially when it came to access to government information. No one publicly backed up Reid's warning at the hearings, and the bill became law in June 2005 – ironically, without any fanfare. With remarkable efficiency, Library and Archives Canada made the 1911 census records available to the public on its website by the end of July. The records were enormously popular, averaging seventeen 'hits' a second on the census portion of the website in the first months, tapering off a year later to an average of five hits per second, a half-million a day, almost thirteen million a month – and still no complaints filed with the privacy commissioner about the disclosure of this kind of personal information being a violation of government law or regulation! (The new Library and Archives Canada had earlier created the Canadian Genealogy Centre to recognize and serve the interests of genealogists who were so important to the census wars.)

Over the next year, in preparation for the 2006 census and the new 'consent' question it would contain, Statistics Canada added a page to its website entitled, 'the 92-year question – say Yes!'[36] The agency also added a 'Genealogy Corner' to its website and reproduced Bill Waiser's article and an interview with Chad Gaffield, all encouraging a 'yes' response. This site contained exactly the kind of information that respondents needed to understand and appreciate the significance of census records to future historical and genealogical research. But this helpful explanation was nowhere else available to the public, let alone strongly advocated in a media and public-relations blitz. The actual wording of the question on the 2006 census form also did not facilitate a 'yes' response. It began with the rather ominous warning – 'The Statistics Act guarantees the confidentiality of your census information' – and then simply asked respondents whether they wanted 'to make your census information available in 92 years for important historical and genealogical research.' This was not 'informed' consent with the consequences spelled out clearly of what accepting or refusing would mean for their descendants or for Canada.[37]

Genealogists, led by Gordon Watts, tried to muster a high 'yes' vote through an intensive Internet and newsletter campaign. Bill Waiser also published an article in the *Globe and Mail* in April 2006, imploring Canadians to 'Say Yes to History.'[38] Waiser noted that, if only a small percentage of Canadians decided to keep their census data permanently inaccessible, then the integrity of the census as a source for genealogical and historical information would be forever compromised. He also warned that it is impossible today to know what might be historically important in the future and that the descendants of census participants might regret bitterly that their ancestors long before them had said 'no' to the opt-in question. What was perhaps most distressing, though, in the weeks leading up to the census day 2006, was that Library and Archives Canada, a long-time supporter of access to historical census materials, and the very portal for releasing all historical census records, did little publicly to lend its support to the 'yes' campaign, aside from some comments buried on its large website. This is not what had been promised. In agreeing to the compromise, historians, archivists, and genealogists envisioned – and were led to believe – that there would be major radio, television, and print media campaigns run by Statistics Canada and by Library and Archives Canada equal to, or accompanying, the main census advertisements telling Canadians to 'count yourself in' by completing the census forms *and* also telling them, equally prominently, to 'count yourself in to history' by saying 'yes.' By contrast, for the similar consent clause in the Australian census, a

> four million-dollar official advertising campaign was funded by the Australian Bureau of Statistics (ABS) over the two weeks before census day. This included advertisements in capital city metropolitan daily newspapers and on radio headlined 'Want to be Famous?' 'Want to Become Part of Australian History?' and 'Will You Tick the Box?' Posters, stickers and other material were distributed by the ABS to all council and state libraries throughout Australia. The State Libraries of Victoria and Western Australia put up especially good displays. Posters were placed in many additional public venues across the country, such as office and shopping centre notice boards, retail shop windows, and in schools, universities and scout halls.[39]

By March 2007, when the aggregate results of the 2006 census were first being made available, a headline in the *Ottawa Citizen* trumpeted: 'Historians, genealogists to get all the census details – in 2098.'[40] The article then described how the 2006 census allowed Canadians to decide for the first time whether their personal information could be made publicly available in ninety-two years and that 56 per cent, a little more than half, said 'yes.' The outcome was disappointing, if not shocking. Until the 2006 census, the personal information on all Canadians was to be made publicly available after the legislated waiting period. Now, 44 per cent of the respondents had apparently decided that their privacy was more important than access in ninety-two years, and, as a consequence, their census information would be permanently inaccessible for research, at least in any name-identifiable way.[41] Maybe Canadians were wary because of all the recent stories about identity theft. Maybe they feared losing control over their personal information, not understanding the nuances of timed-released information only after long periods of complete restriction. Maybe they responded to a leading and badly worded consent question in a predictable way. Maybe they have no current or anticipated interest in history or genealogy. Maybe they resented being forced by law to fill in the census form and so did not feel inclined to do the government any favours, even finding some small rush of pleasure in being able to say 'no' to big government. Whatever the reason, when it came to tabulating the results from the 2006 census, history, archives, and genealogy were the big losers. But there are larger consequences too in the battles of the census wars.

Assessing the Struggle and the Next Campaign

Historians and archivists, with their genealogical allies, can take a large measure of pride in the victories achieved in the census wars. It was easily the biggest, longest, and most sustained lobbying campaign by either profession, something difficult to mount and continue over almost a decade when using only volunteer participants fully employed in other endeavours, representing organizations with ever-changing executives, operating on financial shoestrings, and facing well-connected and well-financed opponents. The campaign demonstrated that archivists and historians need to fight hard on issues of public policy affecting their professions, rather than adopt their more traditional stance of objectivity and neutrality. It also demonstrated that significant victories can be, and were, achieved by such lobbying: an entire century of census records will be opened for research as the ninety-two-year restriction period progressively expires, census by census.

But the census wars raised worrying concerns that need addressing. The first is the consent clause, which has moral, archival, and historical implications that are highly disturbing. On moral or ethical grounds, the head of the household, when filling in the census form, and refusing consent or conversely granting it, speaks on behalf of a spouse, their joint and any stepchildren, and any other relatives, boarders, or students residing in the residence on census-taking day. One person could thus seal the fate of, say, for sake of illustration, three others, and in the next generation (assuming households of four people thereafter) of those three person's 12 descendants, and in the third generation of those 12 person's 48 descendants-descendants, and of those 48 their 192 direct descendants-descendants-descendants to the fourth generation, and so on and on over the centuries into ever greater multiples:

many tens of thousands of Canadians will thus have been rendered voice-less and history-less by *one* person saying 'no' in 2006, or even by that one person ignoring the box and not answering at all. The same fate pertains to those in nursing homes, senior's residences, and hospitals unable to complete their own forms. By not consenting, the great-granddaughter of a young boy living in the household in 2006 (who had no chance to consent) is precluded from accessing the census record of her great-grandfather (that same young boy) for genealogical or any other purpose. This is not informed consent, or even consent at all, but the unethical hijacking of the consent process, whether by intent or ignorance. One Canadian alone is blocking, without their consent, the fundamental right of access to government information, guaranteed in law, for thousands of other Canadians many generations from now. Multiply that times the 44 per cent saying 'no' just in 2006, and within three generations, hundreds of millions of future Canadians would be so denied access.

The second concern, as John Reid rightly asserted, is that the consent clause sets a dangerous precedent that has the potential to gut Canadian archives and seriously undermine the rights of citizens. This rests on a fundamental misinterpretation of privacy law.[42] Basic privacy principle holds worldwide that personal information collected from citizens for an identified administrative purpose 'A' shall not be used for another, separate, administrative purpose, say purpose 'B,' without the citizen's explicit consent. What must never be conceded by any archivist anywhere is former Privacy Commissioner Phillips's premise that the transfer of a portion of government records created for purpose 'A' to document, historically, in an archives, purpose 'A' is a separate purpose 'B.' Such a position flies in the face of the government's (and thus Canadians') desires as expressed through archival legislation (and government information-management policy) that citizens have a right to full and complete archives as determined by society's professional remembrancers, the archivists. That is what the law says. This precedent, if writ large, renders the Archives Act null and void, and destroys major premises of the Management of Government Information Holdings Policy. By contrast, in parallel jurisdictions, including the European Union, the archival retention of some or all of the records of purpose 'A' is viewed as a perfectly consistent with, and indeed an integral part of, purpose 'A.' In the same way, use of the records of purpose 'A' by an auditor general, investigating the financial probity of purpose 'A,' is a consistent use of purpose 'A,' and not a new-use purpose 'B.' Canadian precedent under the Privacy Act has been to inform citizens through published guides that a portion of their personal information collected on a government form under purpose 'A' may be transferred to the National Archives of Canada, now Library and Archives Canada, but their consent to this transfer has never before been required nor sought, nor their ability ever conceded to speed up, slow down, or preclude access to that archival record, which is contrary to access and privacy laws and regulations. Neither Great Britain nor the United States has such a consent clause as appeared in the Canadian 2006 census, upon which nations Canadian census taking has been historically patterned. The only known exception is Australia in its special 'centennial' census of 2001, which is, within Western census practice, a one-time anomaly because of that country's unique convict-settled past.[43]

The consequences of this unprecedented consent clause within Canadian jurisprudence are very disturbing, and lead to the third major concern. Records in archives are useful not just for underpinning history and heritage and genealogy but also for protecting the rights of citizens and ensuring long-term accountability of government activity. Once established, this 'consent' precedent in Bill S-18 (now the Statistics Act, 2005, c. 31) will surely be insisted on in due course by privacy advocates for other case-level records that contain far more sensitive personal information than does the census. And the Canadian government, more concerned these days with privacy than access, might be sympathetic to such demands. These records could include those that form the backbone of the nation's historical records: the Aboriginal status registry system, Aboriginal residential schools enrolments files, immigrant applications and landing records, Canadian naturalization and citizenship forms, taxation and pensions forms, grants to farmers and scholars and scientists and business owners and women and artists, and hundreds, indeed thousands, more series of such records containing personal information.

Reflect on the likely consequences. Go back in time to analogous situations and imagine parents of Inuit or Aboriginal children being asked to consent to the transfer of forms (loaded with personal information) to the Public Archives of Canada that were then being used to remove their children and place them in residential schools. Imagine Japanese Canadians being asked to consent to the archival transfer of forms used to confiscate their belongings and relocate them forcefully from British Columbia to the interior during the Second World War. Imagine CIA-funded brainwashing victims in a Montreal hospital consenting to transfer their forms to augment the nation's archives. Imagine Chinese Canadians paying head tax, Ukrainian Canadians in First World War internment camps, 'juvenile delinquents' interacting with child-welfare agencies, and endless other very real examples from our history. Angry at intrusive and, they would argue, unjust government actions, the victims in these and similar cases in Canadian history would likely produce a consent level of about zero: Why help an oppressive (in their eyes) government have a nice historical archive? Yet those very same records, containing far more sensitive personal information than does the census, are now in Library and Archives Canada and are used by these same people and their descendants, not just to understand their past, but to pursue successfully legal, ethical, and financial recourse from the government. Even if some few did consent to the transfer of their records when under such duress, the incomplete and thus inaccurate surviving archival record would allow future administrators to dismiss claims filed decades later as mere exceptions. Canada's proud international reputation as a fair and just nation, with the will to settle such past grievances, rests on it having an accurate and reliable archive – one chosen by an arm's-length professional archivist, not one riddled with gaps in records. No one can predict the future, let alone tell what seemingly mundane government form today might be an historically significant document tomorrow: for the citizen, for his or her descendants, for their community, for the entire nation and its identity, for the settlement of human-rights injustices. And what is happening today is the history of tomorrow, and the records created today become the sources for human-rights claims tomorrow – if they are not gutted and sanitized by permanent access blockage.

At the level of Canadian public policy and governance, the census wars also reveal a disturbing trend in society. While archivists and historians certainly had strong beliefs about access to the historical census records and argued them vigorously, it was always done, in every brief, letter, and parliamentary appearance, with an explicit and meticulous recognition of the need for balance between the citizen's twin rights to know and to privacy. Good governance requires a balance between competing interests in modern complex societies. Yet that striving for balance was not displayed by the pro-privacy advocates, certainly not by Phillips nor his immediate successor, George Radwanski, and only rarely so by Fellegi. For them, it was an ideological war where privacy was somehow seen as a greater or more important right that should trump access. That is not what the law says nor what good policy demands nor what Canadians wanted through their parliamentary process. Privacy and access/accountability must exist side by side, in balance. Fundamental human rights are not negotiable. There can certainly be debate about how long personal information in various categories should be restricted, or how broad or narrow exemptions to immediate access to government information should be, but the core balanced principle must not be reduced to a fundamentalist ideological discourse. In the census wars, that threat became a reality in the formation of Canadian public policy. If it becomes widespread, Canada's history will undoubtedly suffer. The bad faith evident in the census wars – blatant stalling tactics, using technicalities of the law to undermine its clear intent and broader purposes, agreeing to abide by decisions of expert panels and then turning a blind eye when it was not the decision desired – undermines a flourishing democracy, deeply disheartens citizens seeking to remain engaged in the political process, and engenders the worrisome cynicism so prevalent about politicians and bureaucrats.

More optimistically, however, major victories were achieved in the census wars using the new technologies of e-mail and listserves. There were no paid lobbyists by those arguing for release of the historical censuses, no massive advertising campaigns, only lots of volunteer labour and personal commitment. Representatives from various associations and communities came together in the virtual world quickly and efficiently, and MPs soon understood the value (or otherwise) of having a gold star beside their names on the genealogists' main website and the significance of being bombarded with endless e-mails. Archivists and historians can effect change, therefore, if there be the will to do so, and if the policy-formation process remains open rather than ideological.

Then-archivist and now-historian Tim Cook has examined the growing societal concerns for privacy in light of the easy linkages now possible with pervasive information or computer technology and of the fears raised by the Cold War legacy of nations spying on each other and, too often, even on their own citizens. The cardinal text most cited in this regard by privacy advocates is George Orwell's *1984*, with its totalitarian 'Big Brother' state knowing and controlling every aspects of its oppressed citizens' lives. Tim Cook offers a telling reading of this classic text:

It is clear that we do not want an Orwellian world where citizens are under constant surveillance and where powerful corporations or intrusive governments know everything about our lives. But overreacting to the threat of privacy infringements also runs the risk of wiping out our collective history and heritage ... In trying to protect ourselves against Big Brother, we might unwittingly be playing into the hands of Orwell's other equally terrifying spectre: the Ministry of Truth, which rewrites history to fit the latest needs of the state. If we demand that certain records with archival value be destroyed [or access to them permanently forbidden, which amounts to the same thing] – for whatever reason – are we not advocating, indeed embracing, the potential for Orwellian truth-twisting? ... This is not simply an academic debate, as the fight over the census makes clear. Archives are in danger and archivists will have to champion the right for all Canadians to have access to our collective history and identity, and ensure that in the process of protecting against Big Brother, we do not end up killing Clio and supporting many Ministers of (Un)Truth. That in itself would be a crime perpetrated against all Canadians, those from our past, those living, and those not yet born.[44]

To avoid that crime, historians and archivists, again with their genealogist allies and others, must do four things, beyond their ongoing advocacy overall of a balanced approach to access and privacy. First, these partners must lobby hard after the 2011 census, using the mandatory statutory review clause, to have the consent clause removed from the act, so that only two censuses (2006 and 2011) are ruined for posterity. As a corollary, should the consent-clause precedent be proposed to be applied to any other kind of information-gathering form, from taxation to immigration to Aboriginal administration, it must loudly and forcefully be resisted. Perhaps with luck, given the disastrous 56 per cent result in 2006, far below what experts, including Fellegi himself, predicted, the consent clause can be removed from the census form before the 2011 census takes place, and while allies like Senator Milne are still in place within government. The CHA, for one, is starting that campaign now.

Secondly, the lobbying partners must insist that Statistics Canada and Library and Archives Canada employ a non-leading question for the 2011 census – indeed, that Statistics Canada adopt wording that strongly encourages the granting of consent. The archivist-historian-genealogist partners must also lobby strenuously so that both agencies adopt, as promised, a very visible public-education campaign for the 2011 census, should the consent clause remain, not unlike what the Australians did in 2001. It must be a media-blitz campaign equal in scale and cost to that which now encourages Canadians to fill in the census itself. That way, consent may indeed be 'informed.'

Thirdly, historians and genealogists especially (archivists are somewhat compromised here) must hold Library and Archives Canada to account that it has obtained, or reallocated internally, the resources in people, money, and technology to process and then preserve across time the born-digital (computerized) versions of the census that have now replaced the paper and microfilm census as the archival record, and that it is indeed keeping the digital census as a robust and readable electronic record across time. They must insist as well that Library and Archives Canada force Statistics Canada to adopt data-processing and machine-reading technology that does not separate (or that permits linkage later) the nominal from the statistical information when census returns are being uploaded into computers. To do otherwise is de facto to destroy the record illegally, and thus break the law.

Finally, and as a corollary of the above three, not just the librarian and archivist of Canada, but archivists (and their historian and genealogist allies) everywhere, need to engage much more in public-policy debates, in lobbying, in convincing senior government officials in cabinet and privy council offices of the importance of these information- and records-centred issues. Without strong and well-placed committed allies in the upper echelons of government and politics, archives everywhere, on a whole range of public-policy issues – not just privacy, but copyright, access, electronic-records management, digitization – cannot defend themselves against the likes of a predatory privacy commissioner or a stalling chief statistician that the 'system' can produce.

If these four things are achieved, a peace treaty can be signed. Until then, the census wars continue.

NOTES

1 Robert Hayward, Merle Massie, Jim Miller, John Reid, and Ian Wilson provided helpful comments and corrections on an earlier version of the paper. They are not responsible in any way for the interpretations presented or any errors that may remain.
2 The very influential auditor general of Canada, Sheila Fraser, made this point in a May 2004 keynote address to the Association of Canadian Archivists: the text is at http://www.oag-bvg.gc.ca/domino/other.nsf/html/200406sp01_e.html (accessed 25 November 2007). In their several

annual reports, Information Commissioners John Grace and John Reid eloquently linked the viability of access to information to having good record keeping or records management in place across government. For the value of archives, and archival records, to accountability in democracies, see Sue McKemmish and Frank Upward, eds., *Archival Documents: Providing Accountability through Recordkeeping* (Melbourne: Ancora Press 1993); Richard Cox and David Wallace, eds., *Archives and the Public Good: Accountability and Records in Modern Society* (Westport, Conn., and London: Quorum Books 2002), containing numerous case studies; David Bearman, *Electronic Evidence: Strategies for Managing Records in Contemporary Organizations* (Pittsburgh: Archives and Museum Informatics 1994); Chris Hurley, 'Recordkeeping and Accountability,' in Sue McKemmish, Michael Piggott, Barbara Reed, and Frank Upward, eds., *Archives: Recordkeeping in Society* (Wagga Wagga, New South Wales: Charles Sturt University Press 2005); and John Dirks, 'Accountability, History, and Archives: Confliciting Priorities or Synthesized Strands,' *Archivaria* 57 (spring 2004).

3 Section 19.2c of the Access Act permitted disclosure of personal information in accordance with section 8 of the Privacy Act. In other words, the handling of the census was consistent in both pieces of legislation.

4 See Information Commissioner of Canada, *Access to Information Act: An Indexed Consolidation* (Ottawa, 1994); Privacy Commissioner of Canada, *Privacy Act 1995 Edition: An Office Consolidation and Index* (Ottawa, 1995). Both available online on the website of the Department of Justice (http://www.justice.gc.ca).

5 National Archives of Canada Act, 1987, c. 1, ss. 5 and 6, then 4. The Public Archives of Canada, existing since 1872, was renamed the National Archives of Canada in 1987 and in 2004 merged with the National Library of Canada (established 1953) to create Library and Archives Canada. The versions of the institution's name cited in the text of this essay are correct for the relevant time periods.

6 A retrospective review (and summary) of the policy is available on Library and Archives Canada's website: http://www.collectionscanada .ca/012/010/012010-1012-e.html (accessed 1 October 2004). For a good overview, see Michael Nelson, 'Federal Information Policy: An Introduction,' *Government Information in Canada* 3, no. 1 (1995), http://www .usask.ca/library/gic/v1n3/nelson/nelson.html (accessed 3 October 2004). There had been earlier policies: Chapters 460 and 461 in the Treasury Board Secretariat Administrative Policy Manual of the early 1980s also strongly supporting archival activity within a public-policy and records-management framework.

7 For the history in these two paragraphs of Public/National Archives and Statistics Canada relations and these census transfers, see Jean-Stéphen Piché and Sheila Powell, 'Counting Archives In: The Appraisal of the 1991 Census of Canada,' *Archivaria* 45 (spring 1998): 28–30. The compromise included having relevant archivists being sworn in as employees of Statistics Canada for purposes of viewing census records prior to their transfer to the Public Archives.

8 Both published by the Public/National Archives of Canada in, respectively, 1987 and 1992, and compiled by the archivist responsible for the census records, Thomas A. Hillman.

9 See Piché and Powell, 'Counting Archives In,' 30–1, for the facts that follow, if not for the narrative that surrounds them.

10 Editors' note: Prime Minister Stephen Harper announced that Fellegi would be designated chief statistician emeritus upon his retirement in June 2008. See http://pm.gc.ca/eng/media.asp?id=1990 (accessed 14 August 2008).

11 Piché and Powell, 'Counting Archives In,' 31.

12 Suzanne Morton, 'Separate Spheres in a Separate World: African-Nova Scotian Women in Nineteenth-Century Halifax,' *Acadiensis* 22, no. 2 (1993): 61–83.

13 See P. Baskerville and E.W. Sager, *Unwilling Idlers: The Urban Unemployed and Their Families in Late Victorian Canada* (Toronto: University of Toronto Press 1998).

14 See Terry Cook, *The Archival Appraisal of Records Containing Personal Information: A RAMP Study with Guidelines* (Paris: International Council on Archives 1991), also in French and Spanish versions.

15 See *Appraisal Methodology: Macro-Appraisal and Functional Analysis. Part B: Guidelines for Performing an Archival Appraisal on Government Records* (Ottawa: National Archives of Canada 2000), approved by the national archivist of Canada in 2001. Part A (available at the same site) discusses the theory and concepts of appraisal. Both documents were written by Terry Cook and edited by a team of archivists at the National Archives. The policy and guidelines are at http://www.collectionscanada.gc.ca/information-management/007/007007-1041-e.html (accessed 10 November 2007).

16 Piché and Powell, 'Counting Archives In,' 34–9, 41. Powell and Piché did the actual appraisal research and analysis and wrote the appraisal report; Terry Cook was then the director of the appraisal function within the National Archives of Canada for all government records, and thus supervised this work.

17 'Consultations on Future Role of National Archives and National Library Announced,' *Canadian Heritage News Release*, 12 March 1998.

18 See John English, 'The Role of the National Archives of Canada and the National Library of Canada,' http://www.pch.gc.ca/pc-ch/pubs/johnenglish/english.html.

19 Association of Canadian Archivists (Terry Cook, author), *Written Brief on Bill C-54 Personal Information Protection and Electronic Documents Act*, 12 January 1999.

20 See *Canada Gazette*, 23 April 1911.

21 The CHA brief to the expert panel can be found at http://www.statcan.ca/english/census96/historic.htm.

22 *Globe and Mail*, 12 November 1999.

23 I.E. Wilson to I.P. Fellegi, 16 November 1999.

24 The full report can be found at http://www.statcan.ca/english/census96/finalrep.htm.

25 I.E. Wilson to I.P. Fellegi, 1 September 2000.

26 *Globe and Mail*, 11 January 2001 ('Show Us the Data'); 20 June 2001 ('Don't Muzzle Our Past'); 19 November 2001 ('Come to Your Census, Stats Can').

27 Environics Research Group, 'Consultations on the Release of the 1906 and 1911 Census Data,' 15 February 2002.

28 Both the Canadian Historical Association (Colin Howell) and the Association of Canadian Archivists (Terry Cook) had prepared briefs for, and then testified in Parliament in the spring and summer of 2001 to, MP John Bryden's Ad Hoc Parliamentary Task Force on Access to Information Review, each arguing for a stronger Access to Information role and the release of the census in that connection. Thus, both associations and these issues were doubtless on the radar of the Office of the Information Commissioner.

29 J.M. Reid to B. Waiser, 11 December 2002.

30 *Globe and Mail*, 18 December 2002 ('The Agency That Stole History').

31 See, for example, the *National Post*, 25 January 2003.

32 'Minsters Rock and Copps Announce the Release of the 1906 Census Records,' *Government of Canada News Release*, 24 January 2003.

33 In fact, the case was dismissed in June. Mr Justice Frederick Gibson of the Federal Court found that the chief statistician had legal care and control of the 1911 census records and could not be compelled to transfer them unless there was a negotiated agreement between the National Archives and Statistics Canada. While the National Archives of Canada Act can absolutely preclude destruction of any record without the archivist's authorization, transfer cannot be compelled. Yet the intent of the archives

legislation (as well as all good records-management practices) is clear: records having archival or historical value, and no longer any active or dormant operational uses for their creating department, should be transferred to the Archives. Fellegi was using the 'negotiated transfer' rubric as a stall tactic. But events, as will be seen, overtook this legal distinction made by Gibson, for the spirit of the archives legislation and public pressure demanded another solution.

34 Industry Canada press release, 2 November 2004.
35 J. Reid to B. Waiser, e-mail communication, 1 January 2008.
36 http://www12.statcan.ca/english/census06/reference/info/92yearquestion.cfm.
37 Robert Marleau, interim privacy commissioner of Canada, on 18 September 2003, asserted that 'informed consent requires complete and detailed information on the issues of necessity, purposes, uses, access and disclosure rights, sharing privileges, appeal mechanisms and oversight' (http://www.privcom.gc.ca/media/nr-c/2003/submission_nid_030918_e.asp) (accessed 10 November 2007). The 'informed consent' approach, mechanism, and wording on the 2006 census form fell far short of these standards. We thank Robert Hayward for this reference.
38 *Globe and Mail*, 14 April 2006.
39 http://www.affho.org/news/flash4.pdf (courtesy again of Robert Hayward) (accessed 10 November 2007).
40 *Ottawa Citizen*, 14 March 2007.
41 Thirty-two per cent of the respondents said 'no,' while another 12 per cent did not answer the question. This 12 per cent included close to a third of a million Canadians in institutional collective dwellings (seniors homes and other related institutions) whose information was gathered from institutional records and who were never asked about the informed-consent clause.
42 The argument here closely follows 'Written Brief and Speaking Notes for Presentation to Committee on Social Affairs, Science and Technology, the Senate of Canada, respecting Bill S-13, An Act to Amend the Statistics Act, presented by Terry Cook for the Canadian Historical Association and the Association of Canadian Archivists, 27 February 2003.' English and French versions were tabled with the committee.
43 On the Australian case, see Mary Neazor, 'Permanent Retention of Name-Identified Census Records in Australia and New Zealand,' *Archives and Manuscripts* 34, no. 2 (2006): 40–61. The Australians implemented a consent clause because, before 2001, all census records were destroyed, a curious by-product of the nation's long desire, until very recently, to prevent its

convict-settlement past being connected to individual citizens. So, asking
Australians to consent meant that approximately one-half of the centennial census would be preserved, a very happy result for Australian archivists, going from zero to 50 per cent. This Australian precedent is often
cited by privacy advocates in Canada; unfortunately, the result here was to
take the archival preservation rate from 100 per cent for all past censuses
down to a dismal 56 per cent for the 2006 census. Happy as Australia's
experiment may have been for their archival record, it established a disastrous international precedent.

44 Tim Cook, 'Archives and Privacy in a Wired World: The Impact of the
    Personal Information Act (Bill C-6) on Archives,' *Archivaria* 53 (spring 2002):
    108, 112, 114; Cook was considering the issue of archives and privacy in
    light of the then-draft PIPEDA, not the census per se. For an analysis of
    the archives-privacy interconnection across several countries, including
    others not mentioned in the title, see Livia Iacovino and Malcolm Todd,
    'The Long-Term Preservation of Identifiable Personal Data: A Compara-
    tive Archival Perspective on Privacy Regulatory Models in the European
    Union, Australia, Canada, and the United States,' *Archival Science* 7, no. 1
    (2007): 107–27.

PART THREE

The Digital Age

6 Search vs. Research: Full-Text Repositories, Granularity, and the Concept of 'Source' in the Digital Environment[1]

ROBERT COLE and CHRIS HACKETT

The advent of the digital revolution has raised fascinating questions about the relationship between computer technologies and traditional practices in the organization and analysis of information. One of the presumed benefits of the digital revolution has been its fundamentally egalitarian nature – the availability of resources online will, to a large extent, free researchers from the intervention of librarians, archivists, and other traditional gatekeepers of the cultural record. In one sense, this has come to pass. Digital resources have liberated researchers from many of the limitations imposed by libraries and archives, both innate – the physical location of the institution – and administrative – hours of operation, loan periods, and other arbitrary policy decisions. Barring technical difficulties, online researchers can access documents from around the world at the time and in the circumstances of their choosing. Yet the fact that these documents are no longer tied to a distinct physical space has not meant that access to them has been completely detached from traditional library or archival practice.

One of the essential questions surrounding the development of digital resources is that of the type and intensity of human mediation required to allow the information to be used widely and efficiently. The digital revolution aspires to grant researchers autonomy in accessing relevant materials, but the reality is more complex. The specific models of organization and description traditionally used to structure collections of print documents are no longer completely applicable to the digital environment, but the need for such work is by no means eliminated. Although online researchers have greater flexibility in terms of the strategies that can be used to identify materials, controlled vocabulary and structured points of access remain perhaps the most effective means of aggregating information. Indeed, as the volume and variety of digital documents increase, so does the need for the imposition of some sort of bibliographic control. The centrality of metadata schema – and the work of the metadata specialist – to any digitization project provides eloquent testimony to the need for sophisticated organization and detailed description of online repositories.

The enduring influence of traditional cataloguing practice – albeit under a new name and somewhat refined guise – does not seem to be completely atypical. In many spheres, old and new have co-existed quite comfortably in the age of digital revolution. Yet such mutual compatibility is obviously not inevitable. Revolutions, by definition, carry with them enormous momentum for change, but the transformations they bring about are not always foreseen and often engender unintended, and even undesirable, consequences. The digital revolution is no exception. Certainly, the relationship between online information technologies and traditional models of research and practice is somewhat ambiguous. The digital revolution has provided innumerable benefits to scholars and its overall value to academic research can hardly be denied. Yet, despite the enormous changes that this technology has spawned, its influence on traditional research methodology and approaches – what will, for the purposes of this paper, be termed traditional research culture – is mixed.

The proliferation of online resources over the last few years has provided scholars unprecedented convenience in conducting their research. Countless library catalogues, archival finding aids, and even complete digital versions of relevant sources have become available. These digital reproductions can typically be searched on a word-by-word basis. Such technology offers many obvious benefits, but the argument might be made that the advent of full-text searching also carries potentially problematic aspects in regard to academic research and teaching. Obviously, digital resources are used for such activities in a variety of non-scholarly contexts, but comprehensiveness and methodological rigour are not necessarily valued to the same degree in such cases. For academic disciplines, however, such issues are of paramount importance and, as a consequence, the place of full-text searching is more vexing. The situation is perhaps most evident in regard to humanistic – and, more specifically, historical – research, where close scrutiny of a wide array of texts is a central tenet.

The massive list of hits that are almost inevitably retrieved in full-text searches confronts a researcher with the Faustian bargain of limiting results through the use of complex Boolean chains of terms or relying on the cryptic judgments of 'relevance' rankings. In either case, he or she is left in doubt as to what has been excluded in the process. While the advent of searchable full-text digital collections presents some practical dilemmas for researchers, perhaps the deeper problem lies in the implicit messages that this technology conveys about the nature of research and the requirements of scholarly engagement with texts. It could be argued that digital resources – and more specifically the very powerful tool of full-text searching – sometimes undermine the unity and coherence of the sources they are presenting. Consider the concept of 'granularity' that stands at the heart of full-text searching. This concept – which holds that textual and other items can be dissected and reduced to their component parts for the purpose of categorization and searching – is somewhat at odds with some traditional verities of historical research, most notably the need to examine sources in their totality and to understand them in the broader context of their creation.

The emergence of the so-called semantic Web will likely exacerbate these tensions. Theorists developing this new generation of search tools posit a future in which machine-based evaluation of documents will even more explicitly favour the individual elements of a text as the focus of intellectual engagement. The semantic Web is to be made up of two components – websites broken into discrete metatagged fragments and sophisticated algorithms that will search, sift, and sort those fragments from across the Web to create the pool of information used by the user. Such a system would be able to understand the substantive 'meaning' of these distinct data elements and to adjudicate their relevance to a given topic with considerable precision. Whether these lofty goals can be achieved has yet to be fully tested. Nonetheless, the significant resources already invested in the system's development and the prominence of many of its key advocates (a roster that includes Tim Berners-Lee, the inventor of the World Wide Web) suggest that the semantic Web will likely be implemented in some form.

Given these circumstances, will traditional disciplinary assumptions be seen as antiquated as digital resources come to play a larger and larger role in the research process? Questions must be posed about how digital resources support and reinforce the methodological demands of their users. The essential nature of a discipline's methodology cannot be easily distilled, but, for the purposes of this discussion, perhaps two concepts are central to research in the humanities and, in particular, history: source and context. Sources are, in a general sense, the materials that a researcher marshals as evidence in support of the thesis that he or she is presenting. The process by which the historian identifies and evaluates these sources is, however, ideally an intensely rigorous one. Documents are not to be understood as sources simply because they have information relevant to the historical question being posed. Having content related to the topic at hand is, of course, essential, but that content is always to be interpreted and evaluated in light of the specific context of its creation and dissemination.

Historians constantly strive to contextualize the documents they are evaluating – this process is perhaps exemplified in the categorization of primary and secondary sources so central to historical research. The historian's search for context, however, goes far beyond the dichotomy of primary and secondary materials. Sources should be examined in relation to other works written by the author and similar accounts written by others to evaluate the credibility of the information being offered. Similarly, points within a given source must be understood within the broader context of the document as a whole. The idea that sources are to be viewed as integrated entities rather than simply an aggregation of facts and commentaries is a central tenet of historical methodology. Sources are – as it were – pieces of whole cloth and individual threads must be interpreted as part of the greater pattern. Sources must, therefore, be scrutinized with considerable care and, ideally, always read in their entirety. To limit the examination of a document exclusively to the material that seems most directly associated with the topic at hand would be considered very poor practice.

How well do digital documents lend themselves to this sort of close reading of sources? Online journals and reference works seem to function quite successfully in a research context since articles are generally brief enough to be read on screen or printed simply and without incurring exorbitant costs. Engagement with monographs, however, is more problematic. Working through dozens and even hundreds of pages of text on screen appears to be a very onerous task for most researchers, even younger scholars who presumably have more experience assimilating large amounts of text online. Moreover, even well-designed sites will have difficulty surmounting the inherently fragmentary nature of digital entities. Books, pamphlets, and other printed matter provide a very tangible and constant reminder that each component part – paragraph, page, chapter, etc. – is inextricably tied to a larger physical and intellectual entity. This is not necessarily the case with online materials where the cues to understand works as integrated wholes are not quite so obvious.

Indeed, in many cases, the individual elements of a work can easily be perceived as disembodied from the whole. This sense of fragmentation is perhaps most easily discernible in regard to the powerful tool of full-text searching. The user is, to a very considerable degree, able to 'atomize' the text and reorder the information in a manner more amenable to his or her specific research interests. Many full-text repositories enable users to search a specific term or set of terms and retrieve all the pages on which the word or words appear. In this way, researchers are able to select passages related to their topic without necessarily having to read or even skim other parts of the source. This is obviously a very powerful tool, but it also provides a shortcut that may – if used uncritically – circumvent one of the key tenets of research: seeking to understand the source in its broadest possible context. Indeed, the argument might be made that full-text searching significantly lessens the imperative to read the text in its entirety.

The full-text searching of digital collections potentially blurs the traditional line between 'searching' and 'researching.' These two activities have, of course, always been inextricably linked, but there has traditionally also been a distinction between searching – the identification of sources for study – and research – the evaluation of those documents for relevant material. The former is an absolute prerequisite for the latter – good research cannot be done in the absence of excellent searching – but the processes have been understood as separate. Research – or at least a significant portion of the task – has required working through large bodies of text seeking out relevant material. Library catalogues, bibliographies, and other tools could be consulted to gather potentially useful documents, but the assessment of the specific contents of these works – aside from the rather imprecise guidance of indexes and tables of contents – generally required detailed engagement with the texts.

The advent of full-text searching of digital collections, however, has allowed these processes to occur simultaneously or, perhaps more accurately, allowed them to be perceived as occurring simultaneously. The full-text search in this sense not only identifies possible sources but provides a de facto evaluation of the specific information contained in documents. Indeed, the evaluative component of digital-search technologies has become quite explicit in the form of 'relevance-based' analyses of search results, systems using various algorithms to rank lists of titles in order of their presumed significance to the search topic. Reliance on such a mechanistic form of document evaluation is, on a philosophical level, deeply problematic for traditional research culture. Identifying, reading, and ultimately sorting a wide range of material have always been viewed as essential to building the context necessary to interpret what has been found. Circumventing that process through mechanical rather than human evaluation of documents would require an enormous shift in perspective.

This distinction between identification and evaluation defines the paradox of full-text searching in academic research and teaching. As a search tool – an instrument solely of document retrieval – the benefits of full-text searching are vast and absolutely undeniable. Indeed, in terms of simply compiling a list of potentially useful titles, the impact of digital resources has undoubtedly been transformative. Full-text searching allows researchers to identify potential sources among documents that might not ordinarily cross their paths or whose usefulness might not be discerned simply by looking at a table of contents or index. This search process, however, is one of accumulation of potential sources, whereas the actual assessment of content and the degree to which any given source requires engagement is a research process. Full-text searching potentially becomes much more problematic as an instrument of active evaluation.

This is not to indulge in a crude technological determinism dictating that, because a system allows a researcher to engage a document in a fragmentary manner, he or she will inevitably choose to do so. If sources are mishandled, this is ultimately the responsibility of the researcher and not the medium in which the information is presented. Nonetheless, the fact that digital technology exists in a somewhat adversarial relationship with traditional research culture is a matter of some importance. The fundamental principles and assumptions that appear to animate engagement with digital texts are fairly deeply at odds with traditional practice. The organizational principle of 'granularity' that lies at the heart of digital information provides the most basic point of conflict. This concept defines the digital environment both functionally and philosophically, but it runs completely counter to historians' traditional understanding of sources as organic and fundamentally indivisible entities.

As digital resources become more and more a staple of research activity, what does this tension mean in terms of the enduring viability of traditional scholarship? Are long-standing disciplinary values and assumptions being undermined? In regard to established researchers, the answer to this question is most likely no. Already immersed in traditional research culture, this community will likely avoid the potential pitfalls of utilizing digital resources. In many cases, scholars will simply apply traditional methodologies to the new technology. Where they do choose to deviate from these practices and use the digital technology in different ways, they will likely do so with a full understanding of the limitations and implications of these decisions. Perhaps far more problematic for scholars, however, will be coming to terms with this technology as a pedagogical tool. How do these online resources fit into their efforts to teach students proper methodology and practice? For individuals just learning their craft, the messages that are subtly, and perhaps not so subtly, conveyed by digital technologies may resonate more deeply and have more serious consequences.

The concept of granularity, and frankly many of the intellectual shortcuts that it tacitly promises, will undoubtedly be extremely seductive. The promise of a positive outcome – a list of relevant sources – without the tedium of traditional process – careful examination of the texts – will obviously be enticing. To be sure, the challenge of communicating proper research methodology to students has always existed. These skills and attitudes are not innate and have to be developed. Yet the process of assimilating these skills likely poses even a greater challenge in the digital environment. Anyone working at a university or college library reference desk can testify to the resistance of many students to search retrievals that extend beyond a modest number of titles. Under such circumstances, they will often ask if there is another search term that can be added or some limitation imposed that will reduce the results to a more 'manageable' total. Such responses are doubtless partially driven by pragmatism, but perhaps they are also indicative of a conscious epistemological choice. Why wouldn't a generation of students whose daily life entails constant interaction with Google searches, wikis, and hyperlinked websites believe in the complete malleability of information?

Indeed, why wouldn't students view research in this way when the evaluative power of digital-search tools is accepted as a given – or at least a deeply cherished goal – by many people involved with this technology. A maxim that seems to have some currency in contemporary library debates about the creation of information systems is that 'only librarians like to search, everyone else likes to find.'[2] In one sense, this statement is undoubtedly true. Most people would prefer to acquire a set of relevant sources without the difficult and time-consuming process of reading and evaluating a wide range of documents. From a traditional research perspective, however, the pithiness of the aphorism is exceeded only by its fatuousness. For instructors, the question is not what students 'want,' it is what students 'need' to learn. Abdicating the process of serious and intensive evaluation of sources is not a luxury that can be enjoyed by scholars or students seeking to work seriously within the discipline. For students, this dissonance between the explicit demands of their instructors and the tacit promises of the information systems on which they are increasingly dependent may have significant intellectual consequences.

Current trends in information technology seem to offer little encouragement that this dilemma will be easily resolved. As was discussed earlier, the emergence of the semantic Web offers the promise of computer processes that can interpret documents with ever-increasing sophistication. Research, as it is traditionally understood, will become the domain of 'automatic agents' that will be able to evaluate the substantive content of texts and determine their relevance to a given topic. People will ask natural-language questions of the computer, which will parse that information into queries, select appropriate databases based on contextual information about the query and the person asking it, run the queries, and aggregate and analyse the data retrieved. Semantic Web theorists even propose that these systems will also understand the research question with such nuance that the agents will be able to modify continually the parameters of the search in response to the data being recovered.

The promise of the semantic Web has, of course, yet to be fully realized. Undoubtedly, the various scholars and organizations – including the W3C Consortium, the body that sets standards for Web development – participating in this enterprise face formidable barriers in achieving these goals. The amount of content metadata necessary to support these complex processes will be vast. Descriptors will need to be created to represent almost every concept reflected in the massive textual universe being investigated – an enormously costly and time-consuming enterprise. Indeed, the idea that many of these tags will be generated by users seems to be an article of faith among semantic Web theorists. Similarly, the 'ontologies' – the structured set of inferences that determines the relationship between the content being presented – used within the semantic Web would have to be almost infinitely complex. This is certainly true if these systems seek to meaningfully engage the multifaceted questions posed in scholarly research.

Questions as to the feasibility of the semantic Web, however, are far outside the scope of this essay. The authors acknowledge that they do not possess the expertise to make such judgments. Yet, even if the semantic Web is destined to operate largely as has been articulated by its proponents, serious questions can be raised as to its compatibility with traditional historical methodologies. Some of these problems even appear to be tacitly recognized by semantic Web theorists. Tim Berners-Lee, James Hendler, and Ora Lassila acknowledge in a 2001 article that the ontologies driving the semantic Web will be immensely powerful but not without limitations. The authors note that designers of the semantic Web must ultimately choose between answering a finite set of questions well or embracing a wider range of queries, some of which will be beyond the capacity of the system to address. They argue for the latter option, accepting that 'paradoxes and unanswerable questions are a price that must be paid to achieve versatility.'[3]

Their candour is admirable, but the statement is likely to disappoint historians hoping to use the semantic Web in their research. The unanswerable and paradoxical queries that Berners-Lee and his colleagues are willing to sacrifice in order to achieve 'versatility' are the very ones that historians are most likely to pose. Historical questions are – at least to the standard of rigorous logical proof – generally unanswerable. History is an interpretative discipline. Scholars marshal evidence and their rhetorical skills to put forward persuasive arguments, but the adjudication of the value of any proposition is ultimately subjective. The questions they pose are often paradoxical. Historians generally are not seeking simply to decide between proposition A or B but to examine the interstices between them or, more accurately, to explain how both can exist together and, in many cases, with a multiplicity of other propositions. Will, for example, the semantic Web be able to engage the relatively straightforward thesis 'The French Wars of Religion were not about religion'?

Whatever functional capability the semantic Web possesses when it ultimately arrives, however, this technology will present tremendous challenges in the education of new scholars. If current search tools can be perceived as undermining traditional historical methodologies, the semantic Web will undoubtedly be an even more corrosive force. The promises as to the quality of computer-based evaluation of information will be much grander, and the exhortation to abdicate this activity to machines far more explicit. Students will doubtless find the blandishments of a system that offers comprehensive and sophisticated document selection – with constant adjustment of search parameters – highly alluring. Implicit in such an endorsement of the semantic Web would be a rejection of some core tenets of traditional historical methodology. The ability of researchers to adjudicate the processes by which documents are being selected is likely to be highly circumscribed. The algorithms driving current relevance-ranking systems are often obscure to users and, in some instances, very consciously protected from public view. The ontologies and other core elements of the semantic Web will probably be no more transparent.

The metadata that will serve as the foundation of the semantic Web provide one potential arena of conflict. Although the semantic Web's emphasis on human-created descriptors as a means of content evaluation clearly enhances its research utility, the process of 'crowdsourcing' by which this metadata are to be generated raises serious issues in terms of provenance and consistency. These descriptors will not be selected from a standard lexicon and according to established guidelines, nor – presumably – will the identity of their authors necessarily be accessible to future users. These circumstances make a critical assessment of the validity of a given set of metadata almost impossible. How can the credibility of descriptors be evaluated when their authorship – or even the general intellectual assumptions that framed their creation – cannot be determined? The careful planning and coordination that existing text-encoding projects undertake to ensure the coherence of their tagging suggests that crowdsourcing would be unlikely to produce a consistent and reliable research set.

Even the elimination of crowdsourcing, however, would not completely surmount the dilemma that the semantic Web presents as a tool of historical research. The more intractable difficulty is that the semantic Web – and perhaps all computational-based models of information evaluation – rests on assumptions about the nature of 'relevance' and of research in general that are alien to traditional models of historical study. The semantic Web clearly works on the twin premises that it will be able to replicate the capacity of a researcher to evaluate and select documents and that, in delegating these activities to an automated system, nothing substantial will be lost in the terms of the nature and quality of his or her work. While the first proposition may ultimately prove to be true, the second is – at least in the context of historical investigation – demonstrably false. For historians, the act of engaging documents that ultimately prove outside the narrow scope of their topic is not simply a necessary evil but an indispensable component of the research process.

In the same way that context is essential to evaluating sources and the specific information they contain, a broad perspective is necessary to interpret historical events and forces. Obviously, some arbitrary limits must be imposed – a study on the trial of Louis Riel will likely not strictly require an intensive examination of horticulture in Sri Lanka – but the parameters must be set as broadly as possible. Limiting the array of sources to a pre-selected set of items narrowly related to the topic area would not be sound practice. For historians, the purpose of working through documents is not simply to eliminate material that falls outside the scope of their work – the process itself, not only the outcome, is significant. In separating 'the wheat from the chaff,' benefit is derived not only from the kernels of grains that are gathered but also from the material that is ultimately discarded. Indeed, the capacity of the researcher to determine what is ultimately 'relevant' to his or her work is ultimately dependent on this process. Relevance is not determined a priori but evolves organically as the researcher engages a wide variety of potential sources.

What the semantic Web ultimately seems to offer, therefore, is merely an ersatz form of research. The question that remains is whether such limitations will preclude its use in historical investigation. The argument can be made that the modern research environment has already rendered the strict observance of traditional methodological standards untenable even for professional academics. The sheer volume of material now accessible and the inexorable pressure to publish have made the adoption of certain expedients almost inevitable. Obviously, the decision as to whether – and in what manner – tools such as the semantic Web should be used will ultimately be up to the individual researcher. Nonetheless, the risks of sanctioning such a minimalist definition of 'research' would, at least in a teaching context, appear to carry significant risks. For students just learning their craft, heavy reliance on such systems would offer only a distorted view of the nature of research and an experience that would hamper the development of the critical thinking skills that are ostensibly the hallmark of training in the humanities.

These criticisms are not, of course, intended to undermine the fundamental legitimacy and utility of digital resources within scholarly research and teaching. Only the most passionate Luddite could, at this point, seriously call for a return to the presumed purity of a pre-digital information universe. This would not only be impossible but would also be manifestly undesirable – digital resources are an incredibly powerful tool. The power of digital resources, however, is exceeded only by the demands and expectations that are placed on them. The term often associated with digital technologies is 'transformative,' and this is – at least from a research perspective – a profoundly heavy burden. While the impact of digital resources on research is undeniable, whether that influence is destined to be as extensive or as benign as is sometimes suggested is still a question demanding serious evaluation. This is particularly true in regard to issues of pedagogy. The erosion of traditional research practice may not be an intended consequence of the digital revolution, but it is one that must be addressed nonetheless.

Libraries and other cultural repositories have always been forced to deal with the thorny question of where considerations of access and researcher convenience should fit among the various imperatives that these institutions must address. The digital revolution has, along with other factors, given these considerations a very high standing in recent years. Presented with a delivery system that allows an unprecedented level of access, libraries and other cultural institutions have firmly embraced digital resources and devoted considerable attention to their development. In so doing, they have also adopted a very specific sense of what constitutes appropriate digital access. Certainly, the digital revolution is defined not only by technological change but also by the specific user expectations that it created. Libraries and other custodians of digital repositories have largely endorsed these expectations, articulating a 'user-centred' development model. There is undoubtedly much to recommend this approach, but it has also helped create a potential disconnect between digital resources and traditional research culture.

This dissonance is naturally of most pressing concern for cultural repositories that are directly associated with educational institutions. Yet even repositories that do not possess explicit pedagogical responsibilities may still be compelled to engage this question on some level. During the 2007 meeting of the Canadian Historical Association, Cheryl Avery of the University of Saskatchewan Archives presented a wonderful paper on the place of archives in Canadian public life.[4] In her conclusion, she set out a number of differing perspectives on the role of archives and archivists and offered a quote which described them as 'servants of evidence.'[5] The phrase captures perfectly the dilemma facing all cultural repositories in the digital age. While the imperative to develop digital tools applicable to a broad range of researchers is obviously important, 'usability' should be only one consideration among many. The question of how these tools fit with the methodological demands and assumptions of disciplines must be addressed as institutions strive to make their collections not only better servants of users but also better servants of evidence.

NOTES

1 Elements of this essay were presented at the Annual Meeting of the Bibliographical Society of Canada, Montreal, June 2007. The authors would like to thank Susan Dahl, information analyst, EnCana (Calgary); Jim Bohun, student affairs officer, Office of the Dean of Students, University of Alberta; and John Harris, assistant professor, Department of History and Classics, University of Alberta, for their insightful commentaries.
2 The phase has doubtless been articulated in a variety of forums, but one of the most notable proponents is Roy Tennant. See, for example, Roy Tennant, 'Avoiding Unintended Consequences,' *Library Journal* 126, no. 1 (2001): 38.
3 Tim Berners-Lee, James Hendler, and Ora Lassila, 'The Semantic Web: A New Form of Web Content That Is Meaningful to Computers Will Unleash a Revolution of New Possibilities,' *Scientific American* 285, no. 5 (2001): 38.
4 Cheryl Avery, 'Archives and Public Policy' (paper presented at the Annual Meeting of the Canadian Historical Association, Saskatoon, May 2007).
5 Terry Eastwood, 'Towards a Social Theory of Appraisal,' in Barbara Craig, ed., *The Archival Imagination: Essays in Honour of Hugh A. Taylor* (Ottawa: Association of Canadian Archivists 1992), 74.

7 Preserving Digital History: Costs and Consequences[1]

YVETTE HACKETT

Archivists have been discussing digital technology and its potential impact on the archival record for more than thirty-five years. Sometimes, it seems that all this effort has had little practical effect inside many of the archival institutions mandated to deal with changes to the processes of records creation, maintenance, and preservation. In large part, this difficulty in integrating digital records into existing archival work stems from the fact that digital technology is a moving target, developing new capabilities and upgrading constantly while simultaneously becoming obsolete at the same rapid pace. Digital technology is multifaceted, affecting most of the tools used to perform archival work, the environment archivists operate in, the standards and practices available to them, and the records themselves.

Archivists must focus a great deal of time and attention on money, specifically on available budgets and their frequent inadequacy to fund the job at hand. Over the years, the lack of human and financial resources has been addressed in a number of ways – by allowing a backlog of unprocessed material to grow; by introducing technology and streamlining procedures to improve productivity; or by narrowing the scope of an archives' acquisition mandate. Fewer records acquired meant less material to process and describe, fewer fonds to make available to researchers.

It seems unlikely that any of these methods will successfully support the integration of digital records into the acquisition, preservation, and reference responsibilities of archivists. In the transition from analog to digital technology, it appears even less likely that the automation of another archival function, like workflow control, will allow archivists to accomplish more with less, at least to the degree required to address digital records.

Analog vs. Digital Life Cycle

Among the myriad changes brought about by digital technology, one of the most significant is that it has altered the timing of the archivist's involvement in the life cycle of the record. While paper records could be safely left with the creator for long periods of time with little danger that they would be destroyed or become unreadable, this is not the case with digital records. The time period during which records can be left without intervention has shortened considerably, with at least some action required at early stages to prevent loss and destruction. Just as there are differences in the longevity and stability of analog records, be they vellum, papyrus, acidic paper, or magnetic or optical media, so there are similar variations affecting the many components of digital records – be they hardware, software, operating systems, physical carriers, logical formats, or the complex interrelationships that must be reproduced to maintain the readability of records and to provide on-going access to them. Chemical composition and environmental conditions remain key factors in longevity, as they were with analog records. However, with digital records, survival can also be affected by the maturity of the technology, the economic well-being of its inventor, and the success or failure of national political interventions or even global business alliances.

One can also discuss whether the record life cycle still has three distinct phases in a digital environment, or whether the traditional active, semi-active, inactive equation has been replaced with a two-phase model, where the semi-active period merges into the active period and the main distinction in the life cycle of the record is the shift in custody from the creator to the unit or organization responsible for its long-term preservation.

In the early phases of computer-technology development, online storage was so limited and expensive that most data were kept offline. The ratio of online to offline storage could not be interpreted to consistently represent active and semi-active phases of the life cycle since even active records were kept offline. Today, the widespread online/near-line/offline storage configuration might suggest a three-phase cycle, but these all exist within the creator's environment, with a second possible online, near-line, and offline storage environment available from the preserver. Generally, the trend seemed to be that, as the reliability of the technology stabilized and storage costs dropped, record creators perceived major benefits in maintaining the immediacy and ease of access which resulted from keeping records online for increasingly longer periods of time, especially in database applications. In the more fragmented desktop world, with records spread among hard drives, back-up media, and a variety of allocated personal and shared network spaces, as well as dependent on a wide range of software programs, the practice of moving records from the technological environment in which they were created to a more standardized record-keeping environment gained prominence. But, here again, the distinction between active and semi-active phases was increasingly blurred, reflecting storage choices as much as operational requirements. In recent years, the rapid increase in the amount of digital material being created and the growing size of digital objects that can be created (especially non-textual products such as graphics, photographs, audio, and moving-image files) are once again straining storage budgets.

What is inescapable in this transition from the analog period to the digital environment is the effect of the current situation on archival operations. Paper-based records continue to operate on their traditional long-term schedules, while digital records demand attention in the much shorter term. Both groups of records are expanding exponentially, as the paper period hits the post-Second World War period of growth and every new development in the technology seems to facilitate steady increases in the volume of digital records requiring appraisal, at a minimum, if not acquisition, preservation, and access services as well. This essentially represents a doubling of archives' responsibilities, which so far they have been expected to absorb without an equivalent doubling of their human and financial resources.

The technical challenges of digital technology require research and testing of solutions, and archival theory and practice requires review and possible adjustments to address digital issues. These activities demand funding and take time, but many of these have been successfully undertaken over the years, offering a multitude of recommendations, best-practice guides, and bibliographies to the archival community. The primary reason archives are having such a difficult time coming to terms with the digital era is the complete inadequacy of resources to deal simultaneously with the parallel requirements of the old paper and the new digital records.

Non-textual but still analog media – photography, recorded sound, and moving images – were early harbingers of both this shortened life cycle and the preservation problems associated with rapid technological obsolescence, but few archivists made the connection, focusing instead on the progression from textual-analog records to textual-digital records. It is also interesting to note that the situation for libraries is somewhat different because the bulk of their acquisitions have not traditionally taken place thirty years after a book's publication, but address contemporary publications in the current market. As that market moves from an analog to a digital environment, one side of the equation will diminish, albeit slowly and with a 'hybrid' period, while the other increases. This is unlike the archival world, where both sides of the equation are growing simultaneously and will continue to do so for the foreseeable future. In fairness, this apparent balance in the library world has been upset by the explosive growth of the World Wide Web, providing a widely accessible platform for the public dissemination of digital materials for which libraries are primarily responsible.

Records Creation and Management vs. Archival Functions

The introduction of digital technology into both government and corporate workplaces also had another unexpected effect on archival institutions and the profession. It served as a major trigger to dismantle or seriously weaken the existing records-management systems in departments and businesses. In order to purchase new information technology, funds had to be found elsewhere in the organization. The promises of the information technology industry were, first, that the desktop computer would make typing pools and secretaries obsolete, and, later, that the network environment would make filing clerks and most records-management staff unnecessary, their functions apparently taken over by the 'find' command. All this salary money could therefore be reinvested in information technology which would be faster, cheaper, and more efficient. This proposed paradigm shift appeared accurate until the volume of material to be searched, on storage media with ever-increasing capacity, overwhelmed the simple free-text search method. This led to the next proposed solution – the increased use of the 'delete' key, usually based on the date and time stamp on a digital file since this was one of the few pieces of consistently available metadata in the desktop environment. Old files could be identified and deleted, or moved to offline storage which could quietly become obsolete in a desk drawer.

If no records survived the new, digitally based records-creation environment, there would be little left for archivists to acquire and preserve. Many archivists became involved in the development of these systems. Initially, these were individual automated applications – databases – many of which were intended, if not actually designed, to replace traditional case file series. This chain of events pulled even more archivists from their traditional duties and presented them with an enormous learning curve about digital technology and its many potential business applications – all being developed by an industry famous for its uninformative error messages, its incomprehensible user manuals, and its very short-term definition of the 'long-term' as a time period not to exceed eighteen months.

The role of archivists in the design and deployment of automated-records-creation systems proved to be problematic. The process was time-consuming, spread over long periods of time, and required an extensive knowledge of the operational activities and workflows of the creating organization. The ability of an archivist to contribute to this process varied enormously, depending on circumstance. If they worked within the creating organization, their contribution could be valuable if they learned the technology as well. Archivists responsible for multiple creating organizations, or archivists who developed relationships with records creators after the fact, could deal only with increasingly hypothetical situations.

Archivists who were able to observe or even participate in a system-development project found that plans and designs changed frequently, with functions being removed owing to cost overruns or functions being added as an afterthought. How a system would generate records, and which records it would in the end contain, could usually be ascertained only after the system was built and working. While this potential role for archivists in system design occasionally simplified subsequent appraisal, transfer, and description work, it could not replace it and turned out to be another new role to be performed in addition to existing duties, thereby further draining resources.

As the technology continued to develop, this new role grew to encompass the development of today's records-management systems, which were designed to identify and control the massive volume of small digital objects being generated in today's desktop environment. These activities too, as with the asymmetrical development of the analog and digital life cycle, required additional human and financial resources to help archivists and any surviving records managers to participate. Archives needed to implement records-management applications for the control of their own records, as well as learn how to appraise them, and extract and take custody of records within them. But, again, few substantial budget increases were forthcoming. Funding was inadequate to turn pilot projects into programs, or to transform recommendations into practical solutions. Just as the records' creators had found money to buy computers by dismantling their records-management systems, so archives attempted to find money to fund these new functions by discontinuing services that were not valued by their stakeholders – as long as they did not affect the essential services of providing storage space for semi-active records, or appraisal, or transfer, or re-boxing, or arranging, or the development of descriptions to facilitate retrieval, or preservation activities, or reference services, or ...

Digital Records Cost More: Storage, Preservation, and Access

There seems little need, at this stage, to offer evidence that it costs archives more to handle records created and used in digital form than to preserve their analog equivalents. Digital technology pushes almost every type of cost earlier in the life cycle of the record, and consistently requires more frequent interventions to ensure long-term preservation and accessibility.

The obvious exception to the above statement might appear to be storage space, since bytes on digital carriers occupy far less shelf space than boxes of textual records, containers protecting glass-plate negatives, or cans of film negatives and soundtracks. Environmental conditions are of at least equal importance, though some digital-storage media might require more limited ranges of temperature and relative humidity than analog records can accommodate. These restrictions always come at higher costs. Offsetting any savings on storage space is the fragility of many of the physical carriers and their data-encoding methods. These media characteristics, with the ease of replication of the digital-bit stream, have combined to create the now standard practice of producing and maintaining duplicate preservation copies, preferably in widely separated geographical locations and, preferably too, relying on two different types of technology to reduce the likelihood of catastrophic failure of the stock.

Copying equipment and physical carriers cost more than acid-free file folders and archival storage containers. Obsolescence cycles are shorter – moving from potentially centuries to the current maximum of eight to ten years. And even the single-decade time frame faces many obstacles. The archives must have managed to select a 'winning' technology from among many competing formats and then have the internal knowledge and resources to maintain it several years beyond its disappearance from the mainstream consumer market, into that marginal existence where manufacturers will offer only one or two additional years of technical support before production of the stock is halted and the playback devices can no longer be repaired.

Analog records do require conservation work, sometimes as individual projects, sometimes as more widely required processes like de-acidification. Digital records require ongoing refreshing cycles of their physical format, for the foreseeable future. Depending on the preservation strategy being used, digital records may also require conversion of logical formats, that file structure and encoding scheme imposed on every digital object by its creating software. If emulation is chosen as the preservation strategy instead, this approach requires layers of emulated environment to be developed and maintained on top of a constantly changing technical platform.

Analog records frequently require intensive manual conservation work whereas the processes surrounding digital records lend themselves to automation. However, as the earlier automation of descriptive systems in archives demonstrated, attempts at automated processing or automated workflow never seem to deliver the promised saving, and always cost more than the previous method, though they often introduce a range of valuable benefits to those institutions able to pay for their in-house development or purchase.

From an access perspective, the ease with which digital records can be transformed to provide rapid access and ease of use to researchers has also dictated the production of one or more reference copies, in a variety of consumer-friendly formats, to be made available online or produced on demand.

Digital Records Cost More: Appraisal, Processing, and Description

Archival appraisal must take place sooner after the creation of digital records than was the case with analog records because maintaining ongoing readability requires ongoing attention, even while in the hands of the creator. The appraisal process also requires additional steps. As well as identifying the records selected for long-term preservation, the archivist must explore the technical feasibility of preservation and its potential long-term costs, which will be based, in part, on an understanding of which preservation strategy would best serve the records. This technical evaluation frequently involves a fairly detailed investigation of the technology used to create and maintain the records, the technological dependencies of the various digital components which constitute the record, and the documentation on how the components must work together to reproduce the record. All this information is required to document successfully the records' technological context of creation, to transfer digital records from their creation or maintenance environment to a long-term preservation system, and to reproduce them over the long term.

This need for detail may, to many, appear to run at cross-purposes to the concept of macro-appraisal which begins at a higher, less detailed level by analysing administrative-juridical, provenancial, and procedural contexts of creation rather than the records themselves. In an effort to interpret this approach as a time-saving measure, some may overlook the fact that the hypotheses developed during these analyses must eventually be tested against the records themselves to be validated. If macro-appraisal texts tend to focus on the intellectual rather than the technical aspects of the process, it is certainly because the range of preservation strategies available for analog records is fairly limited and widely known by both archivists and records creators.

As well, the appraisal process requires a documented analysis of the measures in place in the record-creating and record-keeping environment designed to ensure the authenticity of the records. Again, these requirements were widely understood for analog records, depending strongly on the unbroken chain of custody and the documented work processes of the records creator. As a result, this aspect of the appraisal might not actually be discussed extensively in the report, unless the authenticity of the records was seriously in question. The ease with which digital records can be altered requires a more overt identification of the elements which were in place where the records were being created and maintained.

Early appraisal also creates a requirement for a consistent monitoring process to ensure that the appraisal remains accurate over time as the technology generating the records and the organization producing and using the records change and adapt. Applications may migrate to new software platforms, requiring alterations in the system's design. Organizations may subtract from the existing content of the record to reflect changes in their mandate, or add to it if a secondary use for the records is suddenly discovered.

Processing and description of records for long-term storage can also be more time-consuming than similar work on analog media. Some metadata must consistently be collected at the level of the digital object, whereas item-level control remains rare for all but a limited number of very important analog records. With digital records, the software dependency of the record, and the interrelationship of digital components, must be recorded or the archives will not know when access to the content of the file, or the ability to reproduce accurately the form of the content of the record, will be permanently lost. Processing of digital records may run into further obstacles such as compression, encryption, digital signatures, or the presence of other measures designed to protect copyright or to meet security requirements. Each of these additional layers of technological complexity must be undone, removed, or, at a minimum, documented during processing.

The development and maintenance of an infrastructure appropriate to the processing and preservation of archival digital records may also run into resistance from those responsible for the technical infrastructure supporting the day-to-day operations of the archives. The fact that both the institution's day-to-day work and its archival work use computers seems to have generated much confusion about the differences between the current systems vs. preservation systems. Current systems provided by IT units support archivists in the word-processing, accounting, and public-speaking activities of their job. Preservation systems include the obsolete technical environments required to appraise, process, and describe archival records. Current systems require short-term backups while preservation systems require redundancy and stringent environmental conditions to support long-term preservation, without catastrophic loss or failure. Finally, these specialized systems frequently require higher privacy or security requirements than the archives' own business records. Though both current and preservation systems use computers, the similarities end there. They should not be run by the same unit, nor should they ever be merged.

Finally, the processing phase may include the production of more than one version of the records, including temporary working copies which are subsequently destroyed, multiple copies of preservation-master formats, and various versions of reference copies to ensure accessibility. Unless carefully controlled, this may result in confusion about which copy or copies should be retained.

Despite the many obvious similarities between analog records and their digital equivalents, the above review of some of the standard archival functions illustrates the steady accretion of exceptions, variations, and extra steps which the digital era requires. As with the additional costs already noted in relation to the current overlay of the 'late paper' with the 'early digital' periods, and the archivists' increased involvement in records management, almost every aspect of archival activity, from appraisal through transfer, processing, description, preservation, and reference, is affected by the digital-technology layers. And, despite the promises of increased efficiency and improved productivity which always accompany the introduction of automation into the workplace, in the end costs only seem to go up while funding only seems to go down.

Digital Records vs. Digitized Copies

The most recent digital issue to have developed within archives is the competition, and occasional confusion, between records created and used in digital form, on the one hand, and digitized copies of analog records, on the other. This tension is fed by the internal competition for funding within archival institutions, which, with existing budgets, are trying to develop programs to acquire and preserve the recent generations of digital records and to meet the growing demand to produce digitized copies of their analog records. Today, digitization of high-profile or high-demand records is the top priority of archives, libraries, museums, and most other cultural institutions and funding is being reallocated to meet that demand. The argument can be made that this funding has been released from microfilming and photocopying activities, which are being discontinued, as well as from the on-site provision of researcher services, which have been moved to the Web. But, given the dearth of archival programs around the world currently acquiring and preserving digital records, it seems fair to suggest that digitization has attracted funds which might otherwise have been used to build digital capacity for records preservation in archives.

The need to compete with digitization projects can be construed as the fourth major delay in integrating the preservation of digital records into the traditionally analog archival landscape. Initially, digital-record programs were promised funding after the archival-description systems were automated, an undertaking that required the development and adoption of standardized descriptive practices. This particular automation exercise has never ended, moving steadily forward from stand-alone systems using in-house standards to the adoption of shared standards such as the Rules for Archival Description and Encoded Archival Description, the development of national shared-access systems such as

Archives Canada, federated search capabilities, global networks, and portals, and, today, the idea of participatory cataloguing which will include archives' users in the description process.

The second event started somewhat later, but also proved to be on an endless development loop. This was the automation of the desktop and its constant need for upgrading – new software packages, increased processing speeds, in-house and external networks, more storage space. In some types of organizations, this process included the automation of work processes and the digitization of current records to improve efficiency. This environment eventually led to the third event – the need to design and implement records-management systems for the digital objects being created and used on that desktop. This use of scanning technology created a new category of digital record for archives to deal with – the digitized version of an analog record which was subsequently destroyed by the creator. If the analog version survived, it was frequently not classified and filed. During this era, resource-allocations choices might be made between developing digital archival capacity and buying a colour printer; or implementing records management for digital records or just increasing server space. All technology expenditures seem to come out of the same pool of resources.

Today's digitization programs in archives are not only absorbing significant amounts of funding, the copies are filling the newly developed Trusted Digital Repositories. If archives develop a single infrastructure to handle digital objects, will the components of digital records find themselves backlogged behind high-volume digitization projects? Or does a digitized copy of an analog record require the same degree of security, environmental control, and verification as a digital record with no analog version to fall back on? The copy can, after all, be recreated if necessary with only the same minor threat to the original record that existed the first time it was removed from storage, handled, and scanned, assuming, of course, that the originals have not been destroyed.

In audio-visual archives, the segregation of masters and reference copies of films and videotapes is a long-accepted storage practice. It is too early for a solid cost analysis of whether it will be less expensive and more efficient to store digitized copies and digital-preservation masters all together in an environment, and according to procedures, meeting the preservation standards required for records, or whether two systems would be more appropriate – a premium system for the records and another based on a proper cost and risk assessment for the

copies. One danger would be if standards had to be lowered to accommodate the volume contained in a combined repository. Near-line and
offline storage technologies exist because online storage is a relatively
more expensive option.

Archives on the Digital Road

Mainframes

From an archival perspective, the history of the computer era can be
divided into a number of segments, each with different implications for
the profession. Furthermore, the timing of these implications will be
very different for the many types of archival institutions that exist, with
their varying mandates, budgets, and users.

While every broad generalization will have its exceptions, one can
argue that the initial mainframe-computer period produced two types
of digital records – one requiring preservation and one not. Data, such
as the information collected during the 1960 U.S. census, offered a
degree of manipulability and the promise of long-term reuse as part
of an important time series. Scientific data collected during non-
replicable experiments like Apollo space missions, or the types of
climatological observations that included measuring the amount of
ozone over the Antarctic (before the hole formed), offer similar long-
term value. Whether appropriately defined as records or not, this
material was worthy of preservation but much was lost and is still
being lost.

Less important, perhaps, were early database applications in government departments and corporations which seemed poised to replace
traditional case-file series. Searching for a solution to the well-known
storage problems of large case-file series, archivists hoped that these
databases would make the need for selection criteria and sampling obsolete. Careful appraisal showed, however, that they were more like
tracking systems, containing little data from the case file except dates
and deadlines of work processes. Initially developed at a time when
digital records carried no evidential weight, these databases could
serve as little more than automated finding aids to paper case files containing transaction records such as forms, memos, and correspondence.
It would take years, and a major injection of digitized copies into the
workflow, before digital case files could begin to match the archival
value of their analog predecessors.

Desktops

Early word-processing equipment, and eventually early desktop technology, introduced the 'big typewriter' period of records creation, where computers were used to create textual records, but such records were consistently printed to paper and used, signed, classified, and filed as paper documents. Document size was limited because digital storage capacity was small and logical file formats were highly proprietary. There is no archival reason to maintain the digital version of documents from this era in a word-processing software, since there is no value added at all.

As desktop word-processing software, spreadsheets, and database packages became ubiquitous, it remained reasonable to ask, at least in institutional settings like government departments and corporations, whether documents that existed only in digital form were likely to belong to the 1 per cent to 5 per cent of records normally selected by an archivist for long-term preservation. With personal records, this equation is not relevant because individual creators could easily choose to keep important material in digital form only, including, for example, draft versions of correspondence or manuscripts. Other individuals might just as easily choose to print to paper, however, to avoid dealing with a hybrid filing system.

E-mail and Networks

In its early days, e-mail was an immature technology used to organize meetings and lunches or to ask quick questions that earlier would have been asked over the telephone. But as attachments were added, and network access at least within an organization became the norm rather than the exception, e-mail replaced various forms of memos and announcements and became the preferred method to distribute documents. As more and more people became part of global communication networks, individuals also moved their correspondence, and many of their phone calls, into e-mails. As with the desktop environment, it is essential to know the point when a record creator's 'print to paper' system became an online system. And, finally, the World Wide Web allowed everything imaginable, including records, to move into the digital realm – a environment with no analog equivalent.

Each technology reached a tipping point when the paper copy became an unnecessary relic of the analog past. Each user then had to decide when to accept this transition, and to what extent. Compression allowed increasingly large digital objects to move through communication networks; digital solutions were developed to address the need for signatures and non-repudiation; and legislation was passed giving digital records standing in various types of transactions. Courts of law began considering the admissibility of digital evidence, and practices to ensure authenticity were developed.

Are We There Yet?

Are we losing important records? We are well past the tipping point where the preservation of digital records should be understood as an integral part of the archival landscape, rather than a cutting-edge pilot project. The much-discussed threat of the digital dark age remains possible but unproven. Doom-laden announcements of lost digital records, or lost access to digital records, are frequently followed by revelations that somebody had a copy after all, or the necessary device to read it.

The overwhelming volume of digital material and the many new forms of widely available communication and publication suggest that the difficulties are just beginning. Some archives are ignoring these difficulties, and some are confronting the fact that the digital revolution has reached their users but are not actively adjusting to the reality that it has reached their donors as well and must be dealt with now rather than later. Still others are studying the situation as it applies to their context, while a very few are forging ahead, trying, failing, testing, and establishing best practices.

On the institutional side, among governments, corporations, and archival institutions, the only thing that seems to remain constant is the absence of adequate funds to deal with the digital transition and the many changes it is bringing to the entire spectrum of records creation, maintenance, and preservation. Archives cannot weather these changes without assistance, or something will be left out. At the moment, it is too often the digital records documenting the late twentieth and early twenty-first centuries. Public archives and their public funding sources, and private archives and their private funding sources, must learn to recognize which digital activities can be undertaken later and which will offer archivists only one, often early, chance at intervention.

Records produced by private individuals present an interesting problem for archives. Appraising and acquiring digital records earlier in their life cycle is only a partial solution to the need to overcome the

inherent obsolescence of the digital environment. There is no legislated relationship between the archives and the majority of its private
donors which might simply be rescheduled to an earlier date. There is
also a limit to how early an archives can decide whether the records
of an individual donor, family, or even small organization or association will meet their criteria for acquisition. In the interim, disks will
become unreadable, file formats will be come undecipherable, e-mails
will be deleted, and websites will be overwritten. While benign
neglect often ensures the survival of the analog record, only active
intervention will generally carry digital records forward across time,
space, and multiple, incompatible computing environments. As was
the case earlier with government and corporate records-management
environments, archivists must take an active role in developing
and widely disseminating good record-keeping practices for the
private-record creator.

Archives are badly understood and too often absent from the public
eye. As a result, their needs are not recognized or understood during
decision-making processes like budget allocation. Within archives,
digital records are similarly misunderstood and too often absent from
archives' business-planning and resource-allocation exercises. It is
eerily reminiscent of the long struggle that non-textual media endured
before the value of photographs, sound recordings, and moving images was accepted in many archives. A great deal of material was lost
during that wait. Digital records' stability and longevity, from the beginning of the digital era to today, is even shorter. Archives must move
past studies, tests, and pilot projects and into a period of long-term
implementation and maintenance of digital-preservation programs
supported by ongoing research and analysis of the constantly evolving
technological base underlying today's record creation, maintenance,
and preservation systems.

NOTES

1 Yvette Hackett has participated in the International Research on Permanent Authentic Records in Electronic Systems (InterPARES) Projects 1
   (1999–2001), 2 (2002–6), and 3 (2007–12). Initiated in 1999 at the School of
   Library, Archival and Information Studies, University of British Columbia,
   these projects study the theory and methods of ensuring the preservation
   of records; assess the reliability and accuracy of records during their life

cycle; and aim at 'putting theory into practice,' specifically in the case of small and medium-sized archives. See http://www.interpares.org.

The ideas expressed in this article reflect the findings and recommendations of the InterPARES Projects as well as the author's experience working with digital records at Library and Archives Canada since 1993.

PART FOUR

Accountability and the Public Sphere

8 Archives, Democratic Accountability, and Truth

TERRY EASTWOOD

In the Broadway production of *Beyond the Fringe*, a reporter interviews a pedantic police inspector about the Great Train Robbery. After quibbling that it was not really a train robbery because there was 'no loss of train, it's merely what I like to call the *contents* of the train that were pilfered,' the inspector, when asked who he thought did the deed, replies that the police believe that 'the tell-tale loss of property, the snatching away of money substance ... all point to thieves.' The reporter then says, 'You feel that thieves are responsible.' The inspector replies: 'Good heavens, no! I feel that thieves are totally *irresponsible*, ghastly people who go around snatching your money.'

Michael Harmon, in *Responsibility as Paradox: A Critique of Rational Discourse on Government*, uses this theatrical episode to illustrate that 'each of responsibility's dual, indeed opposing, meanings is logically necessary for comprehending the other. That is, the belief that people's actions *cause* events to occur ... is a precondition for their *answerability* to others for those actions.'[1] The propensity in contemporary society to ask people in all walks of life to render an account of their actions, to judge those actions, and to reward the actor or, as is more often the case, to demand some measure of redress, recompense, or punishment for failure suggests that as a society we are becoming increasingly preoccupied with responsibility and with unravelling its meaning in specific instances.

The core idea of accountability is responsibility. At the simplest, the term accountability means the obligation to render an account or answer for discharge of duties or conduct. Jane Parkinson ably summarizes this essential meaning. 'For the purpose of conceptual clarity,' she says, 'we must distinguish accountability from the system to guarantee it, but also from the effort to compel observance, or act on it by whoever is holding someone to it. The latter is difficult to characterize abstractly, since it depends entirely on the tactics of those with power. That there are persons with the power to hold other persons accountable is all that can be implied by the concept of accountability.' As Parkinson also observes, 'accountability … is a condition attached to the person who is to give account, not the person calling for it.'[2] In Gerald Caiden's summary of its nuances, 'to be accountable is to answer for one's responsibilities, to report, to explain, to give reasons, to respond, to assume obligations, to render a reckoning and to submit to an outside or external judgment.'[3] But events in which accountability is at issue are rarely simple. The complexities of organizational arrangements and societal interactions are such that it is often difficult to decide who is responsible for what and to whom, and, *if the facts of the matter are known*, what is often even more difficult, to judge actions and, if necessary, deal with their consequences. Establishing the facts becomes very much establishing the truth in any given case where accountability is at issue. This is hardly surprising: whoever judges actions or deals with their consequences will necessarily seek to understand the truth of the matter. As the philosopher Bernard Williams observes, modern culture exhibits two attitudes towards truth. On the one hand, we are all suspicious of being deceived, for no one wants to be fooled. On the other, we have grown sceptical that objective truth exists at all, for no one wants to be naive, to be seen to accept explanations or justifications for actions or events as the truth of the matter.[4]

With these difficulties registered, what part do archives and archivists play in the pageant of accountability, in the public comprehension of the often paradoxical tangles in which actors' responsibilities manifest themselves in events? To ask this question implies another question: For what and to whom are archives and archivists accountable? Before dwelling on these questions, it is necessary to explore accountability's core concept, responsibility.

The Paradoxes of Responsibility

Harmon argues that there are three contemporary meanings of responsibility. The first, the idea of agency, is 'the idea that freedom of the will makes people, in Jean Paul Sartre's phrase, the "incontestable authors" of their actions.' The second, the idea of accountability, is 'the idea that people are answerable to a higher, usually institutional, authority for their actions.' The third, obligation, is 'the notion that moral action is determined by its correspondence to principles and standards deriving from sources external to the agent.'[5] In his analysis of responsibility as paradox, Harmon borrows theologian H. Richard Niebuhr's depiction of the responsible self as one who is responsible *for* one's actions and who is accountable *to* other members of a moral community. In Niebuhr's terms, responsible individuals are both makers and answerers.[6] Harmon's paradoxes are easy to state in a fairly simplified form. Although he discusses them in the context of public administration, they surely apply to some degree in any bureaucratic setting.

The first, the paradox of obligation, is this. If public servants are free to choose a course of action but must act only as others authoritatively choose for them, practically speaking they are not free. If they do choose freely, their actions may violate authoritative obligations, in which case their exercise of free choice is irresponsible.[7] The paradox of agency is a little more complicated. For there to be responsibility, there must be blameworthiness for morally faulty decisions, but most rational arguments put blame and guilt on individuals and are suspicious of collective responsibility, which if regularly asserted would undermine institutional stability and social control. Blaming someone tends to imply the blamer's innocence. But blaming invites the blamed one, in a paraphrase of Harmon, to deny guilt, justify the action, dispute the facts of the matter, claim an inability to control the events in question, or protest that he or she was just following orders. As Harmon says, all such claims of innocence are 'endlessly arguable.'[8] The paradox, in a simplified version, is that individual acceptance of responsibility undermines institutional answerability, and claims of innocence as the answer given for actions can be achieved only by the individual's denial of moral agency or responsibility. We sense this contradiction when we feel, as we often do, that something is horribly wrong when demands for accountability are made, for the paradoxical quality of obligation and agency in a bureaucratic setting makes it difficult to assign blame or innocence in incidents when some institutionalized failure seems to have occurred. Bureaucratic environments invite us to separate moral agency from authoritative obligation, but neither can we act effectively without being responsible agents, nor can we, as individuals, answer completely for institutional behaviour.

Harmon's third paradox, the paradox of accountability, is this: 'If public servants are accountable solely for the effective achievement of purposes mandated by political authority, then as mere instruments of that authority they bear no personal responsibility as moral agents for the products of their actions. If, on the other hand, public servants actively participate in determining public purposes, their accountability is compromised and political authority is undermined.'[9]

Harmon's statement of the paradox of accountability refers to democratic accountability. In the broadest sense of the term, democratic accountability aims to have public officials render an account of their actions in order to allow citizens to be well informed on the performance of government so as to make intelligent political choices. Accountability is closely associated with two other concepts: transparency and responsiveness. Transparency refers to the degree to which the actions and activities of an organization are in the open, are accessible to the public at large. Accessibility in this sense requires that the public be able to see what happened through adequate documentation of actions and activities. In the public sphere, it is difficult to imagine citizens of a democratic society knowing what their government is up to without there being a high degree of transparency. Responsiveness refers to the degree to which the agent's performance of actions and activities serves the interests of those to whom it is accountable. Responsiveness of governments refers ultimately to their ability to respond to the collective will in delivering effective public programs. When responsiveness is at issue, accountability is frequently extended from the simple responsibility to render an account for actions to a greater responsibility to render an account for the results achieved. In the sphere of public education, for example, accountability often refers to the extent to which schools achieve outcomes thought proper either by the political authorities or by parents.

In a classic in the literature of public administration, Carl Friederich argued, as summarized by O.C. McSwite, that '"the complexity of modern governmental activities" renders it inevitable that there will only be an approximate understanding between the people and their elected representatives and their agents, public servants, "concerning the action at hand or at least the end to be achieved."'[10] Hence, irresponsibility is an inevitable result of the impossibility that the principal and the agent will have a common understanding of what appropriate action is. For Friederich, responsible conduct stems from officials taking the *initiative* necessary to achieve the goals of government. As he puts it, 'the responsible administrator is one who is responsive to two dominant factors: technical knowledge and popular sentiment. Any policy which violates either standard, or which fails to crystallize in spite of their urgent imperatives, renders the official responsible for it liable to the charge of irresponsible conduct.'[11] In an equally famous response to Friederich's article, Herbert Finer argued that the only way for people to govern themselves democratically is for them to express their individual preferences through the vote, and that these preferences together constitute an expression of popular sentiment which elected representatives can use 'to hold administrative officials accountable and to punish them when they go wrong.'[12] Where Friederich puts his faith in technical expertise and aims to create room for public officials, both elected and not, to take initiatives so long as they act in response to popular sentiment, Finer reflects the view that administrators will naturally tend to be self-interested, conspiratorial, and ideological in their motives. Accordingly, he takes the very common position that accountability is needed to prevent abuse of government's power, which he sees as deriving from the people in a democracy. It is true that, as Paul Thomas notes, 'preventing the potential abuse of power is the ultimate goal of numerous accountability arrangements and procedures.'[13] Still, it is clear that both Finer and Friederich see a distinction between political leaders and public servants, who, as agents, are at one remove from the sovereign people and subject to account through elected officials to the people.

Canadian political scientist Donald Aucoin argues that the proper seat of democratic accountability in the Westminster parliamentary tradition is the cabinet. In his view, accountability is secured when three conditions are met. The executive must 'report on the conduct of public business in ways that promote transparency' about its political decisions, its policy instruments, and its performance; the elected assembly must have the capacity to question the executive on all the same matters; and the accounts of government must be subject to public audit and evaluation.[14] As he sees it, the ability of ministers of the crown in Canada to account to Parliament and therefore to the people for the decisions and actions of their administration is being eroded by the expanding role of the auditor general to evaluate management practices, program effectiveness, and policy outcomes, as well as by the tendency to have public servants testify before parliamentary committees.[15] In short, Aucoin believes that the traditional doctrines of cabinet solidarity and ministerial responsibility demand that ministers must regularly account to Parliament for the decisions and actions of the agencies for which they are responsible. Aucoin's view is but one of many lamenting the diffusion of responsibility in organizations. In this he appears to be like Finer, for he seems to want to preserve the ability of ministers of the crown to take responsibility not only for policy but also for the actions of the agencies for which they are responsible.

Commenting on the famous Friederich-Finer exchange about the role of public administrators, McSwite observes that the difference between the two comes down to the assumption each makes about human nature. Friederich takes the position that people can be trusted to do what is good or right, whereas Finer takes the position people cannot be so trusted. McSwite also observes that the two differ mainly about the point at which, in practice, policies as value statements can be separated from facts as administrative techniques. It would appear that most people agree with Finer. Public-opinion polls in many democratic states indicate that trust or confidence in public officials is very low. Democratic or political accountability is often cast as a matter of the public being able to know the decisions of government, to reflect on them, and to respond to them. In this view, political accountability plays itself out mainly as a dialogue about policy. However, the public appetite for knowledge of the details of public mismanagement and scandalous behaviour would indicate that both matters of policy *and* questions concerning how policy is administered are important when it comes to making a judgment about government performance. It is a reasonable assumption that most people in our society come to know about both present and past decisions and actions of government (or, for that matter, of other organizations like business corporations) through various forums of public discourse and news rather than from records, that is, indirectly in some mediated way, mainly, for many, through the popular media.

Archives and Accountability

The stage is now set to examine the role of archives and archivists in accountability. Laws provide the highest statement of policy and, presumably, express the collective will as regards the role of archives in governance. Traditionally, Canadian archival laws aimed mainly to establish the authority of archival institutions, what they can do rather than why they do it. They did not explicitly mention accountability. Rather, they tended to emphasize the cultural role of archives. For instance, the Ontario law passed in the 1920s and existing until a new law was passed in 2006 described the overarching object of the Ontario Archives as being 'the discovery, collection, and preservation of material having any bearing on the history of Ontario.' Another object, obviously long outdated before the change in 2006, directed the Archives to conduct 'research with a view to preserving the memory of pioneer settlers in Ontario and of their early exploits and part taken by them in opening up and developing the Province.'[16] It might be argued that the popular understanding of the object of public archival institutions has tended to favour something like this celebratory view expressed in the old Ontario law, and that political leaders have long preferred such a cultural, historical role for archives. This may be changing. The two most recent Canadian archival laws do make reference to accountability. The Archives and Recordkeeping Act of the province of Manitoba speaks about accountability in the preamble to the law in these terms: 'whereas good recordkeeping by government supports accountability to the public and enables the preservation by the Archives of Manitoba of government records of lasting significance …'[17] One of the purposes of the Ontario Archives in its new enabling law is 'to foster government accountability and transparency by promoting and facilitating good recordkeeping by public bodies.'[18] Even without explicit legislative mandate, public archival institutions often claim to have a role in furthering democratic accountability. For instance, in 2004, the National Archives and Records Administration of the United States made this claim in its vision statement: '[The National Archives] is a public trust on which our democracy depends. It enables people to inspect for themselves the record of what government has done. It enables officials and agencies to review their actions and helps citizens hold them accountable.'[19] It has since amended its vision statement, making the National Archives appear far less forceful as an agent of accountability, but in its mission statement it says: 'We ensure continuing access to the essential documentation of the rights of American citizens and the actions of their government.'[20] In 2009 its motto on its website proudly proclaimed that 'democracy starts here.'[21] As recently as 2004, a statement now removed from the website of the Library and Archives of Canada (LAC) stated that the records of the federal government are critical 'to the capacity of citizen's to hold government accountable for its decisions and actions in our democratic society.'[22] LAC's website now makes no reference to it having a role in accountability. Its enabling act gives it a cultural role 'to acquire and preserve the documentary heritage' and 'to make that heritage known to Canadians and to anyone with an interest in Canada and to facilitate access to it,'[23] which appears to be something of a retreat to an older role, one quite distinct from that adopted by the governments of Manitoba and Ontario.

The sad situation of the British Columbia Archives illustrates the critical importance of legislative policy. British Columbia has never passed an enabling law for its archives. The only law that has regulated the disposition of public records since it was first passed in the 1920s is the Documents Disposal Act.[24] Amendments to the law in the 1980s allowed agencies to schedule records for destruction. Much headway was made during the 1980s and 1990s by the then British Columbia Archives and Records Service (BCARS) to bring about systematic records classification and disposition of the records of provincial government agencies. Then, in 2003, the Liberal government of the day passed the Museum Act to make the Royal British Columbia Museum a crown trust able to raise its own revenue.[25] This act made the British Columbia Archives part of the new crown trust by giving it responsibility 'to hold and manage the archives of government.' The records-management component of BCARS was renamed the Corporate Information management branch and moved to the Ministry of Labour and Citizens' Services. In a report made soon after this change in the status of the Archives, the provincial archivist reported that 'the new crown trust and the government ministries will be working out memoranda to ensure that government's archival records are protected and transferred to the government archives.'[26] The effort to work out memoranda with ministries has apparently hit a serious snag. For at least the last six years, no records have been transferred to the British Columbia Archives. The new corporation, which must in large measure rely on its own efforts to raise revenues to support its work, has failed to reach satisfactory financial arrangements with ministries for long-term preservation of records deemed to have enduring value.

The popularity of appeals to the role of archives in accountability, it is fairly obvious, is a response to the effects of freedom-of-information (FOI) laws over the last twenty-five years or so in instilling some understanding of the capacity of records to render an account of the actions of public officials and the administrations they serve. Many such laws state that their purpose is to enhance knowledge of the conduct of government and government accountability. A 1994 study found that twenty-two of the then existing sixty-one FOI laws in Canada and the United States had the express intent of enhancing accountability, while another eighteen had the express intent of enhancing democratic principles of a free and open society.[27]

If we look for an expression of the role of public archival institutions in democratic accountability, we could find none better than three statements of Judge Harold H. Greene in his decision in the FBI records appraisal case. After acknowledging that the U.S. Freedom of Information law indicated Congress's desire to foster accountability through access to federal records, Judge Greene wrote:

> That leaves for consideration the public interest. Congress has determined that federal record-keeping shall accommodate not only the operational and administrative needs of the particular agencies but also the right of the people of this nation to know what their government has been doing. The thrust of the laws Congress has enacted is that governmental records belong to the American people and should be accessible to them barring security and privacy considerations for legitimate historical and other research purposes. The thrust of the actions of the FBI, perhaps naturally so, has been to preserve what is necessary or useful for its operations. The Archives, which should have safeguarded the interests of both the FBI and the public, in practice considered only the former …
>
> Hence the direction in the law requiring the preservation of documents having historical or research value and those which are needed for the protection of the legal rights of citizens. The Freedom of Information Act is related to those interests and serves similar purposes … Yet the congressional mandate has special relevancy to the Federal Bureau of Investigation. Its files, perhaps more than those of any other agency, constitute a significant repository of the record of the recent history of this nation, and they represent the work product of an organization that has touched the lives of countless Americans. Many of these have been in public life, others have achieved fame or notoriety of a different sort, still others have merely been the subject of routine investigations (security checks, suspected criminality, or inquiries into background or character). The files of such an agency contain far more of the raw materials of history and research and far more data pertaining to the rights of citizens than do the files of bureaus with more pedestrian mandates. The public interest demands that great care be taken before such records are committed to destruction.[28]

Judge Greene, it seems fair to say, is speaking here in the long tradition of accountability as a measure of watchfulness for government abuse, since he raises, by implication at least, the spectre that the rights of citizens might be abused. It is difficult to divorce accountability from the trends in law, particularly in administrative law, to review administrative decisions and actions for their propriety and fairness. As legal scholar David Rosenbloom puts it: 'Given that indirect channels of evaluation and accountability through elected officials are of limited adequacy at best, the citizen must be afforded some direct and fair means of confronting those who wield the power of the administrative state.'[29] Courts and citizens alike depend on the capacity of records to reveal decisions and actions that have consequences for the subjects of the records. The societal need for records that are faithful testimony of decisions and actions is acknowledged in the U.S. statute laying out the duties of the archivist of the United States in records management. In that statute, the first objective of records management is to promote 'accurate and complete documentation of the policies and transactions of the Federal Government.'[30] Public archival institutions are, we can see, implicated in accountability both in their role to appraise records and approve their destruction and in their role to foster good records-management practice.

Livia Iacovino observes that 'some archivists see the role of archival institutions ... progressing naturally from the traditional view ... concerned with the evidential and contextual nature of records and the impartiality they provide, to ensuring that records do in fact provide these qualities and assist in keeping governments "honest."' She goes on to say that 'this can only be achieved if the archival authority has investigative powers and a records audit role which includes involvement in record-keeping systems from the design stage. Thus some archivists would argue that accountability for record keeping is concerned with the quality of the record in terms of its accuracy, reliability and integrity.'[31] At another point, she observes that 'evidence of the *decision making process* provided by documentation and access to such evidence was seen as fundamental to accountability' in the reforms of administration undertaken in Australia in the 1980s.[32] Arguing along similar lines, Verne Harris states that archival agencies need 'suitably powerful instruments for the auditing of public record keeping.'[33]

Such an aggressive role has never been spelled out for public archives in Canada. In fact, such authority as they are given in records management has for the most part tended to be soft – advisory or supportive rather than investigative. To give public archives in this country a records-audit role would implicate them deeply indeed in an important mechanism of accountability, but is it a role archives are equipped to take on or even should in principle assume? There is little indication of a political will to give archives such authority, and not much administrative will in the quarters, like Treasury Board Secretariat at the federal level, that concern themselves with the regime for information and records management. The Library and Archives of Canada Act gives the institution a role 'to facilitate the management of information by government institutions.'[34] There is little reason to expect that archives could handle enhanced authority to audit record-keeping practices, at least with the resources and expertise they have at hand. Part of the problem with the current soft approach to the records-management authority of archives is that the resources allocated have rarely been adequate to the task. It assumes a great deal to expect that governments, habitually niggardly when it comes to spending on records management, will experience some miraculous conversion to the realization that records management is of such importance that archives should be given an audit role and the resources to do the job. Moreover, federal, provincial, and state governments already have audit offices, and nothing prevents those offices from doing the job of auditing the adequacy of agencies' record keeping. Even supposing that archives were to be given this task, they would have to develop far greater record-keeping and audit expertise than many of them currently possess.

But should archives even take on the responsibility to audit agencies' record-keeping practices? Is such a role compatible with their established responsibility, which, as matters stand now, they strain to shoulder as well as they should, to act as the arbiter of public-records disposition? Government audit offices do not have archives' responsibility to cooperate with agencies to achieve effective and efficient management of records. To perform their role in disposition, public archival institutions strive to maintain a position of disinterest so as not to be swayed in their judgment on the fate of records by the immediate concerns of the records creators. This is critical if they are to carry out their responsibility to decide which records have enduring value. Adding an audit role to the picture would greatly complicate the delicate relationship between the agencies creating public records and the archival institution. Would agencies of government be inclined to cooperate in this often highly sensitive matter of records disposition with the same partner that just exposed their poor records-management practices? For all of its difficulties, the soft approach provides the opportunity to work together with agencies at objectives that serve the interests of both parties as well as the public interest in responsible record-keeping and disposition of records. Christopher Hurley sees a similar reason for separating the role of advocate for and supporter of good record keeping from the role of enforcer of standards and requirements. If a single authority possessing both roles confronts a case of unlawful destruction of records, Hurley observes, 'it may begin by threatening punishment and end by mentoring. That may afford a convenient escape from potential bureaucratic difficulty or the consequences of exposing official wrongdoing, but it is no way to uphold accountability.'[35]

But hidden in this issue of the role of archives in ensuring that adequate and accurate records of government action are made and disposed of responsibly – a role amounting to a bedrock condition of realizing democratic accountability – is the question of the placement of archival authority in the scheme of government. In the Canadian system of government, public archival institutions at the federal and provincial level are agencies in the executive branch. In such situation, it is difficult to see public archives standing up against political, executive power to expose to public understanding poor record keeping or irresponsible destruction of records. In most jurisdictions, it is against the law to destroy records without some due process of approval, which usually, in Canada, means only after the approval of the archival authority. This problem comes into relief most vividly when questions arise, as they often have in democracies, about the disposition of the records of the ministers of the crown. Critics often suppose that public archives are not in a position to ensure that records will be responsibly disposed and made accessible to facilitate what is often called historical accountability, of the kind of which Judge Greene spoke. Years ago, the Canadian historian C.P. Stacey observed: 'Nobody, I am sure, will condone for a moment using denial of access to documents for the purpose of protecting a politician or a political party. Nevertheless, as long as archivists work for governments, and governments are composed of politicians, archivists I fear may be occasionally doing just that.'[36]

Verne Harris argues that 'the structural pull in all record making is towards the replication of existing relations of power,' in which archives and archivists cannot help but be complicit. Governments have a strong motive to control the processes of records making, keeping, disposition, and accessibility, and, in any system of government where the archives is in the position of a normal agent of executive administration, pressure can be exerted on the archives to do the bidding of elected officials. All these processes, as Harris and others have observed, are rife with political acts. Like it or not, then, it is unreasonable to expect that archives can be removed to some independent status outside the accountability arrangements of government. Gordon Robertson, who held the office of clerk of the Privy Council and secretary to the cabinet, puts it this way: 'We seem to have recognized, whether by rational analysis or by intuition, that politics is the governing process of a free society and any solution that rules out politics rules out freedom.'[37] So, if people do not trust governments always to act responsibly and transparently and if archives are agents in some measure to ensure that they do, it is, then, to the tissue of rules governing record keeping and the powers given the archival authority that we must turn for solutions to the conundrums and paradoxes of the matter.

As regards the powers of archival authorities, it might be asked whether greater control, scrutiny, and enforcement in the record making and keeping arena might have an adverse effect on transparency, particularly in the sensitive decision-making quarters of government. Kerry Badgley, Margaret Dixon, and Paulette Dozois provide some evidence to support the notion that access legislation at the federal level in Canada has had little chilling effect on operational records keeping.[38] However, there is also evidence that senior officials have been influenced by the new access regime. Political scientist Donald Savoie's extensive interviews reveal that 'departmental officials in both central agencies and line departments report that Access to Information legislation has made them reluctant to commit their views and their recommendations to paper. The fear is that these [records] could well appear in the media and force [officials] to either support or defend their [ideas] in public.'[39] Tightening control of record making and record keeping might very well have the effect of emphasizing the notion that the primary purpose of keeping records is to catch officials out, to emphasize the view of accountability as watchfulness for government abuses, rather than the view that records promote the responsive quality of backward- and forward-looking reflection on actions, as mechanisms of iterative thinking about the conduct of affairs and their betterment. Good record keeping in support of accountability requires above all an adherence to the ethic of accountable, transparent, and responsive organizations, whether public or private, and greater control, scrutiny, and enforcement are as likely to make agents even more careful and self-protective than they are now as they are to improve the situation.

Alasdair Roberts, who has studied the operation of freedom-of-information laws worldwide, reaches a conclusion that 'the beliefs that government leaders cannot be trusted, that there is too much secrecy, that government is too complicated to be readily understood – all of these may combine to form a powerful *ethic of detachment*, which leads to (and justifies) a failure to engage actively in political affairs or insist vigorously on the accountability of political leaders.'[40] This is another paradox. Greater transparency might just be at the expense of truth. Williams nicely frames this relationship: 'The government's behaviour in information management depends not just on the degree of curiosity but also on the public's expectations of government (which themselves can affect the degree of curiosity). It makes a difference whether the public expects the government to behave badly, and also what it counts as "badly." The best results with regard to truth management are not likely to follow from unlimited intrusiveness combined with unlimited righteousness (no doubt, on the part of the media, feigned) about how government can be expected to behave.'[41]

K.G. Robertson, long involved in discussion of the tradition of secrecy in the Westminster parliamentary tradition, reflects that 'openness then does not guarantee that the government will provide access to all of its thinking and information, but it does provide an incentive to the government to ensure that what the public does have access to is complete enough to protect itself. Without legislation providing for public access to government documents, the incentive for the government not to provide half truths and lies is much less. What open government does is to raise the cost to government of attempting to "fool" the public. It does not eliminate the possibility, but this is not to deny the benefit of increasing the difficulties of governments attempting to do so.'[42]

Before the advent of freedom-of-information laws, many public archives in Canada failed to acquire anything like the range of records needed to provide a historical dimension to government accountability. At the least, the new legal regime of access has created a situation in which public archives are less likely to have access issues mar their work to effect systematic disposition of governments' records.

It is not so evident that the new regime has allowed public archives to assume a role as champion of responsible record keeping and thereby ensure that accurate, reliable, and authentic records exist to facilitate both operational and accountability needs. It is remarkable but not surprising how often investigations that reveal a failure of accountability uncover inadequate record keeping. The Australian auditor general once remarked, as Hurley notes, that 'poor recordkeeping attracts corruption like flies to a carcass.'[43] It is doubtful that anyone intent on corrupt behaviour, which they know to be corrupt, is influenced by poor record keeping, but poor record keeping is often a barometer of poor administration of affairs. In her study of Jamaican bank failures, Victoria Lemieux concludes that 'the Jamaican banking community has tended to conceive of information-related problems only in terms of deliberate avoidance of records creation or tampering with records, information technology failures, and other non-systemic risks. [It] has not recognized the cumulative effect of systemically negligent records creation and record keeping.'[44] In her study of the Fabrikant affair, a tragic incident in which a Concordia University professor shot five of his colleagues, Barbara Craig reveals that one investigative report 'spoke about the importance of clear and consistent record keeping as the grounding of accountability and the best insurance against risk.' The investigators recommended that Concordia take 'steps to create and maintain an institutional memory.' Craig concludes her study with these words: 'In the future, accountability will rest largely, as before, on the foundations of trust built by honesty in a community. The best guarantor of that trust remains the record of actions that provide evidence for the audit.'[45]

Incidents such as the Jamaican financial crisis and the Fabrikant affair, extraordinary though they may be, illustrate very well that records are critical to the understanding of past actions in order to come to terms with how individuals have conducted their affairs and shouldered their responsibilities. All too often, especially in such lamentable institutional disasters as those, investigations after the fact can be seen to be a search for individuals to blame, to salve the outrage and pain the incident has caused. This view of accountability disguises its higher purpose. As Jane Parkinson makes clear, accountability is only at issue when those who can be called to account have exercised some discretion in the performance of delegated duties: 'In delegation, discretion arises from trusting the judgement (the discretion) of the delegated person and makes the difference between a servant and an agent. But some code of conduct, formal or informal, written or explicit, exists to guide the agent and keep the actions from being simply arbitrary. The form and nature of this code varies according to the individuals involved, their capacity, the nature of the actions to be accomplished, and the social context, but its existence implies subsequent evaluation, a comparison of the actions with a standard.'[46]

One cannot eliminate the element of trust from the accountability equation. Attempts to do so, like that of journalist and former politician

Patrick Boyer, often end up feigning the 'unlimited righteousness' of which Williams speaks.[47] They also take us along the path of blame-worthiness. The aftermath of giving an account is most productively a time not for blame but for reflection on how to improve the perform-ance of duties and the outcome should similar circumstances occur again in the future. Niebuhr explains this responsive aspect of account-ability. Accountability is, he says,

> a word that is frequently defined by recourse to legal thinking but that has a more definite meaning, when we understand it as referring to part of the response pattern of our self-conduct. Our actions are responsible not only insofar as they are reactions to interpreted actions upon us but also as [those actions] are made in anticipation of answers to our answers. An agent's action is like a statement in a dialogue. Such a statement not only seeks to meet, as it were, or to fit into, the previous statement to which it is the answer, but it is made in anticipation of reply. It looks forward as well as backward; it anticipates objections, confirmations and corrections.[48]

This responsive quality of accountability is suggestive of the sense in which it operates in an archival context. Records in an archival reposi-tory render an account for actions long after the fact of their being accomplished, and in many cases long after the actors responsible for actions or their outcomes in events can respond. But another response mechanism, another kind of dialogue, to sustain Niebuhr's analogy, takes place when records are examined to understand the past. We are still interested in how responsible agents conducted themselves, and painful questions that reverberate today may come up, but the passage of time usually allows us to reflect, in a way unfettered by concerns to reward, blame, or punish, on what past events mean for the present. Such reflection has Niehbur's responsive quality. This is especially true where democratic accountability is at issue. When we examine records to understand what our governments did long after the deed was done, we are rarely (there are important exceptions) interested in achieving some redress or recompense for misdeeds. Rather, we seek to under-stand what those past deeds, as they were answered and responded to over time until our day, mean to us now, and how we respond to them now. As Richard Rorty puts it, 'the appropriate intellectual background to political deliberation is historical narrative rather than philosophical or quasi-philosophical theory.'[49] 'The need to make sense of the past reasserts itself,' Bernard Williams says, despite the efforts of theorists to impress us with the difficulties of that exercise. 'It is,' he says, 'particularly so when the smooth order of things is disturbed by violence, if only to answer the questions "Why?" "Why us?" "Where from?" ... But even in less fraught circumstances ... the need is there to make sense of one's situation, and that requires an appeal to the past. If it is not to the historical past, then it will be to some kind of myth about it.'[50]

Of course, records themselves do not reveal either all the facts of any matter or speak its truth. We know enough about the dangers of trying to separate fact from value or interpretation to be sceptical that records can render an account of past actions in some straightforward way, but the archival faith is inevitably a faith in the possibility of making sense of the past, a faith in the power of rational discourse resting on evidence of past actions. The aim is to make our sense of the past, at the least, true to our society's needs, and none of us concerned with justice, fairness, and honesty would want to rest our understanding on manifest falsehood about what happened in the past. Williams thus says: 'Germans in the last half century have had a special task, of losing a past without forgetting it.'[51] This is one sense in which we can speak of historical accountability in the realm of public governance, the sense in which public records preserved in an archival institution can be used to render an account of the past in order to make our historical experience manifest in the present, to know it, to learn from it, maybe to leave it behind.

There are occasions when understanding past decisions and actions and their consequences does lead us to seek redress or recompense long after the fact. These are also occasions when, in another sense, we may speak of historical accountability, when we ask for an account of past actions of our governments and attempt to devise some redress or recompense in the present for historical wrongs. Several historical episodes in Canada that have touched archives fall into this category: the search for Nazi war criminals, the trampling on the civil rights of Japanese Canadians during the Second World War, the resolution of First Nations' land claims, or the tragic case of abuse of children in Indian residential schools, to name a few. Such occasions meet the difficulties of which Harmon speaks, that it is very difficult to accept collective responsibility for past actions, particularly those alleged to have done harm to groups, without undermining institutional stability and social control. Backed by a fabric of law to support them, governments instinctively steer clear of accepting responsibility for actions of their predecessors or for actions for which they claim individuals are both responsible and liable, and they therefore resist calls for compensation or retrospective justice of some kind for the harm alleged to have been done people by those actions, that is, to accept responsibility for them. Hence, the relief many felt when, finally after dodging responsibility for years, the Canadian government in some measure acknowledged its complicity in the matter of residential schools. All such cases have the quality about them of being, in Harmon's phrase, endlessly arguable. Still, whatever the difficulties of arriving at a just resolution of such cases, records provide the evidence on which to establish some elemental understanding of the facts of the matter upon which, in any reasonable view, just resolution partly depends, but only partly, of course. As Heather MacNeil remarks, 'the pursuit of justice, historical truth, and accountability are important and socially necessary endeavours and the pursuit of all three requires a commitment to the value of accurate fact-finding.'[52]

The case of the search for Nazi war criminals in Canada was very much a search for justice, historical truth, and accountability. But, as Terry Cook explains, the destruction of immigration case files, far from being 'a monumental blunder' that compromised investigation of Nazi war criminals, as was alleged, probably destroyed no evidence critical to that exercise. This episode reveals how little understanding exists both within and outside government of the role of archives and archivists in records disposition, but also how quick people are to believe and expect that records will help us discover the truth and establish who is responsible for what. Despite all the misunderstanding, which Cook nicely walks us through, this episode raises serious questions about just how far archives and archivists are accountable for the decisions made about records disposition. In discussing the position the National Archives took in the Nazi war criminals case, Cook says: 'Establishing retention periods *for legal (and operational) purposes* is the responsibility of the creating department accountable for the function involved. Establishing which records have permanent *"archival and historical" value* to the nation well beyond the operational (including legal operational) lifetimes of their subjects is the responsibility of the National Archives.' While recognizing that some records will have both long-term legal value and archival or historical value, Cook goes on to say that 'overlap must not be allowed to blur the line between the operational and legal accountability of the creator to retain records having any continuing (non-research) use and archival accountability for appraising records which will form the national memory.'[53] Many other archival institutions in this country and the world over take the same position as our federal archives authority, that is, they accept that it is the creating agency's responsibility to judge primary value,[54] the capacity of the records to serve the agency's own needs (which, of course, includes living up to its own obligations), and that the responsibility of the archives is to judge secondary value, the capacity of the records to serve the needs of others than the creator. In this regard, as Hurley reminds us, Theodore Schellenberg long ago assumed that one aspect of secondary value is preserving information on the government's observance of the rights and obligations of citizens.[55] Certainly, Judge Greene took that view in the case of the appraisal of FBI records. It is easy to see that this approach of sharply dividing primary and secondary values is in keeping with the Canadian constitutional, political, and administrative traditions and with the mandate of public archival institutions as spelled out in federal and provincial enabling legislation. However, considering the trend in the Canadian juridical system towards greater accountability, transparency, and responsiveness of public agencies, is it any longer acceptable to speak vaguely of 'archival and historical value' and sharply distinguish its determination from that of operational or legal value?

The Heiner affair in Australia and the recent report of the auditor general of Canada on archival heritage illustrate what is at issue here. In the Australian episode, the Queensland State archivist assented to a request by the Queensland Cabinet Office to approve destruction of records of an incomplete investigation into alleged abuse of inmates in a youth centre, access to which was wanted by a party against whom accusations were being made. Various arguments in defence of this destruction of records were offered during subsequent investigation of its legality and propriety. One such argument is apposite to this discussion. It was argued that the state archivist 'had no role to consider the interests of potential litigants in her appraisal; she was concerned solely with whether or not the records had enduring "historical" value.'[56] Given the silence or vague generality of Canadian archival laws and supporting policy and regulations as to the role of our public archives as agents of accountability and as to the criteria to be applied during appraisal beyond vague statements about historical value, and given the status of archival institutions as executive agencies in a political system of centralized political authority and decentralized responsibility for record keeping, it is not unreasonable to ask whether public archival institutions in this country are equipped with sufficient authority and direction to act on behalf of the public interest as the disinterested arbiter of disposition of public records of which Judge Greene spoke. One can take Finer's (and in essence Aucoin's) view that it is none of archivists' business to pull upstream against the flow of authority from the people through their elected representatives, that to do so undermines democratic accountability. This essentially conservative viewpoint is quite defensible, if professionally unsatisfying. Or one can take Friederich's view that it is archivists' business to proffer their expertise to influence public policy to increase the capacity of public records to serve accountability needs. One can buttress the argument with reference to the evidence of public preference for government accountability to the people and to the role that preservation of public records over the long term plays in the commonweal's interest in knowing how it has governed itself. This essentially liberal view is also quite defensible, if politically troublesome. This is no mean concern. Archivists have for good reason walked softly in the corridors of power to maintain the delicate position they aspire to occupy as disinterested arbiters of disposition of public records, a position that has them serving the interest of the public in knowing and reflecting on what its governments have been up to.

A relatively recent report evaluating the role of the National Archives in disposition of public records by the auditor general of Canada illustrates some of the complexities of the matter. Her report is perhaps a singular document in the history of Canadian archives, for never before has a similar office probed so closely into the role of an archives authority in disposition.[57] The report found the following problems with the regime of records disposition then in place:

- disposition authorities of the twenty-one main agencies covered only 67 per cent of their operational records;
- a majority of disposition authorities were obsolete;
- authorities calling for selective retention resulted in 'a massive transfer of records of little historic value';
- poor records management in departments and agencies impeded the work of cost-effective disposition;
- established retention periods are not acted on by agencies, and the Archives has no authority to enforce them and no program to monitor compliance;
- 'the increasing use of electronic records, which require little space, will probably not further encourage [agencies] to transfer their records on a regular basis';

- attempts to improve the Archives' performance have resulted in no assurance the Archives can fulfil its mandate; and
- the Archives does not have any performance measure to apply to its selection of federal records for enduring preservation.

The report then goes on to discuss how the government's information- and records-management policy gives the National Archives a 'leadership role in the records management field of the federal government,' but the policy spells out the record-keeping responsibilities of agencies in such a way that 'could lead information managers to interpret the policy as being a low priority in government administration.' It is also critical of Treasury Board for having no business case backing up the policy. The auditor general concludes:

> In summary, the National Archives of Canada has no assurance of obtaining all government records that are of historic interest or archival importance. Despite the efforts and progress made over the past decade, the National Archives is still struggling with a situation outside of its control that is growing and becoming more complex. Its capacity to carry out its legislative mandate is restricted, and the measures it is considering are far-reaching and will require validation. Without the appropriate tools, a cultural shift in the government administration, and regular accountability on the part of each stakeholder, the risks to the federal government's archival heritage will only increase.

None of these problems are new or peculiar to the National Archives. They are perennial bread-and-butter issues of every public archival authority. In considering them here, I am interested mainly in what the auditor general says about the accountability of public archives. To begin, there is the question of whether archives authorities have the resources to carry out their obligations as regards records disposition. A condition of being accountable is that a person or agency has the resources adequate to do the job. But whether resources are adequate depends, as the auditor general indicates, on there being clearly stated goals and objectives together with performance indicators against which to judge effectiveness. In this regard, we are in the realm of responsiveness of archival authorities to the public interest in effective governance, in the effective disposition of records to ensure that the public knows, to the extent that mechanisms of transparency and public discourse allow, what its government has been up to. The demands of effective and efficient management of records in an era of freedom of information have seriously eroded the comfortable notion that the determination of primary and secondary values can be responsibly assigned respectively to agencies and the archives. Arguably, the public, as the Nazi war criminal cases showed, are little interested in who does what inside Leviathan government; it simply wants to know what happened. If public archives are to assume, as all the trends that the auditor general outlines strongly imply, a prominent role as agents of accountability, it needs to be articulated more precisely than it has in general statements of information policy that the aim of the exercise of records disposition, like the aim of records-access policy, is to enhance democratic accountability, and how precisely duties to that end are assigned, what standards are to be met, and how resources are allocated to achieve effectiveness. As the auditor general also strongly urges, public archives need to do a lot of work to articulate appraisal strategies, methods, and criteria that can be justified as ensuring the accountability of government, including its historical accountability in terms I have outlined here. Whether you take Friederich's position that it is archivists' task to provide the expert embroidery to public policy or Finer's view that they await authoritative policy and simply implement it under direction, a strong case can be made that there is a public will and a deep-seated public interest in preservation of government records as a vehicle of democratic accountability. We know that to be the case if we listen carefully to the public dialogue that occurs as citizens learn about and respond to attempts to manage their understanding of what government has done, as they try to determine who was responsible for what, who was obligated to do what, and who was affected by what was done, what was right or wrong, just or unjust, true or false. If talk of archival and historical value means anything where public records in the context of democratic governance are concerned, it means that the public has the wherewithal to ponder rationally the endlessly arguable outcomes of its governance of itself. In the end, the very highest purpose that preservation of public records serves is to allow a democratic people to grasp what the past means for the present by enhancing their ability to review and consider the decisions and actions of their governments as they plot their present and future course.

None in the archival profession would underestimate the enormity of this task, particularly the difficulty of articulating how appraisal decisions, which have such a strong discretionary leaven to them, enhance accountability of government. No sensible observer would underestimate the difficulty of wrestling with the paradoxical quality of archivists' task as responsible agents each day as they assume their obligations, which may seem to be such a small part in the elaborate machinery of government or, for that matter, in any organization. In that regard, such are the connections between public and private endeavour that every archivist has a responsibility to the larger society to ensure that in the future we will be able to puzzle out how we have lived and what it means for how we will live. It would be helpful if this trust, as the mission statement of the National Archives of the United States once characterized it, was spelled out in some definitive statement of purpose for public archives, along with, as the auditor general says, some validation of archival plans to achieve the purpose. The almost overwhelming task of deciding which records should survive in our society should never blind archivists to the responsibility of trust they bear to the organizations they work for and to the individuals affected by those organizations. Archivists everywhere stand for accountability, transparency, and responsiveness of organizations through responsible record keeping from the moment records are conceived and so long as they exist. That archivists often labour with little external understanding of their highest aims, with slim means, and in the face, sometimes, of countervailing pressures to act irresponsibly is but part of their paradoxical and noble obligation in a democratic society.

NOTES

1 Michael M. Harmon, *Responsibility as Paradox: A Critique of Rational Discourse on Government* (Thousand Oaks, Calif.: Sage Publications 1995), 1–2.
2 Jane Parkinson, 'Accountability in Archival Science,' Master of Archival Studies thesis, University of British Columbia, 1993, 10.
3 Gerald Caiden, 'The Problem of Ensuring the Accountability of Public Officials,' in Joseph G. Jabbra and O.P. Diwendi, eds., *Public Service Accountability: A Comparative Perspective* (Hartford, Conn.: Kumarian Press 1981), 25.
4 Bernard Williams, *Truth and Truthfulness: An Essay in Genealogy* (Princeton, N.J.: Princeton University Press 2002), 1–2.
5 Harmon, *Responsibility as Paradox*, 6.
6 Ibid., 5, 156.
7 Ibid., 101–2.
8 Ibid., 140–1.
9 Ibid., 185.

10 O.C. McSwite, *Legitimacy in Public Administration: A Discourse Analysis* (Thousand Oaks, Calif.: Sage Publications 1997), 33.

11 Quoted in ibid., 34–5.

12 Ibid., 43.

13 Paul G. Thomas, 'The Changing Nature of Accountability,' in B. Guy Peters and Donald J. Savoie, eds., *Taking Stock: Assessing Public Sector Reforms* (Montreal and Kingston: McGill-Queen's University Press 1998), 348.

14 Peter Aucoin, 'Accountability: The Key to Restoring Public Confidence in Government,' *The Timlin Lecture*, 6 November 1997, University of Saskatchewan, Saskatoon, Sask., 2–3.

15 Ibid., 12.

16 S.O. 1990, c. A.27, s. 5.

17 S.M. 2001, c. 35.

18 S.O. 206, c. 3, Sched. A, s. 1.

19 See http://www.archives.gov/about_us/vision_mission_values.html#vis (accessed 10 August 2004).

20 See http://www.archives.gov/about/info/mission.html (accessed 30 September 2009).

21 See http://www.archives.gov/ (accessed 30 September 2009).

22 See http://www.collectionscanada.ca/information-management/0620_e.html (accessed 10 August 2004).

23 SC, 2004, c. 11, s. 7.

24 RSBC 1996, c. 99.

25 SBC 2003, c. 12.

26 'BC Archives Moves Forward: Extract of a Report from the Provincial Archivist to the Archives Association of British Columbia,' http://www.bcarchives.gov.bc.ca/general/bcarbcm.htm (accessed 12 October 2009).

27 David Allen Weber, 'Access to Public Records Legislation in North America: A Content Analysis,' Master of Archival Studies thesis, University of British Columbia, 1994. See 'Appendix A: Purpose of Access Legislation: Types and Characteristics.'

28 *American Friends Service Committee et al. v. Webster et al.*, United States District Court for the District of Columbia, 494 F. Supp. 803; 1980 U.S. Dist. LEXIS 12847, Order and Opinion, Judge Harold H. Greene, 10 January 1980, 235.

29 David H. Rosenbloom, 'Constitutional Perspectives on Accountability and Evaluation: The Citizen versus the Administrative State,' in Albert C. Hyde and Jay M. Shafritz, eds., *Program Evaluation in the Public Sector* (New York: Praeger 1979), 69.

30 'Records Management by the Archivist of the United States and by the Administrator of General Services,' 44 U.S.C., Chapter 29, s. 2902 (1).
31 Livia Iacovino, 'Accountability for the Disposal of Commonwealth Records and the Preservation of its Archival Resources,' Part I: The Context, in Sue McKemmish and Frank Upward, eds., *Archival Documents: Providing Accountability through Recordkeeping* (Melbourne: Ancora Press 1993), 58. She cites Glenda Acland, 'Managing the Record Rather Than the Relic,' *Archives and Manuscripts* 20 (May 1992): 57–63, as espousing such views.
32 Iacovino, 'Accountability,' 60.
33 Verne Harris, '"They Should Have Destroyed More": The Destruction of Public Records by the South African State in the Final Years of Apartheid, 1990–1994,' in Richard J. Cox and David A. Wallace, eds., *Archives and the Public Good: Accountability and Records in Modern Society* (Westport, Conn.: Quorum Books 2002), 225.
34 SC 2004, c. 11, s. 7.
35 Chris Hurley, 'Recordkeeping and Accountability,' in Sue McKemmish et al., eds., *Archives: Recordkeeping in Society* (Wagga Wagga, New South Wales: Centre for Information Studies, Charles Sturt University, 2005), 242.
36 C.P. Stacey, 'Some Pros and Cons of the Access Problem,' *International Journal* 20 (winter 1964–5): 49.
37 R.G. Robertson, 'The Canadian Parliament and Cabinet in the Face of Modern Demands,' *Canadian Public Administration* 11 (fall 1968): 273.
38 Kerry Badgley, Margaret J. Dixon, and Paulette Dozois, 'In Search of the Chill: Access to Information and Record-Keeping in the Government of Canada,' *Archivaria* 55 (spring 2003): 1–20.
39 Donald J. Savoie, *Governing from the Centre: The Concentration of Power in Canadian Politics* (Toronto: University of Toronto Press 1999), 290.
40 Alasdair Roberts, *Blacked Out: Government Secrecy in the Information Age* (Cambridge: Cambridge University Press 2006), 237.
41 Williams, *Truth and Truthfulness*, 213.
42 K.G. Robertson, *Public Secrets: A Study in the Development of Government Secrecy* (London: Macmillan 1982), 181.
43 Hurley, 'Recordkeeping and Accountability,' 225.
44 Victoria Lemieux, 'The Jamaican Financial Crisis: Accounting for the Collapse of Jamaica's Indigenous Commercial Banks,' in Cox and Wallace, eds., *Archives and the Public Good*, 281.
45 Barbara Craig, 'The Anchors of Community Trust and Academic Liberty: The Fabrikant Affair,' in Cox and Wallace, eds., *Archives and the Public Good*, 286–9.
46 Parkinson, 'Accountability in Archival Science,' 15.

47 J. Patrick Boyer, *"Just Trust Us: The Erosion of Accountability in Canada* (Toronto: Breakout Educational Network in association with Dundurn Press 2003).

48 Quoted in Harmon, *Responsibility as Paradox*, 161.

49 Richard Rorty, *Philosophy and Social Hope* (London: Penguin Books 1999), 231.

50 Williams, *Truth and Truthfulness*, 262–3.

51 Ibid., 263.

52 Heather MacNeil, *Trusting Records: Legal, Historical and Diplomatic Perspectives* (Dordrecht: Kluwer Academic Publishers 2000), 115.

53 Terry Cook, '"A Monumental Blunder": The Destruction of Records of Nazi War Criminals in Canada,' in Cox and Wallace, eds., *Archives and the Public Good*, 53.

54 For instance, in Norway, continuing operational value is assessed according to criteria 'formulated by the agencies themselves.' Torkel Thime, 'New Approaches to Appraisal in Norway,' *Comma* 1 (2004): 65.

55 T.R. Schellenberg, *Modern Archives: Principles and Techniques* (Chicago: University of Chicago Press 1956), 115–17, 155–7.

56 Christopher Hurley, 'Records and the Public Interest: The "Heiner Affair" in Queensland, Australia,' in Cox and Wallace, eds., *Archives and the Public Good*, 308.

57 Office of the Auditor General of Canada, November 2003 Report, Chapter 6: 'Protection of Cultural Heritage in the Federal Government.' References are to sections 6.65–6.93 on 'Archival Heritage.' Available at http://www.oag-bvg.gc.ca/domino/reports.nsf/html/20031106ce.html (accessed 29 June 2007).

9 Archivists and Public Affairs: Towards a New Archival Public Programming

TOM NESMITH

If you ask most Canadians what links the pursuit of Nazi war criminals, climatology, Alzheimer's research, Aboriginal land claims, LSD medical experiments, chemical-warfare experiments, unsolved murders from the American civil-rights era, South Africa's Truth and Reconciliation Commission, the Stasi secret police, Japanese Canadian wartime compensation, and the Steven Truscott murder case, few would answer *archives* – or even know that these are but a handful of examples of the significant role archival records have played in public affairs. Canadians and people elsewhere do not know much about this role, despite the fact that it has been widely publicized in the mass media.

Oddly, however, archives' public-affairs role has not been widely publicized by archivists themselves, even though they are giving publicity about the holdings and services of archives unprecedented new priority in their public programming. Although the multiplicity of archives' roles in public affairs is one of the most striking recent developments in the archival world, it remains a minor feature of public programming. It does not play the central role it could in pursuing what is arguably the top priority for archivists – changing public attitudes towards archives. Even those who are otherwise knowledgeable about public affairs are often poorly informed about archives and the role they play in public life. The public image of archives still evokes stereotypes of records languishing in dust and largely irrelevant to society's principal concerns. Nothing could be further from the truth.[1]

This essay explores how archivists might engage public affairs to a greater extent, as an expression of a new public programming. This programming would place increased emphasis on addressing society's central concerns (which are not necessarily its hot political topics) and could be a key ingredient of a strategy to improve public understanding and support of archives. This is sorely needed. The governments that do have archives badly underfund them, barely enabling them to fulfil their legal mandates and causing them to scramble to hold on to the minimal resources they have. Their electronic-records programs are thus weak to non-existent, even though archiving the public record now in e-mail and other computerized forms is essential to the very future of archives and to understanding the public-affairs issues such records document. Most municipalities and quasi-public institutions, such as educational and medical institutions, simply have no public archival service at all. Even the woeful underfunding of archives in the rest of the government sector would be a major advance in these particular areas. The personal records or 'manuscripts' side of government archives in Canada is worse off still than government records, and that means that most of the immense archival riches of family, work, spiritual, and other social experience (now increasingly computerized as well) are frittered away. And the vast majority of private-sector institutions such as major corporations lack meaningful archives.[2]

The recent increased emphasis by archives on public programming is a response to this lack of support.[3] It takes important advantage of new tools such as the Internet and reaches out to new or expanding user groups of many kinds. But in many respects it does traditional things, albeit with greater investment and imagination. Archives still focus on creating basic descriptions of records and on mounting exhibits of documents on particular historical themes, without much discussion of the relevance of such records and exhibits to contemporary concerns, and on preparing certain digitized documents for the casual Web browser rather than presenting records of broader public-affairs interest.

This still largely conventional approach to public programming parallels the conventional nature of the other principal aspect of public engagement by archives – involvement in public-*policy* matters. This second aspect holds to the familiar ground of lobbying on archival funding and on laws and policies governing archives, records management, access-to-information and privacy concerns, cultural property import and export, and copyright. These crucial interventions by archivists in public affairs must continue to be made, but archivists can broaden this work in their archival and professional institutions.

In the last few years, inklings of a new public programming can be seen. The new view maintains that archival actions help create records and knowledge and thereby shape societal understanding and conditions, rather than simply document society by receiving and keeping records and knowledge. This view emphasizes that records are a product of often lengthy histories, stretching back into the ideas, values, and conditions of the societies that made them and on through their handling by archives and subsequent users down to the present day. Work on rethinking core archival concepts such as provenance and the various archival functions in light of the new view of records and archival work is well under way. But one function that has yet to receive much attention is public programming.[4]

How should public programming be conceived if archival records have long, complex histories and archivists are not just their neutral, passive keepers and retrievers but are implicated in their histories in ways that shape understanding of the past and thus society? Under a new public-programming model, archivists would be obliged to explain as much as they can of this more complex history of records and archiving and its impact. They would have to acknowledge (and be more accountable for) the power they wield, and be more open about explaining the power that others have wielded over the records. Public programming would then be about more than the now typical and seemingly neutral provision of general information about archival services and records and their possible uses, about more than digitizing records, still done largely without much contextual information about their histories, and about more than mounting exhibits on historical topics, usually without much extrapolation to current public concerns – if such concerns are mentioned at all (more often they are studiously avoided).

The new public programming would thus have two interrelated dimensions: greater commitment to the history of records and archives and more active pursuit of a wider role for archives in public affairs. The two come together as archivists employ their knowledge of records and archiving to help identify and contextualize records for public-affairs purposes. This greater commitment to the history of records and archives is needed if archives are to play a serious role in public affairs. Only that commitment provides the fullest possible understanding of the records, and that is essential to any meaningful participation in the resolution of what is often at stake – disposition of vast amounts of money and property, adjudication of human rights, including even personal freedom, the fate of public reputations, and protection of public health and safety.

Archivists have probably shied away from this wider role for fear of appearing partisan in such often highly charged matters. But, if the new understanding of archives suggests there is no position of pristine neutrality, then shying away from it *itself* betrays the inevitable bias affecting anything we do. Archivists can become more engaged in this crucial societal outreach while navigating these tricky shoals. Archives need to be careful and fair in their analyses, not passive in the guise of neutrality. This is something they always have understood. State-funded archives in particular have always had public-policy roles, and, indeed, they themselves are expressions of public policy. For example, since its creation in 1872, Library and Archives Canada (LAC) has existed to foster Canada's national identity and unity as an agency of the national government. In the early years of its history, especially, it was thought that an impartial or scientific historical analysis of the documentary evidence the Archives held would dispel myths and biases fuelling the country's various internal conflicts.[5]

This is hardly a passive or neutral role, as can be seen in LAC's handling of records related to Aboriginal affairs. At the turn of the twentieth century, LAC's predecessor acquired a major body of Canadian government records on Aboriginal affairs administration. These records were then thought to document the government's benevolent concern for a vanishing culture, through such institutions as church- and government-run residential schools for Aboriginal children – which were designed to assimilate them to Euro-Canadian culture.[6] Almost a century later, and as a reflection of the new public programming, LAC endorsed a very different understanding of these records and employed it in public discussion of the now controversial residential-schools issue. LAC joined with Aboriginal groups to prepare an exhibit and related publication that emphasized the harm, including physical and sexual abuse, done to children at residential schools.[7] As the then national archivist of Canada, Ian Wilson, said in June 2002, on the occasion of the opening of the residential schools exhibition: 'Archivists, as custodians of social memory, cannot be spectators, we take part in the creation of memory by the records we preserve. We are active participants.'[8]

Photographs were a key part of the exhibit and accompanying publication. Most had been taken by government or church officials between the 1880s and 1960s to provide evidence of the progress towards assimilation of Aboriginal children in the schools. However, guest curator Jeff Thomas, an Aboriginal person himself, maintains that the photographs tell a different story, arising from the different approach to documentary analysis that is central to the new public programming. By reading deeply into the context of their creation, Thomas points to the racism and suffering the photographs more accurately portray. But more than that, he argues that the photographs are becoming something different again, as Aboriginal people recontextualize or look at them anew today, seeing them now also as symbols of dignity, strength, and survival in the face of oppression and thus as sources of inspiration in their continuing struggle for healing and justice. 'There are new stories,' Thomas says, 'waiting to come out of the photographs shown here in the exhibition. Rather than dismissing them simply as images of colonialism or racism, we can choose, as Aboriginal people, to make them our own, to add them to our stories, and to give the children of residential schools a voice.'[9]

Strong echoes of this opening to a new approach to public programming at LAC, one that draws on much deeper contextualization of records for public-affairs purposes, are also heard at LAC's website in a discussion of the pioneering work of Canadians Harold Innis and Marshall McLuhan in communication studies. LAC asks a question seldom posed at archives' websites: 'To what extent is historical knowledge not merely preserved, but shaped by the archive and its means of selecting, storing, and presenting information? Is the archive an entirely neutral institution with regard to knowledge, or does it, in fact, mediate?' LAC engaged six scholars to outline the ideas of Innis and McLuhan on the impact of communication and to respond to its archival question in that light. Perhaps Terry Cook of the University of Manitoba summoned up their answers best by saying that, across history, 'the societal process of archiving involved a stark exercise of power over who and what was remembered and venerated, and, equally, who or what was marginalized and forgotten.'[10]

In November 2007 LAC began to expand on public-affairs-oriented public programming by launching its 'Forum on Canadian Democracy.' The Forum has hosted a series of activities from exhibits of documents to lectures and public forums (one of which was televised nationally on Canada's Cable Public Affairs Channel). These events are designed 'to promote study and discussion of Canada's democratic experience' and 'improve civic literacy, encourage use of LAC's collections, provide historical context for matters of public interest, and promote democratic diversity across Canada.' Archivists, academics, journalists, judges, politicians, and the general public have taken part in a variety of discussions on subjects such as Canada's Charter of Rights and Freedoms (on the charter's twentieth-fifth anniversary in 2007) and in the less formal 'Political Junkie Café,' where Canadian-American relations was the inaugural topic, as viewed through treaty making from the Treaty of Paris of 1783 to the North American Free Trade Agreement of 1994. It is also noteworthy that LAC places its new Canadian government record-keeping initiative under the Forum's umbrella, thus signalling that record keeping is part of the democratic infrastructure that Canadians should understand. And, reflecting the growing role of digital communication in the new public programming, the Forum's activities have a prominent place at LAC's website.[11]

Despite its excellent work on residential schools, and related efforts to examine Canada's Charter of Rights and Freedoms, LAC could do much more to make public-affairs issues a truly prominent component of its public programming. It could draw consistent attention at its website to its role in providing records and archival services over the years to address a wide range of public concerns – such as the Japanese Canadian wartime compensation case, the pursuit of Nazi war criminals in Canada, and Central Intelligence Agency-funded LSD experiments on Canadian psychiatric patients. LAC could also invest more in identifying and placing in context the types of records that can contribute to discussion of particular public-affairs matters. LAC is typical of Canadian archives in this omission, although it goes much further overall in engaging public issues than they do.

Other major archives elsewhere offer a more explicit focus for linking archives and public affairs in their public programming, but here, too, more could be done to explain and deepen these links. What follows is not a comprehensive review of the world's archives, or archival literature, but a preliminary exploration and report on a topic that merits much further discussion.

The National Archives and Records Administration of the United States (NARA) and the American Library of Congress host talks by well-known public figures, and webcasts of many of these events are available at the NARA and Library websites. As U.S. national archivist, Allen Weinstein hosted the 'American Conversations' series, in which he interviewed political figures such as Hillary Clinton and Lynn Cheney, senior government officials, and leading journalists, academics, and documentary filmmakers. NARA's various Presidential Libraries, which hold the archives of individual American presidents, offer similar forums.[12]

The Library's program is more ambitious, with 262 webcasts available under 'Government, World Affairs' alone, and many more with a public-affairs concern under the themes of 'Religion,' 'Science, Technology,' and 'Education.' Speakers range from former U.S. Secretary of State James

Baker, who delivered the Library's Kissinger Lecture on Foreign Policy and International Relations, to members of Congress, academics, and public officials, such as John Hope Franklin, who spoke on race relations in the United States, journalists, such as *New York Times* columnist Paul Krugman, a sharp critic of the Bush administration, who spoke on economic policy, staff members of the Library explaining the work they do, and at least one archivist not on the staff, Richard Cox, who spoke on archives in the computer age. The Library supports this work with its recently established Kluge Center, which, it says, without much further elaboration, 'fosters a mutually enriching relationship between scholars and political leaders.'[13]

These speakers address a variety of public concerns and make it clear that archives can offer a forum for their discussion. Yet they rarely speak about the role of archival and contemporary records and records administration in public affairs, despite the often central role they play, or about specific archival-policy issues. Like Library and Archives Canada, these American institutions neither make specific links (at least at their websites) to the types of records in their custody that inform analysis of public affairs nor suggest how such public-affairs research can be facilitated.

The State Archives of Vermont, however, has made the link between archives and public affairs the core of its public-programming efforts. It is probably unique among government archives in North America (and perhaps elsewhere) in its commitment to this new style of public programming. This approach is most obvious in the 'Continuing Issues of Government and Governance' feature of the Archives' website and in the *Opinions* publication (also at the website), which contains the reflections of State Archivist Gregory Sanford on the issue of archives and public programming. The Vermont Archives maintains that contemporary public affairs revolve around ongoing 'core issues' affecting the role of government, its various key procedures and functions (such as amending a constitution), civic duties and rights, and attitudes and policies regarding concerns such as taxation, education, the economy, health care, public safety, and the environment. It argues that past experiences, often documented in the archival record, provide guidance to politicians, government officials, citizens, and the media when concerns regarding such issues arise today.[14]

For example, Sanford explains that in 2003, when the Vermont legislature discussed amending the state constitution, the Archives prepared for the legislators an overview of the amendment process, a summary and categorization of all past proposals for amendments since 1880, an explanation of what happened to them, and a presentation of legislative committee minutes outlining the deliberations on each one. Sanford adds that the Archives consults key officials and follows media accounts to learn about developing issues. It monitors current and upcoming legislation and then tries to find relevant information in its holdings. Rather than merely provide finding aids or large quantities of documents for others to sift through, the Archives presents a summary of the information with selected records attached. 'The keys are,' says Sanford, 'gain an understanding of issues of concern in your communities; identify the key players in those issues; and understand what information, in what form, best supports their decision making processes.' He hopes that, by working effectively with key audiences that then publicize the role of the Archives in powerful circles, 'we may eventually reach a tipping point that can change perceptions of the broader society.'[15]

Sanford maintains that the Archives does not try to tell anyone what to decide about a given issue. It strives to present various viewpoints found in the records and 'provide context that can guide deliberations.' He recognizes that some archival colleagues may be concerned about 'a more activist approach,' but argues that archival work is inevitably activist, given that archivists of necessity make countless choices that affect what is kept and how it is made available. Sanford articulates the new approach to public programming by quoting Terry Cook's comment that 'we must think of archives as active, not passive, as sites of power, not as recorders of power. Archives don't simply *record* the work of culture; they *do* the work of culture.'[16]

Sanford says that this approach is enjoying success. The Archives has a higher profile in the media. A new state archives act was passed in 2003, and substantial funding was set aside in 2006 to plan construction of a new archives building. Sanford himself has become a well-known public figure in Vermont. He has participated in the public-policy research program on amending the state constitution at the Snelling Center for Government at the University of Vermont. He has been invited to speak to newly elected state legislators on several occasions as part of their orientation to state government. And the Vermont Archives was honoured for its innovative public programming in 2002 with an award from the Society of American Archivists, as was Sanford himself by the New England Archivists Association with its Distinguished Service Award.[17]

Among other archives checked in this preliminary survey, I could find only one that makes anything like Vermont's attempt to provide links to archival documents related to a range of current issues. The Canadian Broadcasting Corporation (CBC) makes available (at both its English- and French-language services' websites) television and radio clips from its archives that offer insight into the historical context of many current issues, events, and the public figures associated with them. As many as twenty clips may accompany a particular subject. Some are up to thirty minutes in length. The page devoted to the subject also contains links to related subjects in the digital archives (including ones at the other language site), related external websites (including at other archives), resources on the subject for teachers, more 'in depth' background reports on the issue, and recent CBC news reports on it. There are historical documentary profiles of Aboriginal leaders Phil Fontaine and George Erasmus, former Prime Minister Paul Martin, author Margaret Atwood, environmentalist David Suzuki, and controversial hockey commentator Don Cherry, among many others. The federal government 'Sponsorship Scandal' in the 2000s promoted a look back at the history of political scandals in Canada. When Air Canada ran into financial problems in the 2000s, the CBC's digital archives carried a documentary overview of the airline's history. The digital archives has sections on the controversial Atlantic seal hunt, the softwood-lumber dispute with the United States, Arctic sovereignty issues, such as Canada's claim to Arctic waterways including the Northwest Passage, the debate over marijuana use, the development of the Alberta oil industry, the child daycare debate, and the ongoing investigation of the 1985 Air India terrorist attack. There are also many more retrospectives on people and concerns now more remote from the daily news.[18]

The CBC offers a good example of how archives can participate in public affairs, but there are other ways too. While many university archives maintain special collections devoted to public affairs, I found none that match what Vermont or the CBC do to enhance that role. Most, like LAC, NARA, and the Library of Congress, provide useful forums for discussion of public affairs or stress the general relationship between their holdings and public-affairs research, but without linking their records directly to particular public-affairs issues in their public programming.[19]

One university archives that does go beyond this conventional approach into the new style of public programming is the University of California at San Francisco's Archives and Special Collections (UCSF).

This campus's overall focus on medical and health-care education also shapes its archival work. The UCSF has made health issues the focus of its mandate, particularly through the Tobacco Control Archives, which was established in 1994. This program has grown since then to become home to about forty-one million pages of digitized tobacco company records created by major American firms such as Philip Morris, R.J. Reynolds, Brown and Williamson, and the American Tobacco Company. Most of these records were obtained through litigation in the 1990s. They document both the tobacco industry's knowledge of the health dangers of smoking as early as the early 1960s, often before the medical-research community knew much about it, and the industry's subsequent efforts to suppress that information and combat anti-smoking activities. Archivists Robin Chandler, who headed the project, and Susan Storch, who worked for it, note that the Brown and Williamson records, in particular, have spurred informed public debate, successful litigation against the tobacco companies, and government policy designed to reduce smoking in the United States.[20]

There are perhaps few better examples than the Tobacco Control Archives of both the new archival involvement in public affairs and the opportunities that digitization and the Internet now provide to enhance that role. Moreover, the kind of deep contextualization of the records and of the archival work done with them that Chandler and Storch present in a published article reflects the new approach to public programming. The two go hand in hand here, as the central role of public affairs in public programming is accompanied by the deeper contextualization of the records and of the archival work needed to explain their relevance to public affairs.

These North American examples throw light on some of the few archives that make direct connections to their role in public affairs. In England, however, a broader national effort is being made to emphasize that role. English archivists are doing so by joining librarians and museum curators on the Museums, Libraries, and Archives (MLA) Council, which was established in 2000 as a Non-Departmental Public Body sponsored by the British government's Department of Culture, Media, and Sport. The MLA aims to stress its members' social and economic contribution to society and how they can address public-policy concerns. Its ambitious advocacy program, targeted mainly at politicians, policy makers, and funders of archives, museums, and libraries, argues that these institutions contribute far more to societal well-being than is grasped by the typically narrow public understanding of their heritage and cultural role, or conveyed by their own often narrow presentation of it. The MLA recasts this role more broadly to address public-affairs issues and government agendas directly. It maintains that archives, libraries, and museums' support for scholarship and education stimulates the creativity and re-education needed in an increasingly knowledge-based economy. This can help drive economic and cultural regeneration in struggling urban and rural areas. It can help reduce various types of social exclusion and crime, improve health care, and foster cultural identity, citizenship, better and more accountable public administration, and democratic participation through e-government.[21]

Unlike the Vermont, CBC, and University of California examples, the MLA does not draw many specific connections between types of records and their value for public affairs. The council does demonstrate, however, how archival associations can address a much wider range of outreach concerns than their traditional emphasis on archival funding, legal issues, and efforts to improve society's general awareness of archives. Although associations in many countries do valuable work of this conventional kind, I know of no other that is as focused on making the contribution of archives to public affairs the heart of a national strategy for taking archives out of the shadows of societal understanding. The International Council on Archives (ICA) has begun to do this kind of work in areas such as human rights and the archives of indigenous people, but much more could be done by archival associations.[22]

South Africa provides another important example of a national archival community where the new public programming is emerging – with its emphasis on public-affairs concerns and new understandings of records and archives. Since the end of apartheid, a number of archivists, users of archives, and interested citizens have made the point that new conceptions of records and archives are essential to the success of the country's fledgling democracy. The Nelson Mandela Foundation's Centre of Memory and Dialogue now spearheads this effort. A key figure in the Centre's work is archivist Verne Harris, the head of its Memory for Justice Programme, and well known in the archival field as an advocate of the application of Derridean deconstruction to archival records and archiving and of social justice as the overriding goal of archival work.[23] The Foundation's mandate, revised in November 2006, now makes its core function the work of using its archival holdings, such as Mandela's personal archives, to create dialogue on public affairs. The centre's website states that 'we believe that the vehicle for sharing memory effectively, for growing it, and for engaging it in the promotion of justice, is dialogue ... We draw on this memory work in convening dialogue on critical social issues that present a threat to justice in society.'[24] The dialogue program aims 'to provide a non-partisan platform for public discourse on important social issues, and in doing so, contribute to policy decision-making.'[25]

The Mandela Centre has only begun to undertake this mandate. One of its early initiatives involved holding a conference in April 2007 on the serious problems facing the country's various archives. This was done in collaboration with the National Archives of South Africa (NASA) and the University of the Witwatersrand. It resulted in a report to the minister of arts and culture authored by these three conference convenors. The report (*Archives at the Crossroads, 2007*) maintains that the troubled history and contemporary weaknesses of archives and records management in South Africa mean that 'what is at stake is not simply the survival of the inherited documents of the past, but our hard-won democracy itself and our possible future as a cohesive society.' It recommends 'using the opportunity created by the failing system to attend to the nuts and bolts of the records system, while at the same time casting off an out-of-date notion of archive and inaugurating a fully post-colonial one, informed by our unique and complex archival engagements in situations of repression, liberation, negotiation, reconciliation and development. In so doing we have the opportunity to render service to our democracy, and to contribute our ideas of archive to the cause of social justice the world over.'[26]

The old notion of archives assumed the primacy of the textual (and especially state) record over oral accounts, artifacts, landscapes, and conventional documents whose evidential features may have been omitted, falsified, lost, or effaced in efforts to avoid giving information to the apartheid regime. The apartheid state record is obviously not an entirely reliable guide to past understanding, and the post-apartheid state record will also likely be problematic, especially if records management and archives are so weak. Other evidence should be welcomed, as well as a critical historical and contextual approach to all evidence. To enable archives to participate in moulding a new national public life in South Africa, the *Crossroads* report says that the idea of archiving must be reconceived. '"Archiving,"' it says, 'refers to a range of dynamic processes including the processes by means of which some items get preserved and others do not, how choices are made about systems used to preserve items, and the ways in which access to records is determined ... The archive is a conceptual term. It refers to the

circumscribed body of knowledge of the past that is historically determined as that which is available to us to draw on when thinking about
the past.'[27] This new dynamic (rather than static) conception of archives means that what records may say to us depends on understanding as much of their complex histories as we can, and going much far-
ther in that direction than we usually have in archival work. No type
of evidence can thus simply trump other types. No group of people in
control of evidence can exert their will on the basis of its inherent su-
periority. All forms of evidence ought to be critically assessed for their
particular contribution to societal understanding. In this way, memory
can be useful in building a democratic civil society in a country as varied as South Africa.[28]

   The fate of this emerging South African national project to place archives at the centre of public life remains to be seen, but even in these
early stages the Mandela Centre offers inspiration to archivists everywhere to respond in like manner to the complexities and limitations of
records that deal with public issues.

   The recent involvement of archives in sometimes high-profile public-
affairs issues creates broader public-programming opportunities for
archivists that have not yet been explored much. For the most part, archivists have tended to remain in the background of this phenomenon,
while others have been more prominent in mediating the knowledge in
archives about public issues. The various news media, the Internet, academics, and libraries and museums have done much of this mediation.
A recent survey of over 1,000 British people shows that most use the
media, the Internet, and family and friends as their main sources of
public knowledge about current issues. Archives are used the least for
this purpose. Eleven per cent say they had used an archives in the previous six months.[29] At the same time, it is significant that archives are
seen by 25 per cent as important sources of information for understanding current issues. That is still much lower than the media and Internet
or libraries (at 52 per cent) and museums (at 32 per cent), but the figure
may reflect awareness that, even though archives are not used directly
as often as other sources of information, archival material is seen to be
made available through these other outlets and thus understood to be
important.[30] Moreover, like libraries and museums, archives are far
more trusted sources of public knowledge than the more frequently
used news media and Internet *because* of the historical context and varied interpretations they provide to help people go beyond the day-to-
day headlines.[31] People seem desirous of the deeper understanding of

the background to their current concerns that the new public program-ming is capable of delivering.

This British study, which probably reflects attitudes in many other places too, suggests that archives might well benefit from taking a more direct and active role in providing information related to pub-lic affairs. People see archives as holding valuable public know-ledge, but they do not usually receive it directly from archives, if they receive it at all. Others get much of the credit for making it available, including libraries and museums, which hold mountains of publications written from archival records, locate and describe a great many artifacts based on archival research, and often display facsimile documents obtained from archives, while archives suffer from the lowest levels of use, appreciation, and funding.

The examples discussed here show that some archivists are moving in the direction of a new public-affairs-oriented public programming, but little is being done overall. What more could archivists do? Archivists obviously need to continue their efforts in conventional forms of lobbying on archival law and related issues. They should con-tinue to respond to public issues that arrive at their doorsteps, such as the Canadian residential-schools matter. Some of these prominent issues have been discussed in recent groundbreaking work on archives and accountability issues, on political pressures faced by archives, and on the political history of archives.[32] And some of the same issues, again like the example of Canadian residential schools, present major oppor-tunities for special high-profile projects to be developed around them, as LAC has done. Archives should also continue to provide a forum for discussion of public affairs by key leaders, as NARA, the Library of Congress, and other archives do – although these forums could host more discussion of the role of records and archives in public affairs than they do currently.[33]

Associations often organize their work around the special technical problems of managing archives, archival functions, and records, topics that are mainly of interest only to archivists. Archivists could do more in archival associations by taking a page from England and South Africa and moving the various international, national, and local associations towards placing a public-affairs agenda at the heart of their work. Associations could not only articulate this agenda but go a step further by tying records to these concerns. They could also encourage special-interest groups (of archivists and others) to form around public-affairs issues – such as health care, education, the environment, science and technology, human rights, religion, immigration, sport and leisure, housing, transportation, foreign affairs, urban issues, the justice system, defence and security, agriculture, and so on. Associations could give a prominent place at their websites to identification and contextual analysis of groups of records related to various aspects of public affairs.[34]

Individual archives (or groups of them in collaboration) could emulate the Vermont, CBC, and University of California archives in making available records that provide contextual background to public concerns in their particular jurisdictions. The CBC perhaps offers the most useful model for getting started quickly on this work through its presentation of radio and television clips that provide insight into various past attitudes, decisions, and outcomes on a wide variety of still current public issues. At the same time, major related digitization projects like California's may be possible.

University archivists in particular can play a key leadership role in moving forward this public affairs agenda in the archival world. The University of California's work discussed here, including the important contextual analysis of Chandler and Storch, is an excellent example. University archivists are part of educational institutions that have a strong public-affairs interest. Many university archives have formal public-affairs mandates. This academic environment, supported by tenure and the research sabbaticals that many university archivists have, could undergird greater participation in advancing this agenda. University archivists may be among the archivists best positioned to play such a role, not only at their own institutions but also through archival association work.

University archivists and other archivists can shape the new public programming in other significant ways. Some have opportunities to teach at universities. They could offer courses to a wide range of students that focus on the role of records and archives in public affairs. They could thus do much to educate the next generations of civic leaders and researchers to see and use archives in this way and to support much better funding of archives when they come into positions to do so. These archivists could also play a key role in educating others, especially in courses they teach, about the new conceptions of records and archiving that have been outlined here and are central to the overall success of the new public programming.

Perhaps the most promising strategy for moving archives more fully into the public square makes archives the direct mediator of the public knowledge they contain. For the most part, the users of archives, whether academics or others, especially the news media, publishers, filmmakers, libraries, museums, and historic sites, have been the primary deliverers of the information acquired and made available by archives. These users have garnered the public's appreciation and support by doing so, while archives languish by comparison. In contrast, the Vermont, CBC, and University of California archives have sought to be the direct providers of public-affairs knowledge in their custody. LAC, NARA, the Library of Congress, the MLA, and the Mandela Centre and the National Archives of South Africa have built partnerships with these other mediators that make and/or identify archives as the direct providers of such knowledge, whether through hosting public forums, joint publication efforts with academics and other users, LAC's lead role in the residential-schools and Innis and McLuhan projects, the Mandela Centre and NASA's work with the University of the Witwatersrand, or the English archival community's alliance with libraries and museums to bring archives' public-affairs roles to the fore. This may be a key strategy underlying all other efforts by archives to bring the valuable public knowledge they hold more directly to society in a new public programming.

NOTES

1 For a report on such limited views based on an extensive survey of mainly North American, Australasian, and European perceptions of archives and archivists, see Rick Barry, 'Report on the Society and Archives Survey,' http://www.mybestdocs.com/. (This website was accessed on 29 January 2003. All other websites mentioned in this essay were last accessed on 14 September 2009.)

2 Archival issues such as these, although they bear directly on the quality and accessibility of records related to public affairs, have not been a significant concern of public-policy analysts, at least in Canada. A survey of back issues of two leading Canadian public-policy journals (*Canadian Public Administration* and *Canadian Public Policy*) shows virtually no engagement with archival issues. The impact of digital communications may be ending this neglect. An encouraging sign is a recent book published in the Institute of Public Administration of Canada's series in Public Management and Governance: Sandford Borins et al., eds., *Digital State at the Leading Edge* (Toronto: University of Toronto Press 2007). It acknowledges the key role of Library and Archives Canada in addressing the weaknesses in digital-records management and archiving in the Canadian government (289–92, 374).

3 There is now a voluminous international literature arising from this em-
phasis on public programming. It was triggered by Elsie Freeman, 'In the
Eye of the Beholder: Archives Administration from the User's Point of
View,' *American Archivist* 47 (spring 1984). It can be traced in Canada to
Freeman's influence, the 1986 annual conference of the Association of
Canadian Archivists, of which public programming was the theme, and a
special supplement of six key early articles on public programming by
Gabrielle Blais and David Enns, Terry Cook, Timothy Ericson, Ian E.
Wilson, and Barbara Craig in *Archivaria* 31 (winter 1990–1). For an updated
statement by Wilson, who stepped down as librarian and archivist of
Canada in 2009 and became president of the International Council on Archives, see '"The Gift of One Generation to Another": The Real Thing for
the Pepsi Generation,' in Francis X. Blouin, Jr, and William G. Rosenberg,
eds., *Archives, Documentation, and Institutions of Social Memory: Essays from
the Sawyer Seminar* (Ann Arbor: University of Michigan Press 2006). The
Association of Canadian Archivists returned to public-programming issues
for its 2007 annual conference, devoted to the theme 'As Others See Us:
Archivists and Society.'

4 For examples of this work, see Tom Nesmith, 'Still Fuzzy, but More Accurate: Some Thoughts on the "Ghosts" of Archival Theory,' *Archivaria* 47
(spring 1999), and 'Reopening Archives: Bringing New Contextualities into
Archival Theory and Practice,' *Archivaria* 60 (fall 2005); and the double issue
of *Archival Science* 2 (2002) edited by Terry Cook and Joan Schwartz on the
theme 'Archives, Records, and Power.' In addition to articles by Cook and
Schwartz, themselves early contributors to this emerging archival discussion in the 1990s, this theme issue has articles by other pioneers of this
work in archival circles in the 1980s and 1990s, such as Brien Brothman and
Verne Harris.

5 Ian E. Wilson, 'Shortt and Doughty: The Cultural Role of the Public Archives of Canada , 1904–1935,' *Canadian Archivist* 2 (1973): 4–25.

6 Bill Russell, 'The White Man's Paper Burden: Aspects of Records Keeping
in the Department of Indian Affairs, 1860–1914,' *Archivaria* 19 (winter
1984–5).

7 'Where Are the Children? Healing the Legacy of the Residential Schools,'
LAC, 18 June 2002–3 February 2003, http://www.collectionscanada.gc.ca/
native-residential/index-3.html.

8 As cited in J. Keri Cronin. 'Assimilation and Difference: Two Recent Exhibitions of Archival Photographs,' *Archivaria* 54 (fall 2002): 131. See also
Wilson's similar comment in Cape Town in 2003, as president of the International Council on Archives' International Conference of the Round Table

on Archives (CITRA), on archives and human rights in 'Foreword,' *Comma* 2 (2004): 5–6. Wilson's comments should be seen in light of a wider discussion at LAC of the degree to which archivists are interpreters of the materials they work with. On 13 February 2007 Cheryl Meszaros, a Getty Museum Scholar and former head of public programs at the Vancouver Art Gallery, spoke at LAC in the 'Leaders in the Field' speakers series on 'Interpretation in the Reign of "Whatever."' See http://www.collections canada.ca/whats-new/013-281-e.html, and 'Interpretation in the Reign of "Whatever,"' *Muse* (January/February 2007), where Meszaros welcomes critical thinking about the interpretive work museums do. It is significant that LAC thought that Meszaros's topic would be controversial among archivists. In a notice publicizing her talk in the archival community, it said: 'The extent to which LAC interprets the collection as we make it accessible to Canadians, via exhibitions, via our website, or via other means is an important and difficult one. Some might argue that a library and an archives is not in the interpretation business; that our role is to help others discover items in the collection and allow them to provide their interpretations of that material. While others might counter that any act of selection, whether for collecting or for display purposes, is inherently an act of interpretation and so we are always interpreting and cannot avoid doing so. Let Dr. Meszaros inform and provoke you on these issues and many more.' See 'Leaders in the Field / Chefs de file reconnus dans le domaine,' posted to Arcan-l, 25 January 2007, by LAC's Jennifer Svarckopf.

9   Legacy of Hope Foundation, Aboriginal Healing Foundation, National Archives of Canada, and National Library of Canada, *Where Are the Children? Healing the Legacy of the Residential Schools/Que sonts les enfants devenus?: L'expérience des pensionnats autochtones* (Ottawa: Legacy of Hope Foundation 2003), 15–17, 29. The residential-schools issue triggered the largest class-action lawsuit in Canadian history; compensation payments to former students are expected to total about $2 billion. The Indian Residential Schools Settlement Agreement also provided for the establishment of a 'Truth and Reconciliation Commission' to facilitate further information gathering, healing, public awareness, archiving, and commemoration. See *Globe and Mail*, 20 August 2007, A5.

10   Terry Cook, 'Archives as Media of Communication,' in 'Old Messengers, New Media: The Legacy of Innis and McLuhan,' http://www.collections canada.ca/innis-mcluhan/002033 4040e.html.

11   See 'Building a Just Society: A Retrospective of Canadian Rights and Freedoms.' LAC invited a variety of commentators to contribute essays on this theme: Justice Michel Bastarache of the Supreme Court of Canada, poet

and professor George Elliott Clarke of the University of Toronto, ethno-ecology student Severn Cullis-Suzuki, former premier of Alberta Peter Lougheed, lawyer Julius Grey, and journalist Irshad Manji. LAC added: 'Although these commentaries do not necessarily reflect the opinions and policies of LAC or the government of Canada, we thank the authors for contributing to open debate and the exchange of ideas that reflect the spirit of the *charter* itself' (http://www.collectionscanada.gc.ca/rights-and-freedoms/index-e.html). For the LAC record-keeping initiative and the Forum, see http://www.collectionscanada.gc.ca/democracy/023023-3404-e.html. The National Archives of the United Kingdom has moved in similar directions to bring archivists and public-policy scholars together in programs such as its February 2009 conference on 'using archival sources to inform contemporary policy debates' (http://www.nationalarchives.gov.uk/events/ahrc-training.htm). Like LAC and the U.S. National Archives, where the Declaration of Independence and the constitution are on display, the National Archives of Australia and Archives New Zealand have also emphasized their key constitutional documents in permanent exhibitions, publications, and websites. See National Archives of Australia, *Federation Gallery: Charters of our Nation* (2001), and 'Treaty of Waitangi – te tiriti o Waitangi' at Archives New Zealand, http://www.archives.govt.nz/exhibitions/permanentexhibitions/treaty.php.

12 For the 'American Conversations' series, see http://www.archives.gov/about/archivist/conversations/. See also, for example, the various public forums hosted by the John F. Kennedy Presidential Library and Museum: http://www.jfklibrary.org/Education+and+Public+Programs/Kennedy+Library+Forums/.

13 For the Library's webcasts, see http://www.loc.gov/today/cyberlc/. For the Kluge Centre, see http://www.loc.gov/loc/kluge/.

14 For 'Continuing Issues of Government and Governance,' see http://vermont-archives.org/govhistory/governance/index.htm; and for *Opinions*, see http://vermont-archives.org/publications/voice/index.htm. See also Gregory Sanford, 'Upon This Gifted Age,' http://vermont-archives.org/publications/talks/pdf/NEA2003.pdf (a paper delivered to a meeting of New England archivists, 11 April 2003), 4.

15 Sanford, 'Upon This Gifted Age,' 4–6.

16 Ibid., 5–7; emphasis in the original. Cook, in turn, is quoting Steven Lubar, 'Information Culture and the Archival Record,' *American Archivist* 62 (spring 1999). For a similar view, see Randall C. Jimerson's 2005 presidential address to the Society of American Archivists, published as 'Embracing the Power of Archives,' *American Archivist* 69 (spring/summer 2006).

17 Sanford, 'Upon This Gifted Age,' 6; Marcel Joyce, 'Gregory Sanford:
    Vermont's CST (Chief Story Teller),' *Vermont Business Magazine* (1 June
    2006), http://findarticles.com/p/articles/mi_qa3675/is_200606/
    ai_n17174058/. See the Snelling Center for Government website for
    Sanford's reports on amending the Vermont constitution, at http://
    www.snellingcenter.org/constitutionalamendment/amendmentprocess/.
18 The CBC Digital Archives is available at http://archives.cbc.ca/.
19 Many of these archives are in the United States. A sample includes: the
    Howard H. Baker Jr. Center for Public Policy, University of Tennessee; the
    Richard B. Russell Library for Political Research and Studies, University of
    Georgia; the University of Kentucky Public Policy Archives; the Archives
    of Public Affairs and Policy, State University of New York at Albany; the
    Hoover Institution, Stanford University; the Carl Albert Congressional
    Research and Studies Center, University of Oklahoma; and the Archives,
    University of Colorado at Boulder Libraries, which has a mandate to ac-
    quire records related to 'Environmentalism,' 'Peace and Justice,' 'Labor,'
    and 'Politics,' in addition to serving as the archives for university records.
    The archives director, Bruce Montgomery, is one of the most prominent ar-
    chivists engaged in public affairs. He has commented in the media and in
    archival and other journals on American presidential-records legislation
    and human-rights records. See his 'Human Rights: A Survey of Archival
    Sources in the United States and Canada,' *Human Rights Quarterly* 23
    (May 2001): 431–63. It discusses the University of Colorado at Boulder's
    archival program 'The Human Rights Initiative.' This program, begun in
    1992, housed the archives of Human Rights Watch and Amnesty Inter-
    national (U.S.), among other records. Montgomery comments: 'The cen-
    trality of human rights in the world political arena makes human rights
    documentation imperative in enabling countries to confront the abuses of
    the past, assist in ending impunity, and reconstructing historical memory'
    (463). The University of Colorado has been seeking to relocate the human-
    rights archives since 1999. Columbia University, which established its Hu-
    man Rights Documentation and Research Center in 2005, is now the home
    for the Human Rights Watch and Amnesty International (U.S.) Archives,
    among other extensive human-rights holdings. The Center serves 'as both
    an archive and a teaching resource ... for current and future generations of
    human rights activists' (http://www.columbia.edu/cu/lweb/news/li-
    braries/2005/2005-05-19.bayandpaul_grant.html). The Thomas J. Dodd
    Research Center at the University of Connecticut hosts another archival
    program that emphasizes human-rights concerns. It also articulates the
    new conception of archives at the heart of the new public programming.

For an exhibit of the university's archival and library materials entitled 'Treasury of the Human Spirit' that marked the dedication of the Dodd Center in 1995 and commemorated the fiftieth anniversary of the Nuremberg Trials, the Center said: 'Books and manuscripts have long been celebrated as preservers of the cultural memory of humankind, and libraries as treasuries of the human spirit. But libraries and archives are active places as well as repositories. They are workshops for teaching and research, for engagement with the documentary sources of issues that are central to our world today. This exhibition is an invitation to that engagement.' See http://doddcenter.uconn.edu/exhibits/humanspirit/index.htm.

20 See http://www.library.ucsf.edu/tobacco/ and Robin L. Chandler and Susan Storch, 'Lighting up the Internet: The Brown and Williamson Collection,' in Richard Cox and David Wallace, eds., *Archives and the Public Good: Accountability and Records in Modern Society* (Westport, Conn.: Quorum Books 2002), 135, 156.

21 See 'Communities' at www.mla.gov.uk/what/policy_development/communities. For archives in particular, see *Archives for the 21st Century* at www.mla.gov.uk/what/strategies/archive. This 'Consultation Draft,' which was prepared by the MLA and the National Archives (U.K.) in order to elicit broader discussion of the future of England's archives, emphasizes the emerging role of publicly funded archives in public affairs. These archives 'have a wider role than simply being custodians of our national memory. The availability of information is an essential part of a healthy, robust democracy. It empowers people to make the decisions affecting their own lives. It promotes a better understanding of how policy is developed and how it applies to individuals. Increasingly, the archives sector has an important role to play in contributing to outcomes of government policies at a local, regional and national level' (1). An innovative example of the new directions in public programming that the MLA espouses for archives is the collaboration in 2004–5 of the National Archives (U.K.) with the mental-health program of the British National Health Service on 'There Be Monsters.' This project used very early archival maps in the National Archives as a source of information for a sculpture of the globe made by the patients. The globe contains many of the symbols and imaginary creatures found on the maps. It is now displayed at the archives. The project has been deemed a great success by the archives and mental-health services. The agency that provided external funding to assist the project concluded that it 'enabled The National Archives to make its collections available in an imaginative way to people with mental health difficulties for the first time. The resulting globe sculpture is a triumph and

we hope that [it] … will inspire further access improvements for mental health and other hard to reach groups to be involved in their archives across the UK.' See *There Be Monsters: A Case Study*, 4, available at http://nationalarchives.gov.uk/documents/tbm_overview.pdf. See also John Holden and Samuel Jones, *Knowledge and Inspiration: The Democratic Face of Culture: Evidence in Making the Case for Museums, Libraries and Archives* (London: Museums, Libraries and Archives Council 2006), 34, available at www.demos.co.uk/files/knowledgeinspiration_fullreport .pdf?1240939425.

22   See the special issues of the ICA journal *Comma* on 'Archives and Indigenous Peoples,' 1 (2003), and 'Archives and Human Rights,' 2 (2004). For the activities of the ICA Working Group on Archives and Human Rights, see http://old.ica.org/body.php?pbodycode=HRG&plangue=eng.

23   Many of Harris's writings have been brought together in his *Archives and Justice: A South African Perspective* (Chicago: Society of American Archivists 2007).

24   See http://www.nelsonmandela.org/index.php/memory/about/.

25   Ibid.

26   *Archives at the Crossroads, 2007*, 1, 13, available at http://www .nelsonmandela.org/images/uploads/NMF_dialogue_ _Archives_at_ the_Crossroads1.pdf. The Malibongwe Dialogue on the role of women in the struggle against apartheid was also one of the Centre's first major events held under the new mandate. An exhibition of historical records and a variety of oral recollections framed the discussion of how past experiences in mobilizing women against apartheid relate to current concerns about achieving gender equality in South Africa. See http:// www.nelsonmandela.org/index.php/publications/full/malibongwe/.

27   *Archives at the Crossroads, 2007*, 2–3.

28   Ibid., 8–9.

29   Libraries had been used by 38 per cent of the respondents and museums by 22 per cent. See Bob Usherwood, Kerry Wilson, and Jared Bryson, 'Relevant Repositories of Public Knowledge? Libraries, Museums and Archives in "the Information Age,"' *Journal of Librarianship and Information Science* 37 (June 2005): 92. There is an odd comfort in the archival figure of 11 per cent, since some, including this writer, would have expected an even lower result.

30   Ibid. Like Gregory Sanford at the Vermont Archives, Usherwood, Wilson, and Bryson make the useful point that respondents' interests should be seen as 'issues of *enduring* social and political concern in a contemporary context rather than as current concerns.' Ibid., 91; emphasis in original.

31 Ibid., 94–5.
32 See Sue McKemmish and Frank Upward, eds., *Archival Documents: Providing Accountability through Recordkeeping* (Clayton, Australia: Ancora Press 1993); Carolyn Hamilton, Verne Harris, Jane Taylor, Michele Pickover, Graeme Reid, and Razia Saleh, eds., *Refiguring the Archive* (Dordrecht: Klumwer Academic Publishers 2002); Cox and Wallace, eds., *Archives and the Public Good*; Margaret Proctor, Michael Cook, and Caroline Williams, eds., *Political Pressure and the Archival Record* (Chicago: Society of American Archivists 2005); Sue McKemmish, Michael Piggott, Barbara Reed, and Frank Upward, eds., *Archives: Recordkeeping in Society* (Wagga Wagga: Centre for Information Studies, Charles Sturt University 2005); Menzi L. Behrnd-Klodt and Peter Wosh, eds., *Privacy and Confidentiality Perspectives: Archivists and Archival Records* (Chicago: Society of American Archivists 2005); and Blouin and Rosenberg, eds., *Archives, Documentation, and Institutions of Social Memory*.
33 In June 2007 LAC also took a step like this towards the new public programming by hosting 'Taking a Stand: A Conference on Activism in Canadian Cultural Archives.' The conference brought together archivists, academics, and others to discuss how social activism across a spectrum of issues related to gender, sexuality, race, and disabilities is documented in archives of various artists, authors, and filmmakers. See http://www .collectionscanada.ca/whats-on/taking-a-stand/014004-1000-e.html.
34 The May 2009 annual conference of the Association of Canadian Archivists on the theme 'Rights, Responsibilities, Trust: Archivists and Public Affairs' and the association's establishment of its Climate Records and Information Special Interest Section in 2007 are important recent Canadian steps in this direction.

PART FIVE

Resource for the Present

10 Reconciliation in Regions Affected by Armed Conflict: The Role of Archives

TOM ADAMI and MARTHA HUNT

As a result of the horrors of the Second World War, the United Nations was established in 1945 for the purposes of preventing war, safeguarding human rights, providing a mechanism for international law, promoting social and economic progress, improving living standards, and fighting disease. The international political climate of the first four decades of the UN's existence made the use of peacekeeping forces and the establishment of protocol for international law a potentially contentious subject, limiting the UN's ability to take action to prevent or prosecute violations of humanitarian law. The changes brought about by the ending of the Cold War led to a more harmonious diplomatic environment and greater cooperation among member states. Since the early 1990s, the UN has increasingly focused on promoting human rights and ending conflict through work done in the areas of peacekeeping and international law. By the first decade of the twenty-first century, numerous UN-sponsored peacekeeping missions and judicial organizations have been created to establish peace in regions affected by armed conflict, and to promote the cause of justice in post-conflict communities.

The records and archives of peacekeeping missions and international tribunals and courts have the potential to make many important contributions to world history and memory. In order to live up to this potential, however, it is essential that administrative and financial support is provided for various long-term information-management and archival programs. Funding must be made available for the resources and staff needed to implement and run compliant record-keeping systems, ensure the intellectual and technical control of audio-visual materials, provide public access to the records, and develop outreach and capacity-building policies. Administrative support is required to develop plans for the deposition of copies of archival records in affected communities and the long-term preservation of these records. Support for such activities must be made available from the earliest days of the institution's existence through the completion of its mandate to ensure the success of these programs.

The maintenance of reliable, accurate records of an institution's operations is a crucial component in ensuring its transparency and accountability. The accessibility of records to internal users provides for efficient and effective work practices, and the accessibility of the records to the general public is necessary for educational and outreach purposes. The long-term viability of the records will ensure that the information is accessible to future researchers and historians and will contribute to the formation of a comprehensive record of human-rights violations, as well as providing a roadmap for the development of future institutions with similar mandates. And, finally, the availability of the records in communities affected by armed conflict can aid in the process of reconciliation in those communities.

The primary goals of the UN's Department of Peacekeeping Operations (DPKO) are to alleviate human suffering and to create conditions for self-sustaining peace. In 1948 the first UN-led peacekeeping operation, the UN Truce Supervision Organization (UNTSO) was established in Jerusalem. In the ensuing forty years, only thirteen other peacekeeping missions were established worldwide. However, in recent years, from 1988 to 2007, the UN has proved its commitment to ending armed conflicts and human-rights violations by establishing forty-eight new peacekeeping operations on four different continents.[1]

Several peacekeeping missions have resulted in less than successful outcomes. The 1993 peacekeeping and relief mission in Somalia resulted in a bloody battle on the streets of Mogadishu and failed to save the lives of thousands of Somalis. The genocide in Rwanda in 1994 and the massacre in Srebrenica in 1995 both occurred despite the presence of peacekeeping forces. Accusations of sexual abuse by UN peacekeepers committed against the very populations they were meant to protect have been made since 2004 in the Democratic Republic of the Congo, Haiti, Liberia, and Sudan, compromising the integrity and credibility of the missions.

Yet, despite these setbacks, the increase in resources devoted to peacekeeping has yielded many positive results. An independent study[2] documents a sharp decrease in the number of human-rights abuses, armed conflicts, and genocides committed since the end of the Cold

War. As of January 2010, there were more than 121,000 personnel serving in seventeen different DPKO-led missions worldwide, operating with a budget of over US$7.7 billion.[3] Another independent study has found that UN-led military intervention is the most cost-effective method of preventing risk in post-conflict societies.[4]

Because of the amount of resources devoted to peacekeeping, the provable veracity and integrity of the records generated in the completion of a mission's mandate are essential for the purposes of accountability and transparency. Further, because of the volatile nature of the political climate in which peacekeeping missions are established, the security of all public and confidential documents is an important concern. It is a bleak reflection on the nature of humankind that there will undoubtedly be a need for the establishment of future peacekeeping missions; the records of past and present missions will provide insights into lessons learned, enhancing the efficiency of the operations of future missions. The DPKO Best Practices Section plays an important role in enhancing the already established procedures for all aspects of a mission's administration, including information management. There is a large pool of knowledge and personal experience within the DPKO and it is continuously growing and built upon through discussions forums, meetings, and staff mobility.

Prior to 2006, there was little standardization among the various missions operated by the DPKO regarding electronic-records management. In most cases, the record-keeping responsibilities belonged to the mail and diplomatic pouch registry staff of the mission, with different missions making use of a variety of electronic record-keeping systems. Since 2006, missions have begun employing archival- and information-management professionals to enhance their record-keeping practices, and an enterprise-wide content-management system has been selected that will be deployed in all DPKO-operated missions throughout the world within the next few years. In the interim, some missions have implemented their own solutions to electronic record keeping by acquiring applications to address issues of access, preservation, and risk management. These attempts at managing e-records have had varying degrees of success and were usually led by the IT staff with a focus on digitization and little more. The headquarters-endorsed application, EMC's Documentation product, will be the standard to be used in all missions when the roll-out phase begins around 2013. Smaller pilot projects have been undertaken at UN headquarters. In mid-2009 it was also decided to fully digitize the audio-visual production and archival processes at headquarters, a step that will also benefit missions in that they, too, produce audio-visual records.

It is hoped that all these developments will lead to a more harmonized approach to the information-management practices organization-wide, aiding the missions in completing their mandates through enhanced efficiency and accountability. While an enterprise-wide content-management policy is being developed, lessons can and should be learned from both the failures and the success of the information-management practices of the UN-sponsored organizations devoted to the field of international criminal law.

Few instances of the prosecution of perpetrators of crimes against humanity exist prior to the Second World War, when an individual had no standing in international law and could not conceivably be brought before an international court.[5] The Tasmanian Aboriginal[6] and Herero[7] atrocities are but two cases of genocide that went virtually unnoticed until decades later. In the quasi-national setting after the American Civil War in 1865, Henry Wirz, commandant of the notorious Confederate prison of Andersonville, and Champ Ferguson were charged with mistreatment of Union prisoners[8] and for guerilla-style murders, respectively. Both men were put on trial, with witnesses called and evidence tendered for consideration, in what was possibly the first modern-day attempt to punish gross atrocities. Wirz and Ferguson were both found guilty and hanged.

International war crimes trials, however, got off to a dismal start in 1918, after the First World War. The victorious Allies drew up a list of 4,900 alleged German war criminals but soon thinned the list to 901 names. Of these, twelve were ordered to stand trial by a German court in Leipzig, four years after the war ended. Three of the twelve defendants never bothered to appear in court. Charges against three more were dropped. The remaining six defendants received wrist-slap sentences.[9]

The post-First World War investigation into the Armenian genocide serves as a warning about the negative impact of not maintaining verifiable records in times of conflict. The Peace Treaty of Sèvres required the Ottoman government to deliver 144 officials accused of what the Allied powers termed 'massacres.' The British government transported these 144 Ottoman officials to Malta for trial and appointed Haig Khazarian to conduct a thorough examination of documentary evidence. The investigators could not find sufficient evidence demonstrating that Ottoman officials either sanctioned or encouraged killings of Armenians. The British procurator general finally determined that it was 'improbable that the charges would be capable of proof in a court of law' and exonerated and released all 144 detainees, after twenty-eight months of detention without trial.[10] Apart from this aborted trial by the British to establish the facts of the deaths of countless Armenians living under Ottoman rule, no other legal process has been attempted, leaving the crimes uninvestigated, the perpetrators unpunished, and the issue unresolved.[11] Given that there was no formal judicial process, there is no definitive collection of evidentiary material that is acknowledged as being a true record of the events of 1915–23 with regard to the Armenians in the Ottoman lands. Had a full trial been carried out, a degree of reconciliation may have been achieved. So virulent is the discourse to this day that people have been murdered for their views of the disputed past.[12]

What are generally considered to be the first international war crimes tribunals were held in the aftermath of the Second World War. The unconditional surrender of the Axis powers left the Allies in an unusual position; the United States, the Soviet Union, and the United Kingdom were given the responsibility of trying the German and Japanese individuals accused of war crimes and other crimes against humanity. France joined the three major Allied powers in discussions regarding the issue, and an agreement was reached to establish an international tribunal, based in Nuremburg, Germany, to try the most notorious war criminals of the Nazi regime. In the Trial of the Major War Criminals before the International Military Tribunal (IMT), held between 20 November 1945 and 1 October 1946, twenty-four of the most important Nazi leaders were indicted; two were acquitted and eighteen were found guilty.[13] A secondary set of trials, the Trials of War Criminals before the Nuremberg Military Tribunals (NMT), was held between 9 December 1946 and 13 April 1949. In total, 185 individuals were tried in twelve separate trials and 142 were found guilty of at least one crime. The NMT trials were not an international endeavour, however, being conducted entirely by U.S. government officials.

The International Military Tribunal for the Far East (IMTFE), also known as the Tokyo Trials, was convened on 3 May 1946 and adjourned on 12 November 1948. It was established to try the leaders of the Empire of Japan for crimes against peace, war crimes, and crimes against humanity (referred to, respectively, as Class A, Class B, and Class C crimes). Twenty-five military and political leaders were charged with Class A crimes, and over 5,700 individuals were charged with Class B and C crimes. No member of the Japanese imperial family was charged with any crime. Although ostensibly international, with a chambers composed of judges from each of the eleven victorious Allied powers,[14] the Tokyo Trials have been criticized as having an American bias because, unlike the IMT trials, the prosecution was conducted by only one, U.S.-led team.

The judicial records of the Nuremburg and Tokyo trials were widely dispersed following the adjournment of the tribunals, with selected records housed in the law school libraries of several universities, as well as in the International Court of Justice (ICJ) in The Hague and the National Archives and Records Administration (NARA) in Washington, D.C. Approximately one million pages of documents relating to the IMT and the NMT are housed in Harvard University's Law School Library. A project is under way to digitize these records to make them accessible via the Internet; however, as of December 2009, only 13,904 pages of records from the Medical Case (Case 1 of the NMT trials) were available.[15] This dispersal of the jurisprudence of the Nuremburg and Tokyo trials continues to make accessing the records problematic for researchers.

Following the Nuremberg and Tokyo trials, the UN General Assembly adopted the Convention on the Prevention and Punishment of the Crime of Genocide,[16] recognizing the necessity of establishing an international judicial body to prosecute crimes against humanity. The ICJ was established in 1946 to adjudicate disputes between states, but, in the fifty years that followed, no international court existed to try the individuals accused of serious crimes against humanity. During those years, atrocities were committed that undoubtedly warranted the investigation of the international community. The names Idi Amin, Pol Pot, Mobutu Sese Seko, and Augusto Pinochet have become synonymous with the culture of impunity; despite having committed crimes against humanity, these men were allowed to live out the remainder of their days without ever having been held accountable for their actions. However, important developments have been made in the field of international law since the early 1990s, including the formation of numerous institutions devoted to the cause of international criminal justice.

The fundamental influence of the Nuremberg and Tokyo trials on current international criminal justice has been discussed widely and is indisputable.[17] One thing that is clear from this literature is that, within the various institutions dealing with criminal proceedings, there is great diversity in work practices and procedures but also harmonization, cooperation, and standardization. Owing to the different nature of the crimes being tried, the differences in the historical contexts of the atrocities, and the differences in cultural mores of the affected communities, the lack of standard operating procedures in these various institutions is inevitable. Dispersion of the record, the amalgamation of the records of the complex judicial process – from the indictment to the eventual release or death of the accused – and the definition and selective use of evidence and witness testimonies are but some of the aspects of the management of information in these present-day criminal justice institutions that give rise to differences in procedures. Yet these differences should not necessarily be viewed as a negative. They allow for a community of best practice to analyse the working procedures of each institution in terms of all aspects of administration, including information management.

The judicial records of the ad hoc tribunals and courts established to date form the backbone of international criminal jurisprudence. The precedents set and decisions made by the chambers of these institutions will function as a point of reference for the continuing work of the International Criminal Court (ICC), as well as for the national judicial systems of countries faced with the task of trying individuals accused of serious violations of humanitarian law. The records of an institution devoted to international criminal law provide proof that justice is being served within the organization. By demonstrating that serious violations of humanitarian law will not be tolerated by the international community, it is hoped that the visible presence of the tribunals and courts in affected regions will contribute to the efforts being made to end the culture of impunity.

In May 1993 the United Nations Security Council passed a resolution to establish the ad hoc International Criminal Tribunal for the Former Yugoslavia (ICTY) to deal with the violations of humanitarian law committed in the region since 1991. The main goals of the ICTY are to spearhead the shift from impunity to accountability, to establish the facts regarding the conflicts in the former Yugoslavia in the 1990s, to deliver justice and give a voice to the thousands of victims of the conflicts, to expand the boundaries of international humanitarian law, and to strengthen the rule of law in regions affected by armed conflicts. As of 20 January 2010, the ICTY had concluded cases against 121 individuals in 86 cases, convicting 61 and acquitting 11 others; the trials of forty are ongoing and two accused are still at large. As the ICTY approaches the end of its mandate, resources have been devoted to the implementation of a compliant record-keeping system to manage the vast amount of documents generated throughout the course of its judicial proceedings.

The information-management policies of the International Criminal Tribunal for Rwanda (ICTR), the sister organization of the ICTY, are an example of the harmonized differences between the post-Cold War ad hoc tribunals. The ICTR's mandate is similar to that of the ICTY; both tribunals are scheduled to complete their work by the end of 2013. The differences that have evolved in the information-management policies of the two organizations have shown that, if adequate resources are available for information-management programs such as compliant record-keeping systems, audio-visual intellectual and physical control, public access via the Internet, and senior management support, the archives of an institution can aid in the process of reconciliation.

In April 1994 an airplane carrying Juvenal Habyarimana, the president of Rwanda, was shot down.[18] President Habyarimana was a moderate member of a political party representing the Hutu ethnic majority. He had recently signed a peace treaty with Tutsi rebel leaders in an attempt to end a decades-long civil war that had been ravaging Rwanda since the earliest days of its independence. It remains unclear who was responsible for shooting down the plane; what is clear is that Habyarimana's assassination sparked a genocide that had been carefully planned by extremist Hutu leaders. The motive for planning the genocide was power. The tools used were political manipulation, military intimidation, ethnic tension, propaganda, ignorance, and fear. It was the most efficient genocide ever planned; over the course of one hundred days, an estimated 800,000 people were murdered. That is roughly 10 per cent of the entire population of Rwanda. On average, five people died every minute in this tiny country in central Africa. The victims were both Tutsi and moderate Hutu who opposed the ethnically divisive policy of the Hutu Power government. The killers were their neighbours. The weapons were primarily garden tools.

Recognizing the serious violations of humanitarian law that were committed in Rwanda in 1994, and acting under Chapter VII of the United Nations Charter, the Security Council created the ICTR by Resolution 955 on 8 November 1994. The purpose of this measure is to contribute to the process of national reconciliation in Rwanda, to establish and maintain peace in the Great Lakes region of central Africa, and to end the culture of impunity in Africa. The ICTR was established to prosecute the persons most responsible for the genocide and other serious violations of international humanitarian law committed in

Rwanda and its neighbouring states in 1994. As of January 2010, the ICTR had arrested eighty-one individuals. The trials of forty-eight of the accused have been completed, and those of twenty-six others are ongoing. Twenty-one individuals have either been acquitted or released, have died in custody, or have been transferred to national courts. Approximately eleven accused are still at large. The accused individuals are those deemed by the prosecutor of the ICTR to have been most responsible for planning, instigating, implementing, and financing the genocide and include key figures in the fields of government, the military, the media, business, and religion. The trials of the individuals accused of taking part in the genocide on a lower level are being conducted by the national judicial system of Rwanda.

The judicial records of the ICTR are all documents created or received in support of the judicial processes. They include the written transcripts of the proceedings in both English and French, all exhibits tendered in court, all documents from the case file (motions, decisions, judgments, and so on), all correspondences among parties, and all audio-visual recordings of the proceedings. Taken together, these documents are a comprehensive record of a historically unique organization. From the earliest years of the ICTR's existence, resources have been made available for the long-term preservation, management, and internal accessibility of the judicial records. A professional archivist was hired in 1998, and a compliant electronic record-keeping system, TRIM, has been in place since 2000 to aid in the management of the judicial documents. Access to all public judicial documents is provided via the ICTR's website. Internationally accepted archival standards have been employed to manage the intellectual and physical control of the audio-visual records, and a program is in place to digitize the audio-visual recordings of the court proceedings.

Despite the availability of resources to ensure the long-term viability, management, and accessibility of the judicial archives, it has only been in the years leading up to the completion of the ICTR's mandate that policies have been developed and resources devoted to the outreach and capacity-building responsibilities that the tribunal bears to Rwanda. If the ICTR is to achieve its aims, it is essential that its target groups, in particular the Rwandan people, have a clear understanding of its work. This implies a sustained strategic communication program using a range of techniques, varying according to the audience addressed, to explain the tribunal's work and its relevance to Rwanda and the international community. Beginning in 2005, the ICTR embarked on improving its public outreach to diverse audiences, using various communication channels. The ICTR outreach program has been conceived as a series of projects complementary to the main institutional communication of the tribunal. Particular attention is given to mass media and interpersonal communication in order to convey efficient and persuasive messages to targeted audiences inside and outside Rwanda. Apart from informing the public about its work, the tribunal also holds information seminars for different groups. The outreach program gives particular attention to the availability of printed materials, radio broadcasts, and speakers in Kinyarwanda. Training seminars for journalists and a research-fellowship program for Rwandan law students are central to the outreach program. The program also encompasses a capacity-building initiative aimed at enhancing the legal and information-management skills of the staff of the national judiciary of Rwanda.

In 2002 the Special Court for Sierra Leone (SCSL) was formed through an agreement between the UN and the government of Sierra Leone to try those people most responsible for atrocities during the country's armed conflict since 30 November 1996. In comparison to the ICTR, the SCSL did not devote a large amount of resources to the area of information management. The scaled-back solution in place was deemed suitable for the requirements of the court. The SCSL is scheduled to complete most of its work by the end of 2011. It is only now, at the stage of winding down its operations, that the challenge of legacy systems has needed to be addressed, with extra resources committed to maintaining its archives and other residual legal matters. It is incumbent upon the management of the SCSL to commit sufficient resources to resolving these issues while the court is still operational, and while the institutional knowledge and expertise remain available to ensure legacy systems that are authentic, reliable, and accessible over time. The SCSL planning committee has decided that copies of its judicial archives will be left with the Sierra Leone government, and it is more than likely that the original archive and other collections of court records such as the prosecutors' evidence collection will be maintained in The Hague.

Although the SCSL may be considered the younger sister of the ICTY and ICTR, valuable lessons can be learned by the two larger tribunals in the area of community outreach. Since the SCSL is the first court to be established in the country where the conflict took place, outreach is a critically important aspects of the court's work. A very active outreach effort is in place that includes radio broadcasts throughout Sierra Leone summarizing the weekly activities of court and the establishment of outreach centres located throughout the country to disseminate information. The SCSL has done an admirable job in aiding in the acceptance of the work of the court within the affected communities through its outreach program.

The Serious Crimes Unit (SCU) for East Timor was established in 2000 by the UN Transitional Authority in East Timor (UNTAET) following UN Security Council Resolution 1272. The SCU was mandated to conduct investigations and prepare indictments to bring to justice those responsible for crimes against humanity and other serious crimes committed in East Timor in 1999. The mandate of the SCU ended in May 2005 and, pursuant to UN Security Council resolutions 1543 and 1573, the SCU completed all investigations by 30 November 2004. Unfortunately, the SCU was not successful in ending violent conflict in East Timor; riots in the capital city of Dili in April 2006 led to a nationwide uprising that resulted in the death, injury, and displacement of tens of thousands of citizens. The archives of the SCU were a secondary victim of this violence. Recognizing the potential power of judicial records, machete-wielding mobs broke into the attorney general's office in Dili and looted the SCU archives, stealing an estimated 15 per cent of the records.[19] This theft seriously undermines efforts towards reconciliation by impeding any future investigation and prosecution, as well as compromising the accountability of the SCU and other government offices. The documents stolen pertain to the past investigations of the SCU, including witness statements and trial transcripts that contain information that could reveal the identity of protected witnesses. In the wrong hands, this information could potentially lead to reprisals. Clearly, the looting of the SCU archives was not a random act of violence but rather a carefully planned attack on this powerful yet vulnerable source of information.

Further developments in the field of international law were made in 2006. An agreement was reached between the government of Cambodia and the UN to form the Extraordinary Chambers in the Courts of Cambodia (ECCC) to try the leaders of the Khmer Rouge accused of committing crimes against humanity between 17 April 1975 and 7 January 1979. Also in 2006, the UN Security Council endorsed a proposal to establish the International Independent Investigation Commission (IIIC) to investigate the terrorist bombing that led to the death of Lebanese Prime Minister Rafiq Hariri and others. In both of these organizations, lessons can be learned from both the successes and the failures of the ICTY, ICTR, SCSL, and SCU. The channels of communication among the staff members of the existing courts and these newly established institutions are open and the sharing of knowledge is encouraged by management.

Despite the important work that has been done by these various ad hoc organizations, the UN has recognized that there are serious administrative, diplomatic, and financial deficiencies inherent in such institutions. Because these deficiencies threaten to soften the political will to establish future tribunals as the need arises, an international conference was held in Rome in July 1998 to discuss the creation of a permanent international court. One hundred and twenty nations voted to adopt the Rome Statute of the International Criminal Court.[20] By the beginning of 2001, the required number of 139 nations had ratified the treaty, and the ICC's jurisdiction officially commenced in The Hague on 1 July 2002. After more than fifty years since the Convention on the Prevention and Punishment of the Crime of Genocide was adopted, the world's first independent and permanent international court was finally established.

The effectiveness of these complex international judicial institutions is difficult to quantify; success in a relatively new and developing system is difficult to define. The heinous acts of murder, rape, slavery, and torture have long been recognized as the worst types of crimes, and the international community has put tough measures in place to bring perpetrators to justice and to halt the continuation of these crimes. When such offences are committed by one group of people against another, international courts and the international community have not always been consistent in their approach, and the international tribunals and special courts established over the past decade to deal with genocide and other crimes against humanity have achieved mixed results.[21]

Most observers in international law believe that a coherent system is evolving that will, over time, bring justice to the people who have suffered at the hands of their own or other governments, but that the process of finding the best approach is a matter of trial and error and could take decades. This applies not only to legal methodology and policy but also to the management of information systems and the archival legacies of the institutions. There has been and continues to be a degree of inter-tribunal cooperation. A recent fact-finding mission to the offices of the ICTR of those responsible for information-management processes at the ICC demonstrated the close working relations that exist between the ad hoc bodies and the ICC. The information systems being developed to assist the judicial processes are constantly evolving and can be described as living bodies of interrelated knowledge. Cross-fertilization among the permanent, ad hoc, and special courts is a reality, and is one of the positive aspects of the work being undertaken. It is less a matter of trial and error than of the harmonization of differences. The information-management systems that will become an integral part of the archives after 2010 are the product of constant adjustments depending on the needs of users and the organization in general.

Justice should not be the only driving force of these institutions. The prosecution of the perpetrators of crimes against humanity can never compensate affected peoples for the suffering, or erase the international community's culpability for the failure to prevent genocides and other violations of humanitarian law in the first place. The dead will stay dead, and that is beyond question. Yet, though it is no substitute for preventing atrocities, prosecuting perpetrators is still critically important. It acknowledges the suffering of the victims, and, in the long run, it could help deter future abuses by forcing the rogue leaders of the world to ask themselves if the abuses are worth it, given the increasing likelihood that they will be held accountable for their actions (assuming that the corrupting force of absolute power allows for the luxury of self-assessment and re-evaluation). Additionally, the creation of a system of precedents in the area of international criminal jurisprudence is related to the work being carried out by the ad hoc and special courts. Current international courts refer continuously to the work of the Nuremberg and Tokyo military tribunals, and continually cross-reference each others' preceding jurisprudence. This factor will be important to the success of these institutions and to the ongoing work of the ICC.

In the process of dispensing justice, a large body of information is gathered, analysed, interpreted, translated, digitized, absorbed into systems, processed, copied, printed, and so on. There is a great flow of information into these institutions, and the outcome is another flow of information generated by the institutions themselves. The informational inputs and outputs are clearly not end products in and of themselves, and cannot be seen as a marker of success. Rather, the accessibility, preservation, and legacy commitments of the archives of these institutions can be used, in part, to measure the success of their work. Since these institutions are all closely affiliated with the United Nations, discussions are currently under way to coordinate the management of the archives of these institutions post-closure, under the UN's auspices.[22] This would, in one sense, ensure that the process of justice is preserved, a crucial component to the successful conclusion of the mandates of these institutions.

Justice is aided by the application of appropriate information-management technology and work practices. For example, the pace of the trials of the ICTR increased between 2003 and 2007 to such an extent that only the lack of support staff and courtroom space were limiting further increases in trials; technology has never been an impediment to increased workload projections. One aspect of dispensing justice is the requirement to be as transparent and publicly accessible as possible, and appropriate use of technology can allow for the accessibility, authenticity, and reliability of information – a key contribution to the pursuit of justice, both currently and in the future. The archival legacies of international criminal justice institutions are a critical aspect of the successful application of future humanitarian law as it relates to prosecution of criminal acts of an international scale. But there is also a larger human element being addressed: contributing to the process of reconciliation.

Although the concept of reconciliation is somewhat vague and difficult to quantify, it is one of the main factors in determining the success of the UN organizations devoted to international justice and peace-keeping. It is a complex matter, involving the search for truth, justice, healing, and forgiveness. The level of success in attaining reconciliation can be properly evaluated only after many years. The establishment of self-sustaining peace is an indicator of whether or not true reconciliation has been attained in a community affected by violent conflict. The aim of all peacekeeping missions is not simply to end conflict but to establish peace. The successful implementation of self-sustaining peace in a post-conflict region can be determined by evaluating such criteria as disarmament, government policies, donor demands, internal or external armed interference, and outside political manipulation. But lasting peace can never truly be established without reconciliation. Justice is also a key component in the process of reconciliation. The legal process gives survivors and victims a forum in which to speak and an opportunity to attempt to forgive the perpetrators of the atrocities they suffered.

The accountability of peacekeeping missions and legal bodies is a crucial component in the process of reconciliation. There appears to be little doubt in the professional literature or in practical experience that record keeping does aid the reconciliation process. As can be seen in the example of the Armenian genocide, lack of verifiable documentary evidence can seriously undermine international and local efforts to attain the goal of reconciliation. Because accountability leads to trust in the rule of law, the archives of international courts and peacekeeping missions can benefit the process of reconciliation, assisting in the return to normality in the affected communities and nations.

The work being undertaken in support of the judicial and peace processes is by definition a dynamic one owing to a sustained – albeit uncommon within the profession – focus on a largely international, interdisciplinary, and victim-centred methodological approach. It has been said that, whereas 'lawyers are particularly interested in the minutiae of technical questions ... what matters to most people is a bigger question: is the emerging system of international criminal justice fulfilling its objectives?'[23] The question can also be asked of the information managers of legal and peacekeeping institutions. Are the records fulfilling their intended objectives? Will the archival legacies of these institutions be of a calibre that will support future research and the process of reconciliation?

Although it is ultimately the courts that determine whether records are telling the truth, archivists should, in conjunction with the courts, be part of the process, neither conceding nor abrogating their role in this regard.[24] There is a gradual but nevertheless perceptible change, almost on a daily basis, in the collective archival fond of the UN peacekeeping missions and judicial bodies. The record, as described in the records-continuum model developed by Frank Upward and Sue McKemmish of Monash University, is constantly ebbing and flowing, and is perhaps also transfigured, according to the various influences and uses attributed to it.[25] The archives of a peacekeeping mission may have future use as documentary evidence in the legal process. For example, documents created or received by the UN Assistance Mission for Rwanda (UNAMIR) in 1994 are often tendered as evidence in court at the ICTR. In fact, the archives of a single organization may contain many copies of the same document serving different, sometimes conflicting, purposes. A transcript of a racial-hatred broadcast by the Rwandan Radio Télévision Libre des Mille Collines (RTLM), the national radio station of Rwanda, may be submitted as exculpatory material by one of the parties in a case heard at the ICTR, and may again appear as an exhibit in subsequent cases. The same transcripts may later appear in another case defending or refuting a set of actions attributed to a different defendant. Records are used, reused, interpreted, and reinterpreted according to a complex set of requirements of the users. The records can exist within the different vectors and dimensions of the continuum model, thereby serving multiple purposes and attaining different values. Amalgamation would not be possible, practical, or desirable. The purposes and resultant end uses of these records are too varied even to contemplate such a development.

There is another fundamental issue surrounding information management in the international judicial and peacekeeping environments: historical revisionism. On the issue of revisionism and the concept of minimization of the evidence, it has been said: 'As every attorney knows, it is often easier to create doubt and win than it is to prove what actually took place.'[26] The concept of burden of proof and evidential value of the record should be the fundamental raison d'être of any record-keeping program in the legal field. As was proven by the looting of the archives of the SCU in East Timor, the documentary evidence of crimes against humanity is greatly feared by the perpetrators of these crimes, and is therefore susceptible to destruction or alteration by individuals who believe they have something to hide. The security of the archival holdings of peacekeeping missions and international judicial bodies must be vigorously maintained, especially when they are housed in regions of unrest. Historical revisionism is a great threat to the establishment of peace and justice and is more damaging to the process of reconciliation than the complete lack of record keeping that, to this day, has allowed the denial of the Armenian genocide.

The archives of peacekeeping missions and international tribunals and courts need to be preserved over time as a testament to the survivors of the worst possible crimes. The five main responsibilities of a human-rights archives are ensuring historical accountability, retaining memory of the victims and survivors, supporting prosecution, documenting the extremes of repression, and chronicling the individual's power against the state.[27] In the case of the Rwandan genocide, Human Rights Watch, a U.S.-based non-profit, non-governmental organization dedicated to the protection of human rights worldwide, has stated:

Accurate accounts of the genocide must establish in all their complexity the roles of the leaders, the followers, and the dissidents within Rwanda as well as the parts played by various international actors. This is essential both for assessing fairly the behaviour of individuals and for creating strategies for the future. We must understand how local and international protest can resonate back and forth to create the swell of outrage that will prevent or halt future genocides. This work is one of the many that must come to establish the historical record, to lay the groundwork for justice for Rwandans and accountability for all others who failed to respond to the bonds of our common humanity. The story must be told.[28]

It is somewhat ironic that repressive regimes do, in fact, have a habit of maintaining vast amounts of records which invariably end up in the archives of post-conflict governments or judicial organizations. For example, the Khmer Rouge regime had a fascination with keeping documentary records of their victims.[29] These records are now used to prosecute the perpetrators of the human-rights abuses of the Khmer Rouge regime at the ECCC. The legacy of the Khmer Rouge archives highlights the potential transfiguration of one archival function into another. A tool of repression can, at times, become a tool of reconciliation.[30] This is one aspect of the transformation of the archives of institutions devoted to the promotion of human rights. Over time, the value of the information shifts, grows, takes on new meaning, enlightens, and ultimately becomes immutably fixed in temporal and physical location and composition. Its purpose may then, at a later stage, be changed again as the users' needs evolve. The archive evolves from a mass of separate records into a body of information that points to a time and place that no longer exists, except in the memories of those individuals with the fortune, or perhaps the misfortune, to have survived.

NOTES

1 See http://www.un.org/Depts/dpko or http://www.un.org/en/ peacekeeping/ (both accessed 14 January 2010).
2 Human Security Centre, Liu Institute for Global Studies (University of British Columbia), *The Human Security Report: War and Peace in the 21st Century* (2005), http://www.humansecurityreport.info.
3 According to figures available at the end of December 2009, there were 98,197 troops and police plus over 21,000 civilian staff in the 15+2 UN DPKO-led missions. See the UN document detailing budgetary allocations for the DPKO: http://www.un.org/ga/search/view_doc.asp?symbol=A/ C5/63/26. UNOMIG, the UN observer mission in Georgia, was closed in 2009. UNAMA, the assistance mission in Afghanistan, is a political mission supported by the DPKO, as is the Burundi operation. UNMIN in Nepal is a UN Department of Political Affairs (DPA) peace-building and support mission, and so are six others in Guinea-Bissau, Iraq, Central African Republic,

Sierra Leone, Somalia, and Lebanon. These DPA missions are run in collaboration with the UN Peacebuilding Support Office. They are not included in the figures given here.

4 Paul Collier and Anke Hoffler, *The Challenges of Reducing the Global Incidence of Civil War* (Oxford: Oxford University, Centre for the Study of African Economies, Department of Economics, 26 March 2004).

5 M. Drumbl, 'Pluralizing International Criminal Justice,' *Michigan Law Review* 103 (2005): 1295.

6 Jesse Shipway, 'Modern by Analogy: Modernity, Shoah, and the Tasman Genocide,' *Journal of Genocidal Research* 7 (June 2005): 205–19.

7 H. Lundtofte, '"I Believe That the Nation as Such Must Be Annihilated ...": Radicalization of the German Suppression of the Herero Rising in 1904.' In S.L.B. Jensen, ed., *Genocide: Cases, Comparisons, and Contemporary Debates* (Copenhagen: Danish Centre for Holocaust and Genocide Studies 2003), 15–53.

8 See http://en.wikipedia.org/wiki/Henry_Wirz and http://en.wikipedia.org/wiki/Champ_Ferguson (accessed 2 July 2007).

9 Joseph E. Persico, *Nuremberg: Infamy on Trial* (New York: Viking 1994), 11.

10 Taner Akçam, 'Anatomy of a Crime: The Turkish Historical Society's Manipulation of Archival Documents,' *Journal of Genocide Research* 7 (June 2005): 255–77. See also http://www.turkey.org/politics/facts.htm.

11 'Genocide and Human Rights – Lessons from the Armenian Experience,' Special issue of *Journal of Armenian Studies* 4, nos. 1 and 2 (1992).

12 Turkish Armenian journalist Hrant Dink was murdered in January 2007 for what is believed to have been his comments on the Armenian 'genocide.'

13 One defendant committed suicide prior to the commencement of the trial, and one was found medically unfit to stand trial.

14 United States, Soviet Union, United Kingdom, Republic of China, the Netherlands, Provisional Government of the French Republic, Australia, New Zealand, Canada, British India, and the Philippines.

15 http://nuremberg.law.harvard.edu/php/docs_swi.php?DI=1&text=overview (accessed 14 January 2010).

16 http://www.un-documents.net/cppcg.html (accessed 15 January 2010).

17 T.A. Adami and K.S. Khamis, 'Legal Recordkeeping in an African Context: The Rwandan Genocide,' ATLANTI 13 proceedings (2003); Tom A. Adami, Jones O. Lukose, and Khamis S. Khamis, 'Legal Recordeeping in an African Context – The Case of the Rwandan Genocide Archives,' *ESARBICA Journal* (Eastern and Southern Africa Regional Branch of the International Council on Archives) 23 (2004): 3–16; Tom Adami and Martha Hunt,

'Genocidal Archives: The African Context – Genocide in Rwanda,' *Journal of the Society of Archivists* 26, no. 1 (2005); T.A. Adami, 'The Management of International Criminal Justice Records: The Case of the Rwandan Tribunal,' *African Journal of Library, Archives and Information Science* 13 (2003): 1–10; Allan Connelly-Hansen, 'The International Criminal Tribunal for Rwanda – A Case Study Verifying the Utility of the Australian Records Management Standard AS4390 and the DIRKS Manual in the International Arena,' *Convergence* (Australian Society of Archivists and Records Management Association of Australia, 2001).

18 For background of and events surrounding the assassination, see http://www.youtube.com/watch?v=ObRJbPL1d3Y (accessed 15 January 2010).

19 http://www.wsws.org/articles/2006/jun2006/lett-j06.shtml (accessed 15 January 2010).

20 http://www.untreaty.un.org/cod/icc/index.html (accessed 15 January 2010).

21 G.J. Bass, *Stay the Hand of Vengeance: The Politics of War Crimes Tribunals* (Princeton, N.J.: Princeton University Press 2000); M. Osiel, *Mass Atrocity, Collective Memory, and the Law* (New Brunswick, N.J.: Transaction Publishers 2000); S. Power, '*A Problem from Hell': America and the Age of Genocide* (New York: Perenial 2003).

22 By the end of 2009, the issue of archival legacy had gained more importance with all the stakeholders as the deadline of 2013 approached for the ICTY and ICTR to conclude their work. The SCSL will probably be included in some manner in the final decision-making process for the archival legacy of international criminal tribunals when they close in 2011, as will the Kosovo and East Timor records which are already in UN custody. The records of all these institutions were too voluminous for the United Nations Archives Section to accept all of them into custody, and so forced a reconsideration of the archives' mandate and procedures.

It is generally thought that the International Criminal Court will be involved in this development because of its situation as the only remaining international criminal court once all the ad hoc and special courts close. The UN Security Council, at its meeting of early December 2009, noted that its informal working group on archives would make a final decision on location and organizational structure of the 'residual meachanism(s)' by mid-2010. Another issue to be resolved is the right of access for the affected communities and how best to ensure that access is provided given the huge variation in terms of literacy, wealth, Internet access, and so on of some of the stakeholders.

23 P. Sands, *Pluralizing International Criminal Justice from Nuremberg to The Hague: The Future of International Criminal Justice* (Cambridge: Cambridge University Press 2003), xxx.

24 Verne Harris, 'Law, Evidence and Electronic Records: A Strategic Perspective from the Global Periphery' (National Archives of South Africa 2000).

25 Frank Upward and Sue McKemmish, 'In Search of the Lost Tiger, by Way of Sainte-Beuve: Re-Constructing the Possibilities in "Evidence of Me ...,"' *Archives and Manuscripts* 29, no. 1 (2001).

26 S. Totten, W.S. Parsons, and I.W. Charny, eds., *Century of Genocide: Eyewitness Accounts and Critical Views* (New York and London: Garland Publishing 1997), xxi–xxii.

27 Bruce P. Montgomery, 'Fact-Finding by Human Rights Non-Governmental Organizations: Challenges, Strategies, and the Shaping of Archival Evidence,' *Archivaria* 58 (2004).

28 Human Rights Watch Report, 1999, 'Leave None to Tell the Story: Genocide in Rwanda,' http://www.hrw.org./reports/1999/rwanda/Geno15-8-05.htm#P1296_419255 (accessed 18 August 2005).

29 G. Chigas, 'Building a Case against the Khmer Rouge: Evidence from the Tuol Sleng and Santebal Archives,' *Harvard Asia Quarterly* 4, no. 1 (2000).

30 Eric Ketelaar, 'The Archives of the United Nations International Criminal Tribunal for the Former Yugoslavia: A Joint Heritage, Shared by Communities of Records.' Paper delivered to the I-Chora 2 Conference in Amsterdam, 31 August–2 September 2005.

11 Bridging Us to Us: An Argument for the Importance of Archivists in Current Politics and Journalism[1]

ROBERT STEINER

The archivist, to most of us, is a librarian of memory. We picture archivists bridging generations: some guarding old artifacts for current audiences, others guarding current artifacts for future thinkers, each of them with one foot in another era.

What could the archivist possibly tell *us* about *us*?

A lot, I argue.

Archivists are, in fact, *uniquely* able to confront one of the major rots in the popular culture: the literal disintegration of meaning in political communications and in journalism. That's because outstanding politicians and journalists share the instincts of outstanding archivists, and archivists thus have a particular ability to recognize great politics and great journalism.

Great politicians, journalists, and archivists all instinctively invite individuals into a frank encounter with the roots of their current experience. Like archivists, the best politicians and journalists embrace root causes that are messy, ambiguous, complicated, and anxious. Like archivists, they have an instinct for primary sources, and know the delicate art of working with the ore of human experience, unprocessed by historiography and national mythology.

Consider that one of the ways in which politicians signal their quality is in the way that they use historic materials. Conventional politicians use 'history' to simplify decisions; they draft narratives that distract a society away from the complexity of its true situation and instead drive people towards a specific agenda. Such politicians have no appetite for primary sources. They thirst instead for secondary sources that suit political needs.

Great politicians, on the other hand, use history more 'archivally' – they seek out primary sources that expose the messiness underlying a society's current circumstances. Few ever attempt this, to be sure; even fewer succeed in using complexity to inspire. But it *is* possible, and those who succeed in the effort are legend. They share a rare political goal: to expose the meaning of a people's current struggles by helping it encounter the true and messy sources of its current experience.

There is a similar distinction between conventional journalists and great ones. Great journalists have an 'archival' instinct to encounter the root causes of current experience, because it is their only route into truth. This quality is salient in their writing or broadcasting. They do more than recite fact or opinion; they are great storytellers – literal 'correspondents' – rather than reporters.

Journalism and politics are (along with entertainment) the pillars of mass communications in contemporary culture. In both cases, greatness is a matter to which the archivist – with her instincts for the qualities of an authentic source – is uniquely attuned. The archivist can assess far more than whether a speech or body of journalism has lasting value. The archivist can also judge whether contemporary communications have the flavour of primary sources and thus deserve to have *current* value. In a world weary of 'spin,' the archivist – far more than any pundit or 'political analyst' – holds the litmus test of meaning.

First, though, some definitions. I am only an amateur archivist – my passion is eighteenth-century naval charts and my grandmother's well-worn early-twentieth-century Hungarian cookbooks. No professional qualification would warrant my contribution to this literature. Still, let me define archives as any materials – artifact or natural – that invite a person into a frank encounter with the source of their current experience. Archival materials are those that offer an experience of origins (at either a mass or personal level) untempered by subsequent philosophy, historiography, rhetoric, ideology, or mythology. They invite a person to meet roots unworn by the plush sediment of collective memory. Archives by this admittedly broad and amateurish definition are anything that compels a person's current mind directly into the circumstances of their origins.

This can – though only on rare occasions – also be the achievement of politics.

I have a brief history in politics. In Canada's 2000 general election, I managed the national 'new media' campaign for Prime Minister Jean Chrétien and his Liberal Party. In 2002 and 2003 I developed health policy for Paul Martin, Canada's then finance minister and heir apparent to Prime Minister Chrétien, as he campaigned for the leadership of the Liberal Party of Canada and the premiership. That work led me to be Martin's principal speechwriter in the eight months prior to his assumption of the position of prime minister.

Although I worked as a highly tactical political operative, I gained a growing sense that politics should aspire to be a healing profession on a mass scale. 'Anyone who is going to be a truly good guardian of our community, then, will have a philosopher's love of knowledge,' writes Plato, in a chapter of *Republic* whose title one classicist translates as 'Fundamentals of Inner Politics.'[2]

As I flew across Canada on my political work, I came to imagine that Plato would have politicians do for a society what physicians, social workers, psychotherapists, or teachers do for individuals. That is to say: grasp a people's true potential, bluntly diagnose the factors limiting that potential, and coach a people – gently but surely – past those barriers to its true and proper place.[3] The archival perspective is vital to such efforts, because it allows the politician to make the blunt diagnosis from which later healing flows.

Most politicians, including those with whom I worked, don't operate that way. Rather than make a true attempt at diagnosis, political writers craft speeches and platforms to serve a prefabricated, if generally well-intended, policy agenda. The politician's work is thus much the same as that of the harried (rather than thorough) physician, who writes a prescription she's pretty sure should more or less work without her prying too closely into the patient's specific circumstances.

As far as I could tell, politicians often simplify their communications in this way for two reasons. One is to polarize a debate and force people into a false choice between two mythical extremes. Writing policy communications for the Liberal Party of Canada in 2000, I was instructed to ignore our real differences from the leftist New Democratic Party and, instead, exaggerate the differences between all centrist and leftist Canadians and the new conservative parties to our right: 'Polarization is our strategy,' I was told as I sat down at my keyboard.

Such approaches easily encourage an unquestioning devotion to a single ideology alongside an unreasonable, desperate fear of other options. It is no exaggeration to say that political communications of this nature undermine the emotional maturity democracy needs. (Although Canada has by no means flirted with dictatorship in recent times, the widespread sense in 2000 that my party, the Liberal Party of Canada, was in fact Canada's only 'natural governing party' – a far more radical notion than simply presenting it as Canada's best choice – was a troubling sign. The disciplined archivist would undoubtedly have probed deeply into the material origins of a notion that voters ultimately dismissed as contrived.)

There is also a less malevolent, if equally unsettling, reason why many politicians refrain from ushering people into a frank encounter with the complex origins of their current condition, why many instead favour simple mythology in their communications. Quite simply, few have much new to say. Often a politician can squeeze his words into the public ear only by grafting lightly thought ideas onto the weight of imagined history. We know these speeches when we hear them. They are ridden with overblown references to historic figures and moments of which the speaker has only a spattered understanding. In tone, these speeches are usually strident but rhetorically unhinged from their milquetoast substance.

Political communications in either case are far removed from the archival perspective. They are rooted, rather, in myth – the gauzy view of intermediated history. These speeches are remembered, if at all, for their gaffes. (While Franklin Roosevelt confirmed that a shocked America had faced a 'Day of Infamy' at Pearl Harbor, George W. Bush's own day of infamy, in the case of the Iraq War, had only two words: 'Mission Accomplished!')

Politicians who speak this way don't pretend to be helping heal a people through a deeper understanding of its roots. Indeed, they even pervert the cycle of longer memory – because they are conscious of the compromises they made for expediency. Politicians like George W. Bush would prefer that no one know the 'story behind the story' and seek to seal the very records they so obsessively assembled for their own edification. (Hence, deviation from the archival perspective in active politics destroys the work of actual archivists later on.)

How far, indeed, is this whole world from 4 April 1968, when Senator Robert Kennedy rose to address an inner-city Indianapolis crowd from the back of a flatbed truck. In the five years since his brother's death, Kennedy had assimilated the great Athenians – Aeschylus, Sophocles, Pericles – whose stories he had first read during the spring of 1964 in *The Greek Way*, an elegant survey by classicist Edith Hamilton. 'He discovered in her book the mysterious processes by which tragedy and suffering defy so many of man's rational and Enlightened efforts [and] understood that pain is a necessary precondition for any great or worthwhile achievement.'[4]

Aeschylus was the Greek who came immediately to Kennedy's mind in the minutes after he heard that Dr Martin Luther King had been shot. Aeschylus, wrote Hamilton, 'perceived the mystery of suffering. Mankind he saw companioned by disaster. But to the heroic [person], desperate odds fling a challenge ... The fullness of life is in the hazards of life.'[5]

Kennedy spoke for only about six minutes that night. His speech-writer rushed notes up to him, but the senator simply crumpled them into his pocket. He did not eulogize Martin Luther King. He did not start by calling for calm. He did not work the circumstances of that night into the philosophy of his own campaign. He offered nothing we would consider conventional politics.

Instead, Kennedy gently walked his audience of African Americans into a frank encounter with the origins of the emotions they were experiencing at that moment. 'My favourite poet was Aeschylus,' Kennedy said, off the cuff. 'He wrote, "In our sleep, pain which cannot forget falls drop by drop upon the heart until, in our own despair, against our will, comes wisdom to us through the awful grace of God."'

Hearing the tinny recording – eyes closed – forty years later, we still respond to the power of this direct encounter with the truth of a current experience. Kennedy chose words that underscored the psychological legitimacy, and thus the truth, of his audience's current experience of overwhelming pain. 'I don't have to be ashamed of these feelings,' one thinks to oneself, 'because things actually *are* this bad.'

In ushering his audience to such a frank encounter with its impulse to despair, Kennedy muted a far more destructive impulse that could have swept his crowd: survivor's guilt and shame. One might imagine people in the Indianapolis crowd that night asking themselves the kinds of questions that naturally come to any of us on hearing of a tragedy: 'Why do I deserve to cry tonight? Imagine what his family is going through ...' or 'Why do I deserve to cry? I haven't done anything close to what Dr King did and died for.' Any impulse to guilt and shame easily re-bounds as rage. In the summer of 1968, of course, that rage burned cities across the United States. But on one night, in one community and just for a moment to be sure, Kennedy stymied that descent through shame to rage. Instead, he gave meaning to his audience's pain by ushering them into a frank encounter with the psychological roots of that pain.

Any politician can drop a quote, of course, but there is more at play in this shard of speech. Kennedy's appetite for using Aeschylus' own experience of pain in the fifth century BCE as a primary source allowed a wealthy white senator to create meaning for an African American audience whose perspective must otherwise have been radically different. Politicians usually quote great figures or draw on historical data to simplify. Their intent is to distract audiences from complexity. To that end, they present history with an agenda, and use history as a secondary source. Audiences listen for a moment, then feel manipulated and occasionally rebel. Robert Kennedy intuitively did the opposite. In presenting Aeschylus' emotions, he *unmasked* the complexity of the immediate moment. Only that then gave him the licence to ask for calm and be heard.

The question of whether a speaker uses historic materials to 'mask' or 'unmask' the true experience of his audience is the litmus test that binds archival practice to great politics. An archivist, educated in the subtle distinctions between primary and secondary sources, would recognize the *authentic* encounter Kennedy ushered between a primary source (Aeschylus' poem) and a contemporary audience in Indianapolis.

Very rarely do politicians deploy historic materials with such an acute archival perspective. On New Year's Day 1990, the great Czech playwright Vaclav Havel offered a powerful example of this archival perspective at his inauguration as Czechoslovakia's first post-communist president. The thought of the weeks of preparation before that event is unbearably romantic. In my fantasy, imagining myself a Czech speechwriter instead of an anglophone one, I would have turned immediately to paraphrase Tomas Masaryk's own words on his inauguration as Czechoslovakia's first-ever president in 1918: 'The affairs of your government are returned into your hands once more, oh Czechoslovak people.'[6]

President-elect Havel would certainly have recognized the layers of eager meaning in that speech draft. He would know that Masaryk himself had mined those words in the deeper past, from the great seventeenth-century Czech Protestant reformer Johan Comenius. He would have understood the attempt finally to correct, in 1990, Masaryk's mistake in quoting Comenius literally in 1918 – 'The affairs of your government are returned into your hands once more, oh *Czech* people,' he had said, neglecting their Slovak compatriots and seeding resentment that ultimately led Slovak politicians to form a separate Nazi-style state in 1939.

I would have presented the president-elect with the draft, anxious that he not touch a word. I would have paced on the far side of his office as he reviewed the drafts weeks before the event, already hearing in my mind the gasp of an overwhelmed crowd at the moment that words their grandparents had heard reached their own ears to welcome them home from a tyranny they had just survived.

But Havel started differently: 'I assume you did not propose me for this office so that I, too, should lie to you ... Our country is not flourishing. The enormous creative and spiritual potential of our nations is being wasted ... We live in a contaminated moral environment. We have fallen morally ill because we have become used to saying one thing and thinking another.' Rather than recalling Czechoslovakia's wealth of cultural achievement, Havel then turned to more recent source material: the Slovnaft chemical plant and the Petrzalka housing project that entombed Bratislava's once pretty outskirts. He proceeded to catalogue Czechoslovakia's *contemporary* archives: the special farms that produced healthy food only for communist apparatchiks, rather than for hospitals and schools; the Stalinist prisons of the 1950s; the generation of thinkers forced into exile or killed.

'Why do I say all this? It would be very unwise to think of the sad legacy of the last forty years as something alien or something inherited from a distant relative. On the contrary, we have to accept this legacy as something we have inflicted on ourselves. If we accept it as such, we will understand that it is up to all of us, and only us, to do something about it ... If we realize this, hope will return to our hearts.'

Only *after* bringing Czechs and Slovaks to a frank encounter with the roots of their current experience does Havel allow us all to hear Masaryk: 'Masaryk rooted his politics in morality. Let us try – in a new era and in a new way – to restore this conception of politics ... Let us teach ourselves and others that politics can be the art of the impossible, namely, the art of improving ourselves and the world.'

And only then, in the *final* seconds, this: 'The most distinguished of my predecessors opened his first speech with a quote from Comenius. Allow me to end my first speech with my own paraphrase of the same statement: My people, your government has returned to you.'

Imagining myself a conventional speechwriter in Prague on New Year's Day, 1990, I would have instinctively used the archival material at hand to simplify the current moment. President Havel, like Senator Kennedy, instinctively used the archival material to *unmask* the complexity of that moment, reveal its pain, and so begin to heal the current injury.

Havel's and Kennedy's own primary source – morally, intellectually, and emotionally, if not literally – was perhaps the greatest statesman of ancient Athens: Pericles. Pericles himself could draw on no robust source material. Herodotus, the father of Western history, was a fifth-century BCE contemporary; Thucydides, the West's first formal historian, sat in the audience cataloguing Pericles' own speeches.

Yet even in Pericles, the archivist would recognize those same values of frank encounter that inspire the archival profession today. For Pericles, like Havel and Kennedy generations after, understood the powerful art of walking people into a frank encounter with the source materials of their own experience.

In 431 BCE Pericles was as close as democratic Athens had to a prime minister. The city state had just ended the first year of a terrible war against Sparta, and he was called to centre stage at the mass funeral for the war dead. His political task was to inspire persistence.

Around the same moment in history, philosophers were formalizing the rules of argument meant to convince people under just such daunting circumstances. Indeed, those rules were already in wide use in the *polis*, but Pericles set a distinct path. The entire power of his appeal came from his focus on the truth of his fellows' suffering. And that, in turn, came from his appetite to create a frank encounter between his audience and the primary sources of their trauma: their own dead. Like Kennedy and Havel, Pericles refused to simplify the current moment with exaggerated history and instead exposed the complex truth of current circumstances: 'It is difficult to say neither too little nor too much; and even moderation is apt not to give the impression of truthfulness. The friend of the dead who knows the facts is likely to think that the words of the speaker fall short of his knowledge and of his wishes; another who is not so well informed, when he hears of anything which surpasses his own powers, will be envious and will suspect exaggeration.' Pericles delves deeper into the encounter even than Havel's references to the Slovnaft chemical plant. To him, the dead are themselves the archival source of Athens' current circumstances.

For the whole earth is the tomb of famous men; not only are they commemorated by columns and inscriptions in their own country, but in foreign lands there dwells also an unwritten memorial of them, graven not on stone but in the hearts of men … Do not weigh too nicely the perils of war …

To you who are the sons and brothers of the departed, I see that the struggle to emulate them will be an arduous one. [For] when a man is out of the way, the honor and goodwill which he receives is unalloyed.

This frank encounter with the source material of Athens' current circumstances – mass, intimate death – exposes the complex emotions in Athens at that time and gives it meaning. Only with this truth in hand does Pericles have the moral credibility to make an almost impossible appeal: that his fellows persist through further, mass death. He *ends* with the appeal that conventional political rhetoric might have tried to avoid: 'Now let everyone respectively indulge in becoming grief for his departed friends, and then retire.'

Two hundred years earlier, the prophet Isaiah had anticipated the essential sanctity of such communications: 'Woe unto them that put bitter for sweet, and sweet for bitter!' he proclaimed.[7] In this, the prophet illuminated the space that archivists share with history's most moral practitioners of political communications: the instinct to walk a people gently into a frank, archival, encounter with the source material of its own experience.

My roots – like those of some others I met in politics – were in journalism. In my case, they lay as a foreign correspondent for the *Wall Street Journal*. Early in my career, a more senior correspondent gave me an internal handbook, commissioned for young *Journal* reporters by our editors in New York. Upon opening it, I was soon swimming through a moving, 153-page meditation by a legendary colleague named Bill Blundell entitled 'Storytelling – Step by Step.' Storytelling, he noted, was all one word: a formal designation, a calling.

Blundell's book was already scarce by the time I got it and had achieved something of a cult status in bureaus around the world. As foreign correspondents, we had been granted remarkable access to the *Wall Street Journal*'s Page One. It was a unique venue in American journalism, where editors set aside the most prominent space in the newspaper for elegant storytelling rather than breaking news. It was also a profoundly meritocratic space – available to any reporter with a great story, regardless of tenure or experience. Each of us, pushing insane hours in our cubicles across the time zones, yearned to churn out perfect Page One 'leders.'

But Blundell's book struck me as something more than a guide to Page One. It was, rather, a humble primer on some of the elements of a good life. For that reason it remains the single best book I have ever read about the fundamental values of journalism. Blundell's point to young journalists was that great reporting is really great storytelling; that storytelling is, fundamentally, a high calling to witness; and that the attempt to bear true witness is a hard craft and a work of discipline. In the pages of his book, Blundell describes the kind of journalist who can act *archivally* (my word, not his) because she has the discipline of witness.

If the moral politician can initiate the process of healing by walking citizens into a frank encounter with the sources of their own experience, then the most moral journalists are even more thorough diagnosticians. They identify the pathology truthfully, and articulate it in the form of a true story so well crafted that it compels a person's mind directly into other circumstances. This is the rare journalist whose communications complement the work of those politicians like Robert Kennedy, Vaclav Havel, and Pericles.

But, just as the archivist would recognize only a few great politicians in our generation, Blundell asks, 'Why [are] there still so few storytellers in a business whose product is stories?' Perhaps, he notes, it is because 'too many reporters do not see themselves as story tellers, but as something else.'[8] Blundell sees some journalists acting as 'lawyers … fixated on ideas, they lack humanity in their work. They may talk down to the reader or talk at him, but they seldom talk *with* him as the storyteller does.'[9]

Other journalists, he says, masquerade as 'scholastics who, against all reason, try to learn everything about a subject before writing anything. Lacking scope, they report and report and report until their desks are hidden under stacks of papers and notes. When the scholastic finally starts to write he is, of course, overwhelmed … his prose is usually stuffy, he is apt to pay unwarranted attention to petty matters of interest only to insiders, and his epics lack highlights on major points because these are so deeply buried in drifts of irrelevant or marginal material.'[10]

Yet another type, whom he calls the 'objectivist,' has 'a less obvious problem. His work seldom sticks in the memory because he sees himself as a fact funnel. He writes flat prose. He shies away from making firm conclusions dictated by plain sets of facts; instead he gives us timid, weasly ones, or more often drags into the story a source who will analyse the obvious for him.'[11]

Thus, many journalists, like many politicians, wear masks that distance them from frank encounters with the true source material. They interview 'analysts' in their well-removed offices, instead of people experiencing a story for themselves. Or they dip into the midst of a story just long enough to get a few quotes, rather than to obtain a deep experience. Journalists who don these masks actually get in the way of the original material and make themselves secondary sources. And so once again it is the archivist – educated in the disciplines of evaluating witness – who is outstandingly qualified to assess whether a journalist is working through a mask or has resisted the mask in order to work with primary source material.

In my own experience, the masks Blundell describes were almost irresistible aids we needed in order to cope with fear. Most of my colleagues and I were afraid of getting the important stuff wrong. 'When the correspondent approaches a major feature story, phantoms crowd around his desk,' Blundell wrote, very accurately. 'The bureau chief is there, the page editor is there, maybe the managing editor is there. The whole weight of the *Wall Street Journal*'s importance settles on his shoulders like a cast iron yoke. This is no simple story he's attempting – not tomorrow's kitty litter. To him [or her] this is nothing less than the tablets of Moses.'[12]

We were also quite often afraid of getting it right – because getting it *really* right meant stepping into the problem and hewing the distance that we found comfortable. It also meant confronting editorial systems that sometimes smirked at the extra effort and instead recognized the qualities of volume, of 'byline count' – faster, shorter stories with simpler histories.

But it *is* possible for the journalist to be a primary source. Many in fact display the very disciplines that are, again, especially familiar to the archivist. Those who do have an acute sense of the difference between a primary and a secondary source in their own storytelling. They literally yearn for the primary source, even when a casual reader might not know the difference. These journalists go to terrific lengths not just to find that source but to tease from it the full complexity of messy experience, and not just a quote or two.

Jon Lee Anderson, in a recent article in the *New Yorker*, accompanies a team of U.S. agents, mercenaries, and local police on a campaign to eradicate poppy fields in a small part of Afghanistan. He describes being targeted by Taliban in hours of close combat, cut off from most of the team he is accompanying, and then sitting for ten days in forward bases as he gets to know the Americans involved in this mission.[13] We are satisfied that he has attended to what Blundell calls 'the lowest level of the story.' Anderson has brought us to a world far messier than the boardrooms of diplomats back in Kabul and vastly more complex than the analysts' conferences in Western Europe or Washington.

But even that is not enough, for him. He goes back to the poppy fields with a few local police rather than the well-armed American mercenaries who had escorted him before 'so that I could speak to farmers freely.'[14] He aims, presumably, to chat with farmers who would otherwise be aiming shots at him. Though his diligence is rare, Anderson is by no means alone among correspondents in his ethos.

Great journalists also have a sense of humour that the archivist would find familiar: an acute eye for irony, along with a complete blindness to mockery. They retain an honourable nose for the absurd.

In 1989 I arrived in apartheid South Africa to report for an opposition magazine – my first foreign experience as a journalist. The culture shock of southern Africa was multiplied, many times over, by the culture shock of South Africa's institutionalized web of racism. But even within two weeks, I began to adjust. I assumed that Black colleagues could not visit my local pub for a drink after work because they were not allowed to stay in Johannesburg at night; and I began to adjust to the fact that, despite being thoroughly new to the country, I actually could feel more comfortable wandering through a local mall than could my boss – an Indian-South African editor who had lived nearby all his life. My sense of the absurd began to slip away. I started to wedge my daily life around those ugly corners in dozens of minute ways that signal a barely conscious moral compromise.

Around then, someone took me aside and warned me: 'Don't be like all the foreigners who come here. Don't forget that what you're seeing isn't normal.'

Great journalists, like archivists, retain their sense of the abnormal. Their common weapon in this effort is humour. Like shock, humour alerts us to things that stand out. But humour stands a better chance of enduring. Shock wears us out; it yields to numbness and exhaustion in a way that ultimately betrays our ability to notice the absurd. Humour is precisely the opposite: it's addictive. Of course, humour presents its own risks that great journalists must confront with discipline. They draw the line between humour – a sense of the absurd – and mockery, which diminishes another person's experience and obscures the primary source material.

Of the three 'Page One leders' in the *Wall Street Journal* every day, the most sought after by reporters, the most central on the page – always occupying the middle column – and usually the most memorable to readers is a humorous story called the 'A-hed' (after the lines and dots that form a kind of 'A' around its headline). 'The purpose of an A-hed is to entertain readers with good story-telling and clever writing,' one editor explains.[15] In fact, A-heds are often the day's most poignant piece because they offer a thoughtful anatomy of some absurdity that seems funny, at first. They invite the reader to laugh, and then follow the laughter to source material that is complex, messy, and true.

The A-hed was where I could write about a boulder that suburban Vancouverites said sang them lullabies at night. That let me usher readers into a direct encounter with the source material of Aboriginal-White relations in suburban North America, a messy world where Whites and Aboriginal neighbours disregarded one another in daily life but shared the discovery of a nine-thousand-year-old religious site on White-owned farmland.

The A-hed was also the place where I could write about the millions of dollars that Japanese construction companies spend each year designing golf resorts for the moon. That let me usher readers to a direct encounter with the source material of a very important phenomenon in twentieth-century Japan: the personal shame that prevents many Japanese leaders from stopping ambitious projects (like lunar construction, say, or waging war on the United States) long after those ideas had ceased to be practical.

Danny Pearl, the *Wall Street Journal* correspondent whom terrorists killed in Pakistan in 2003, captured the form perfectly in a 1997 A-hed he wrote about hundreds of Iranians employed in hand-weaving carpets the size of soccer fields. From a place called Ben, he wrote: 'This is a small town in search of a really big floor. It should be a bare floor, big enough to accommodate about 6000 people, with no columns breaking up the space. And it should be crying out for the subtle decorative touch of the world's largest hand-woven carpet with a third of an acre of beige, brown and blue swirls with flowers.'[16] This 'mega-rug,' it turned out, was the primary source in a deeper story about boycotts on Iranian exports. Whatever politics surrounded those boycotts, Pearl witnessed how they tore through the heart of traditional Persian crafts – how thousands of people kept weaving carpets even though no one in the world would buy them.

Thus, at their best, journalists try to cultivate three modes of thought familiar to the archivist – the intellectual courage to toss masks away and work up close as a storyteller; a hunger for primary sources; and a sense of humour that exposes the abnormal without mocking it. With those, a journalist may have the mental faculties to be fully conscious of his surroundings, to notice everything, and to bear witness. The same Danny Pearl, on a very different day (exactly a year before he died), started an article this way: 'What is India's earthquake zone really like?

It smells. It reeks. You can't imagine the odor of several hundred bodies decaying for five days as search teams pick away at slabs of crumbled buildings in this town. Even if you've never smelled it before, the brain knows what it is and orders you to get away. After a day, the nose gets stuffed up in self-defense. But the brain has registered the scent, and picks it up in innocent places: lip balm, sweet candy, stale breath, an airplane seat.'[17]

'This is not a defense of personal journalism, which is nothing but arrogance,' Blundell had warned us all, years earlier. 'Wallowing publicly in his own feelings, the personal journalist assumes the license to filter reality and presents without shame a picture of the world as reflected in a fun house mirror. By contrast, the honest storyteller responds emotionally to what *is*.'[18] Our job, he added, was to 'reject the fear of being wrong, this impulse to fudge and hedge to protect' ourselves. Our conclusions and summaries about a situation would be 'the spine of the story and, taken together, impart its central message. When all this is done, the reader gradually becomes conscious of a guiding intelligence within the story, working for his benefit, the close and warming presence of a fellow human being conversing with him in print – not that of a bloodless entity lecturing him from afar – and he responds.'[19]

This is the discipline of witness. And its scarcity – or frequency – in journalism is easy to gauge. Spend one week flipping through your local newspaper. How many articles are 'fact funnels,' written in 'flat prose'? How many pieces 'talk down' to you, or 'talk at' you, rather than with you? How many simply report on press conferences? How many 'profiles' simplify a complex individual and render him into a 'type' or a caricature? How much is mockery and sarcasm?

How often do you feel the 'close and warming presence of a fellow human being conversing with [you] in print'? The archivist, I believe, is professionally attuned to that 'warming presence' because it is the presence of a primary source. Great journalism is written for us all; but finding it amidst the cacophony is the natural province of the archivist.

A number of friends experienced in high politics, even those who are deeply spiritual and well read in philosophy or literature, find my thesis exasperating. 'That's all well and good,' they note, 'but even the best politicians – the ones who might try to usher in what you call this "frank encounter" with the source material – are "intermediated" by journalists who do not share the same perspective.' True. And, for their part, those journalists who do have an 'archival instinct' for primary sources tend to stay away from politicians, preferring the complexity of messy stories to the polish of a public figure. Indeed, it seems society itself works hard to help us *avoid* the frank encounter with the source materials of our current experience. Whole industries invest billions of dollars and employ thousands upon thousands of people to create *simple* stories.

What would happen, then, if the world were filled with politicians and journalists who both strove with equal intensity to the archival encounter? Likely, it couldn't exist. Life would be too intense.

What my political friends might call the 'intermediated encounter' between people and their source material is what the Jewish philosopher Martin Buber calls the encounter between 'I' and 'It.' This relationship with 'It' – the intermediated 'other,' the secondary or tertiary source – is where we spend most of our lives.

What I call the 'frank encounter' between people and their primary source material – the occasional accomplishment of great politicians and great journalists – is far more extreme and something potentially far more painful. It is closer to what Buber calls a sacred dialogue between two whole figures, naked before one another. He calls them: 'I and Thou.' 'In all seriousness of truth, listen,' Buber writes; 'without "It" a human being can't live. But whoever lives only with that is not human.'[20]

It is true that we must water down the pure spirit of painful source materials to ingest any of the drink at all. But the weakness of communications in our generation is, perhaps, that we have watered down things *too* far. We allow ourselves to be distracted into simple explanations. We avoid complexity to such a degree that there is little left in one another's stories – or even of our own stories, about ourselves – for us to really taste.

Against this stands the archivist. The very skills he has honed to bridge generations are the instincts he has to help us, hear us, about us.

NOTES

1 This essay was prepared thanks to Amanda Young, who gave me time; John Fraser and Geraldine Sharpe, who gave me space; and Gordon Bricker, who gave me perspective.
2 R. Waterfield, ed., *Plato's Republic* (Oxford: Oxford University Press 1993), 69, 376c.

3 I am deliberately avoiding the well-worn debates over how Plato would select philosopher kings, or even whether such an intellectual aristocracy would be consistent with democracy. My point is simply that Plato believed a love of wisdom, however derived, to be fundamental for leadership. Plato, of course, equates a love of wisdom – *philo-sophia* – with a hunger for truth.

4 M.K. Beran, *The Last Patrician: Bobby Kennedy and the End of American Aristocracy* (New York: St Martin's Griffin 1998), 91. Editor's note: all subsequent quotations from the speeches by Kennedy, Havel, and Pericles can be found in William Safire, *Lend Me Your Ears – Great Speeches in History* (New York: W.W. Norton 1992).

5 E. Hamilton, *The Greek Way* (New York: W.W. Norton 1930, reissued 1993), 147.

6 *Office of the President of the Czech Republic, Presidential Biography of Tomas Masaryk*, http://www.hrad.cz/en/prezident_cr/masaryk.shtml (accessed 15 January 2010).

7 Isaiah 5:20.

8 W.E. Blundell, *Storytelling Step by Step: A Guide to Better Feature Writing* (New York: Dow Jones and Company 1986), 55–6.

9 Ibid., 56. Emphasis in original.

10 Ibid.

11 Ibid.

12 Ibid., 58.

13 Jon Lee Anderson, 'The Taliban's Opium War,' *New Yorker*, 9 July 2007.

14 Ibid.

15 J. Berentson, ed., *Dressing for Dinner in the Naked City: And Other Tales from the Wall Street Journal's 'Middle Column'* (New York: Hyperion 1994), Introduction.

16 D. Pearl, *At Home in The World*, edited by Helene Cooper (New York: Wall Street Journal Books 2002), 250.

17 Ibid., 4.

18 Blundell, *Storytelling*, 57.

19 Ibid., xx.

20 M. Buber, *I and Thou*, translated by Walter Kaufmann (New York: Touchstone 1996), 85.

Index

Aboriginal peoples, 81, 98, 101, 169, 172–3, 177, 179, 186n9, 190n9, 198, 227

academics, 50, 121, 173–5, 181, 184, 191n33

accessibility, 146, 208; of census materials, 76, 89; of digital records, 111–12, 122, 130; of government records, 44–5, 46, 155–7; of personal information, 72, 97, 99–100; vs. privacy, 72–3, 83–4; of records, 30, 31, 196, 203. *See also* records

Access to Information Act (ATIA) (1983), 40–1, 72–3; amendments, 46, 54; applicants under, 40, 43–4, 51; bureaucratic obstruction, 43–5, 55; and census wars, 90; challenges, 43–51; costs to administer, 48–9; exclusions, 45–6; impact, 52; improvements needed, 53–4; vs. privacy, 72–3, 83–4; and record keeping, 44–5, 46, 155–6; scope, 45–6; security concerns, 50. *See also* FOI legislation; Privacy Act

accountability, 53; in archival legislation, 148–9; in archival work, 81, 158–9, 162–5; ATIA and, 41, 46; as concept, 143–5, 158; and democracy, 145–6, 147, 158; FOI legislation and, 41, 46; government and, 147–8, 150–5, 159–60; government records and, 155, 156–7, 162; historical, 154, 158–60; in reconciliation process, 196, 208–9; record keeping and, 155, 156–7, 162, 196; vs. responsibility, 146; trust and, 157–8, 165. *See also* responsibility

acquisition, 4, 5, 6; of census records, 77, 79; of digital records, 126, 127; narrowing of, 124

adversarialism, 43–5

advocacy, 11, 32, 178–9

Aeschylus, 219

Afghanistan, 211n3, 225–6

agency, 144, 157, 164–5

Air Canada, 177

Alberta, 20

'American Conversations' (NARA), 174

Amin, Idi, 200

Anderson, Jon Lee, 225–6

apartheid. *See* South Africa